MEN AGAINST THE CLOUDS

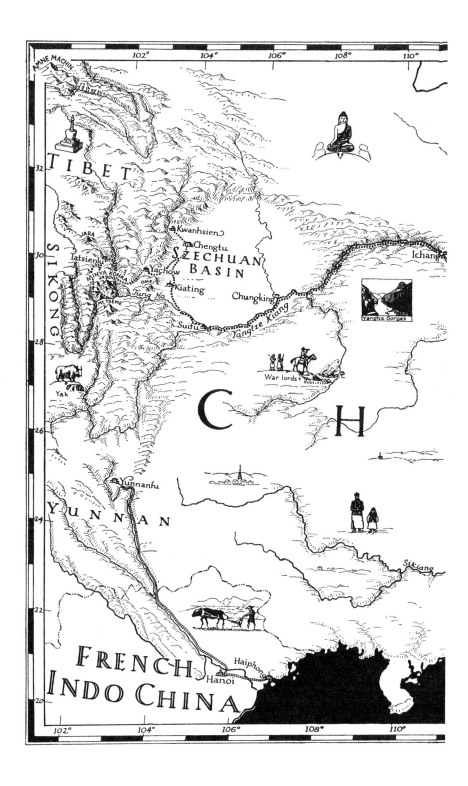

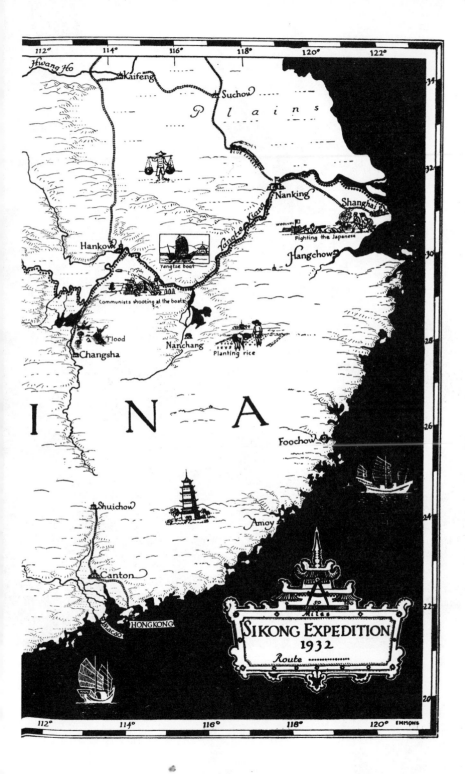

Minya Konka

MEN AGAINST THE CLOUDS

The Conquest of Minya Konka

by
Richard L. Burdsall
and
Arthur B. Emmons, 3rd

with contributions by
Terris Moore
and
Jack Theodore Young

THE MOUNTAINEERS
Seattle

Original edition published in 1935 by Harper & Brothers.

Revised edition copyright © 1980 by The Mountaineers.

Published by The Mountaineers
719 Pike Street, Seattle, Washington 98101

Published simultaneously in Canada by
Douglas & McIntyre, Ltd., 1875 Welch Street
North Vancouver, British Columbia V7P 1B7

.

Cover: Burdsall and Moore on the Northwest Ridge, Minya Konka
Frontispiece: Minya Konka, by Joseph F. Rock © National Geographic
Society

Library of Congress Cataloging in Publication Data

Burdsall, Richard Lloyd.
    Men against the clouds.

    Bibliography: p.
    Includes index.
    1. Mountaineering–China–Minya Konka. 2. Minya
Konka–Description. 3. Sikang expedition, 1932.
I. Emmons, Arthur Brewster, 1910–   joint author.
II. Title.
GV199.44.C552M563   1980   915.15   79-25369
ISBN 0-916890-93-7

Publisher's Note

When the opportunity first arose for The Mountaineers to publish our edition of this mountaineering classic, there was question about the inclusion of the original Hunting Notes: they seemed both out of date with contemporary thinking and inappropriate in a book about exploratory and expeditionary mountaineering. After all, it has been many years, if not decades, since major expeditions have done trophy hunting, or any hunting whatsoever, except in survival situations.

After thorough consideration, we realized that the hunting described here was not for purposes of collecting trophies for anyone's den, but was instead for the loftiest of contemporary scientific purposes: to collect for the Academia Sinica in Nanking the floral and faunal specimens of a then-unexplored region of the world. We trust readers will also consider it in this perspective. In addition — as a minor literary footnote — this book was first published when hunting stories a la Teddy Roosevelt were in vogue, which doubtless influenced the editing style of this volume: there was evidently insufficient excitement in mere mountaineering!

In preparing this edition, we are profoundly grateful for the invaluable assistance of Terris Moore, who provided the Prologue and Epilogue and contributed photographs from his personal collection — several never before published anywhere. The photograph on page iv was made available by the National Geographic Society, which made a rare exception to its policy of refusing such requests.

If you enjoy this book, we call your attention to our other reprint editions; we welcome suggestions for addition to this series.

The Mountaineers

CONTENTS

APPENDICES

Prologue

SEARCH FOR THE WORLD'S HIGHEST
MOUNTAIN

by Terris Moore

"THIRTY thousand feet?" I repeated in astonishment. "Is there really any chance Mount Koonka could be *that* high?" Even allowing for some over-enthusiasm or an error of up to a thousand feet, such a height might cause the new peak to out-top Mount Everest! Could there yet be, so late in the history of exploration as March 1930, any remaining possibility of discovering the highest mountain in the world? My new friend and I were quite skeptical, but we read on.

Allen Carpé, fifteen years my senior, was a distinguished research engineer for the Bell Telephone Laboratories, with numerous recent patents in multiplex telephony to his credit. I was but a beginning graduate student, aged 22. In the old Explorers Club library in New York, where he was a member, we were studying the detailed route map in *Trailing the Giant Panda,* by Kermit and Theodore Roosevelt, Jr., which had just appeared late in 1929. That Christmas I had glanced over the map without noticing this detail, because I was distracted by the Roosevelt brothers' thrilling experiences in the wild, mountainous, and still unknown border region of far west China and eastern Tibet. In

Map of Mount Koonka from the Roosevelt brothers' book

January—a newcomer at the annual American Alpine Club dinner meeting in Boston—I had met Allen.

Now my friend's finger pointed out the meager relevant sentences in the Roosevelts' book, to which high mountains were only incidental. "Early one morning we got our first glimpse of mysterious Mount Koonka, rising high in white majesty... and regretted the lack of time that made it impossible for us to make a reconnaissance.... The altitude of this mighty peak is unknown, but there are those who claim that it rises more than thirty thousand feet and is the highest in the world. A geologist from Chengtu made a special expedition to establish Koonka's height, but after he had taken his observations he refused for some entirely unaccountable reason to divulge them. Perhaps some slip had occurred in his calculations and he was unwilling to dwell upon the error."

We duly noted the route-map-maker's credentials: "prepared by E.J. Raisz of Columbia University. All the country between the Szechuan Basin of China and the Irrawaddy River is mountainous and most is unsurveyed... the altitudes were determined by barometer."

Next, Carpé and I examined the preceding month's issue of the *National Geographic* for its article by Joseph Rock, distinguished botanist of the Arnold Arboretum, titled "Seeking the Mountains of Mystery; an Expedition on the China-Tibet Frontier to the Unexplored Amne Machin Range, One of Whose Peaks Rivals Everest." Now was this Amne Machin yet another unsurveyed range whose highest peak might be in the giant class? Apparently so; for checking back we noted that while "Mount Koonka" was set as the highest point at the headwaters of the upper *Yangtze* River, the leading sentences of Dr. Rock's article stated: "After dangerous, difficult months, I reached the headwaters of the 2,000 mile long *Yellow* River and the towering unexplored range of the Amne Machin."

This range too must still be unsurveyed, for at the end of the article Rock wrote: "Not being supplied with a theodolite, I could not take the actual height; but from other observations... we stood at an elevation of nearly 16,000 feet, yet in the distance rose still higher peaks, another 12,000 feet of snow and ice.... I came to the conclusion that the Amne Machin towers more than 28,000 feet."

Further back in his account he had written: "That it fell to my lot to reach this region was due to a chance encounter, back in 1923, with that famous British explorer,

Brig. Gen. George Pereira. I met the English traveler in Yunnan. He had then recently completed his now historic march from Peking to Lhasa, and during our visit, he told me of an amazing landmark passed on his westward journey—the great snow-capped Amne Machin Range, which he saw from a distance of more than 100 miles. Very likely, he remarked, the Amne Machin, when surveyed, might prove higher than Everest."

One and a half years and two Alaskan mountaineering expeditions with Carpé were to pass before I stood again in the Explorers Club library, studying its great globe and more detailed maps of central Asia. By now a member myself, I was examining with others the realities—insofar as they could be determined—of an expedition specifically to locate and measure the highest mountain in the world. What a discovery if one were indeed found to be higher than Mount Everest!

Chilling this possibility, however, as we now went into it, were the details about our high mountains on the latest and best military map that the library possessed: the General Staff War Office Map No. 2975, dated September 1925, H.M. Stationery Office, London. Seemingly published especially to include the correcting observations available from Pereira's journal of his Peking-Lhasa march in 1921–22, its contour intervals indicated about 25,000 feet for the upper *massif* of the Amne Machin range, but no estimate for the height of its summit peak. We were amazed, however, at the map's presentation of the Mount Koonka region through which he had also passed: no indication of high snow peaks, nor even any blank area there. Instead: explicit contour intervals showing nothing so high as 16,500 feet!

"Just might have been cloud-covered the entire time Pereira was within sighting distance," someone suggested. "But then, since he walked in a semi-circle around it from only twenty-five to thirty miles away, having walked in toward it from a hundred miles east, and then walked out a hundred miles north, you'd certainly think he'd have gotten a glimpse of something like *that* to put on the map!" His finger rested upon the photograph of the spectacular peak that Dr. Joseph Rock had named Minya Konka and published as 25,600 feet high.

We had all become aware of this additional article of Rock's as soon as it had appeared in the October 1930 *National Geographic*. Now, checking and rechecking the latitude and longitude of all three locations—the Roosevelt brothers' 30,000-foot Mount Koonka, Pereira's area of nothing-over-16,500-feet, and Dr. Rock's 25,600-foot Minya Konka, and all supposedly at about 29½° north latitude and longitude 102° east—we became convinced that these three were indeed intended to describe the same place!

The intriguing mystery about the actual terrain at 29½° north, 102° east deepened. We read in Rock's article that the name Minya Konka, which he was the first to publish, meant in the local native language "the Great Snow Mountain of the Minya region," with Konka being pronounced "somewhere between Gungka and Goong-ga." Surely, we reasoned, there must be a very high peak there!

Next we talked privately with the chief cartographer of the National Geographic Society, who told us that in determining his altitude figure for Minya Konka, Dr. Rock had used neither theodolite nor mercurial barometer, but simply a pocket sighting compass to read angles, and only an aneroid to obtain the elevation of his base line. Upon in-

quiring about the Amne Machin range at the headwaters of
the Yellow River, we learned that "Dr. Rock originally reported this to us by cable as being 30,000 feet high; we,
however, advised Dr. Grosvenor not to publish any such
figure until Rock could return and convince us from his ob-
servational data. When Rock did return to Washington we
decided that with sighting compass and aneroid as his only
instruments for determining altitudes, 28,000 feet was the
maximum we were willing to publish."

For those of us at the Explorers Club now definitely
planning an expedition, all this produced a conclusion. If
Dr. Rock found the Amne Machin to be 4,000 feet higher
than Minya Konka, then, crude though his methods may
have been, apparently he used the same method on both.
Since Amne Machin must therefore be the higher, let's head
for it.

It was at this point, late in the summer of 1931, that Allen
Carpé reluctantly bowed out. Nearly forty, married and
with a family, deeply involved in his professional career, he
was now engaged in obtaining a Carnegie grant to pursue
his scientific cosmic ray research in the mountains of
Alaska.

To the rest of us, gathered about the great globe in the old
Clubhouse, the first question—as always, especially in those
years—had to be: Money. Airplanes? No. The best airplane
not only would cost far more money than we could raise,
but in those years would still not be adequate. For at that
time no accurate altitude determinations of high mountains
could be made in flight. Only from the ground could this be
done with the methods of half a century ago. And there was
no place to land a plane anywhere near those remote mountains, nor gasoline to refuel. Indeed the very altitude of the

Tibetan plateau was itself too great for the "aeroplane" of those days to land and take off.

Among our group, long-time Club member Gene Lamb seemed the obvious choice for leader. My initial meeting with him in 1930 had come about because of his arresting idea for a small American expedition to make an attempt on Mount Everest, via an approach from Peking across Tibet, following Pereira's route. "If Pereira could walk that route alone with a small party, and *without arranging his permission* from the Dalai Lama *until he reached Jyekundo* in the middle of Tibet, why not also a small American climbing party?" Lamb himself was not an alpinist, nor did he aspire to become one. But perhaps someday after a successful exploration of the Amne Machin range, he might even lead an American mountaineering expedition to Mount Everest in such a way—thus circumventing British control of the conventional India-Sikkim route to Everest.

In late 1931, Lamb took responsibility for the Explorers Club flag, denoting Club support of his leadership of a Club expedition to first explore the Amne Machin range in detail, then to climb it if possible. Gene Lamb was 37, had made previous successful expeditions into Manchuria, Siberia, and far west China, spoke Mandarin fluently, and had a satisfactory employment record with the U.S. Consular Service; and we observed that he was respectfully treated as an experienced old China hand by Roy Chapman Andrews, the Club's president and Asian expert. Corinne Lamb, his personable wife, was planning to accompany us part way. His friend, Major John Logan, helped with money raising and was to be second-in-command. Lamb also had recruited Jack Young, the engaging, very capable, and well-connected youthful Chinese who had figured so importantly in the Roosevelt brothers' giant-panda-Mount-Koonka-30,000-feet? expedition; Young was now a New York University student. Finally, with our help, Lamb also enlisted Dr. Fouad Al Akl, a promising young medical doctor who declined a Mayo appointment to join our expedition. These excellent choices increased our confidence that the expedition leader would be able to obtain the necessary Chinese Government official permission upon our arrival in Shanghai.

My responsibility was to organize our mountaineering capabilities. I began by recruiting my old friend Lewis Thorne, with whom I had climbed Mounts Sangay and Chimborazo in Ecuador two years earlier. Thorne was a Yale graduate, who entered Johns Hopkins Medical School after our return. The two of us next added Arthur B. Emmons 3rd, a young engineering student in his junior year at Harvard and an enthusiastic member of the Harvard Mountaineering Club, with experience in the Alps and Alaska. And then the three of us persuaded Richard L. Burdsall—a Swarthmore graduate in his mid-thirties, a professional engineer with patents to his credit and some minor climbing experience—to qualify himself at the American Geographical Society for preparing a reliable map and making an accurate determination of the altitude of the highest mountains we might be able to visit.

Hardly had our group been organized and enough money raised—with the greatest difficulty, for two years of collapsing stock market and declining economy had drained most pocketbooks—when, buying the newspapers one fine morning outside the old Clubhouse at 110th Street and Cathedral Parkway, we read: JAPANESE SEIZE MUKDEN IN MANCHURIA! The date: September 19, 1931.

For the next two months, the Lamb Expedition to Northern Tibet, headquartered in New York at the old Clubhouse, continued to collect its equipment and prepare its members while additional northern Chinese cities were falling, one by one, to the aggressive Japanese military machine. With the loss of each city our hearts sank further, for we well realized that the worse the war in China became, the less likely that we would be able to obtain official permission from the Chinese Government when we arrived. But finally, during the last week of November, we sailed from New York on the *Tai Ping Yang*.

She was a slow but modern freighter of the Barber Lines, and the nine of us occupied nearly all her limited passenger capacity. We plodded through the Panama Canal, touched at Los Angeles and Manila, and finally landed at Shanghai about the middle of January 1932. By then the appetite of the Japanese politicians and their military machine seemed to have been sated, for only China's Manchurian cities had been seized so far, and none at all for some weeks. Our spirits rose.

But in Shanghai, two weeks after our arrival, disaster fell upon our expedition—and in far worse degree upon the thousands, and eventually millions, of unfortunate and inoffensive Chinese. All nine of us were lunching in our hotel room on January 28 when the doors to our balcony, which by chance I had just latched, swung inward as though pushed by some giant unseen hand, accompanied by the sound of a vast detonation. We later learned that a powder barge had been exploded in the Whangpoo River. We climbed to the roof of our hotel in time to see the Japanese battleship *Idzumo*, anchored just off the Shanghai Bund, begin firing her shells at point blank range into Chapei, the

Chinese part of Shanghai. Next, while we watched, a wave of Japanese airplanes appeared over the Chinese part of the city; we saw small black objects fall, and soon their bomb blasts added to our sense of outrage.

The sound of machine gun fire from the same part of the city soon told us that Japanese Army units were pushing outward from the Japanese section of the International Settlement into Chapei, where the Chinese Army resisted in heavy fighting. Pandemonium seemed to be sweeping the International Settlement, a closely delimited area of the city that the Japanese, so far, were not attacking.

Within hours it became evident that the small military forces of the western powers occupying the International Settlement—British, American, and French—were putting their military contingency plans into effect. Notices appeared on the bulletin boards of all hotels in the occidental parts of the International Settlement, urging able-bodied volunteers to report to the military of their own nations. For us this was the tiny U.S. Marine Corps headquarters. And soon, after we had signed emergency legal papers (wherein we committed ourselves to obey the orders of the U.S. Marine Captain company commander), Thorne, Emmons, and I were patrolling with rifle, bayonet, cartridge bandolier, steel helmet, and arm-band as substitute for uniform, along a section of the Soochow Creek perimeter of the U.S. part of the International Settlement. Technically we were members of the American Company of the Shanghai Volunteer Corps, and by the exigencies of war were released from our expedition agreements made in New York.

Assigned to separate platoons, the three of us never encountered each other during the first five days of intense strain and uncertainty. The foreseeable future had suddenly become enormously shortened. Now life rushed along from hour to hour only, as during this time, from close-in guard detail, we were obliged to watch the bitter fighting between Japanese and Chinese soldiers immediately across narrow Soochow Creek, and the resulting sad flow of Chinese refugees through our lines.

Our Chinese member, Jack Young, had vanished, but not before telling us that he was hurrying to join his people. During the third night, in the gloomiest part of my patrol beat, a startling but familiar voice spoke out of the darkness: "Hey, Terry? Let me have a handful of cartridges?" It was Jack Young! I thought quickly. Why, of course, he's firing from the Chinese side, badly needing ammunition. As an experienced hunter from the Roosevelt expedition, doubt-less *he* knows how to make each shot count! We had been issued thirty rounds apiece, but not being engaged our-selves, we had not fired any. Wondering what excuse to give later for the missing rounds, I handed Jack ten, and he promptly disappeared.

By the fifth day a British cruiser and transport had arrived from Hong Kong. A thousand or more regular British Army soldiers (the English newspapers said 5,000) paraded complete with field artillery through the streets in-side our perimeter. It was becoming evident that the Japanese were attempting to take over Chinese territory only and not the entire International Settlement as had at first been feared. Tension dropped visibly in people's faces and in their manner. We and others like us could now honorably ask to turn in our weapons and be released.

But what of the Lamb Expedition to Northern Tibet and the Amne Machin range of unsurveyed mountains? Back in our hotel with hot baths, a sleep around the clock, and a restaurant dinner under our belts, we thought the foresee-able future a little brighter. The visibility seemed to have lifted to an outlook of at least a few months ahead.

The disruptive war was still going on, though the sound of shelling was becoming more distant as the defending Chinese, lacking adequate air support and overcome by superior fire power, were being forced to retreat. It was becoming obvious that as long as the war raged on, Gene Lamb, the expedition leader, was not likely to be granted official permission to travel into the interior. Miraculously, however, during the ensuing week, he managed to get our party out of war-wracked Shanghai, obtaining passage for all nine of us aboard a small coastal steamer up to Tientsin, where we were able to catch a train into relatively calm Peking.

Nevertheless, the expedition was beginning to separate into three groups. The Lambs and Major Logan talked increasingly of proceeding with the expedition into the interior of China, even *without* official permission. And indeed in those years casual travel by individuals who were sufficiently fluent in Mandarin, and who had the funds, was entirely possible without government permission: China was still an open society.

Four of us – Burdsall, Emmons, Young, and I – were increasingly drawn together by similar views of our new situation. We joined with Dr. Akl in declining to proceed into the interior of China without official Chinese Government permission; but unlike Dr. Akl and Thorne, his medical student, we had no compelling professional reasons to return immediately to the States. Indeed, a letter just received from home from an old and close family friend of one of our group said: "We're all having the worst 'hard times' in human memory. Nobody has any money left to spare; your Dad and Mother are really hard up but hate to admit it, and there are no jobs for you to find even if you do come home now. If what you write is true, that living expenses for you at this time in China are only a quarter of what they were here when you left, you and your parents are probably better off for you to stay in China for awhile, especially if you have something worthwhile you can do there."

Meanwhile Burdsall, Emmons, and I, urged by Jack Young, had become students at the North China Union Language School. During every bit of our spare time in Peking we were engaged in intensive drill in conversational Mandarin Chinese: *Kwan Hua,* literally translated, "official talk." Written Chinese, the classic ideographic characters, requires about five years to learn; this we were not attempting at all. But conversational Mandarin, the most widely used of the Chinese dialects, and by chance also the one used along the far western Tibetan border region, is no more than perhaps twice as difficult to learn as, say, conversational Spanish. Three to six months, depending upon the intensity of effort, can produce worthwhile results. Jack Young himself, to whom the Chinese languages were mother tongues, helped us with the special vocabulary that would be useful to the sort of expedition of our own that was beginning to shape in our minds.

Before long the inevitable day arrived: Gene Lamb advised us of his definite decision to proceed with Mrs. Lamb, Major Logan, and the Explorers Club flag into the interior —despite lack of official Chinese Government permission— and again invited the six of us to accompany him. But, as expected, Dr. Akl and Thorne formally declined. They felt that official Government recognition of the medical program they had been planning among the natives of the Chinese-Tibetan border ranges was essential for them professionally; otherwise they must return to the States without further delay. The remaining four of us (Burdsall, Emmons, Young, and I) thereupon also declined: we sadly gave Dr. Akl and Thorne a final farewell dinner before they departed. Now entirely on our own in Peking, we resumed the study of Mandarin.

By the early summer of 1932 several months of peace had greatly changed our situation with the Chinese Government; more normal conditions began to prevail at the administrative capital in Nanking. The four of us decided to seek official permission for an expedition of our own. In preparing our petition we confined ourselves to much more limited objectives than had been sought of the Chinese Government by the Lamb Expedition in its approach six months earlier. In effect, we gave up the quest for the highest mountain in the world. We entered a simple application for permission (1) to journey to Minya Konka to determine its height; (2) to climb it, if possible; (3) to collect any previously unknown flora and fauna we might encounter and present the first or only specimens to the Academia Sinica, the Chinese National Academy of Sciences in Nanking.

Why had we changed our objective to Minya Konka? Our youthful romantic interest in discovering the world's highest mountain still continued, of course. We were eager young people in our early twenties, excepting Dick Burdsall, who was 36 but just as keen. We changed to Minya Konka because in the light of more recent information we had become persuaded that its summit would prove to be higher than Amne Machin's, though both still remained unsurveyed. We had learned much from our conversations with scientists at the Academia Sinica, who told us about a 1930 visit to Minya Konka by a Swiss party from the Sun Yat Sen University of Canton. And from knowledgeable individuals in the China Inland Mission at Shanghai we learned that the Mission supported a small western-style university near Chengtu in Szechuan province, where later we would locate the geologist originally mentioned in the Roosevelt brothers' book.

I was delegated to represent our new four-man expedition to the U.S. Minister at the American Legation. Thus, in May 1932, I found myself facing the Honorable Nelson T. Johnson in his legation office in Nanking. He had some sharp questions to ask me before he would present our petition to the Chinese Foreign Ministry. But his action on our behalf would be essential because no foreign ministry of any country would (at least in those years) entertain an outside citizen's petition unless sponsored by that citizen's own embassy or legation.

"Purpose?" asked Mr. Johnson. "We understand your real objective is Mount Everest; but for such a destination in western Tibet the American Legation here in China does not have authority to help anyone." This question was easy. I replied: "The original ultimate objective of the Lamb Expedition was indeed to be Mount Everest *if* the Amne Machin range, for which its specific application was made, proved to be lower than Everest's 29,000 feet. But Burdsall, Emmons, Young, and I will be glad to give you a commitment, if you wish, that under *no* circumstances will we attempt to journey west beyond Minya Konka toward Mount Everest." To my surprise, a written guarantee to this effect really would be necessary; but this guarantee would in no way curtail our revised plan for Minya Konka only, with its three limited objectives described on the paper he now held in his hand.

"Finances? Are you sure they are adequate? Organization? Are you actually planning to set forth without a designated leader, as we hear?" Exactly what I replied to these questions is lost in the memory of how events actually happened. But I have a distinct recollection of his discontent with the shoestring financing from our pocketbooks; and also with the fact that we were but an informal partnership of four, the managing partner for a particular purpose being chosen by action of the other three as occasion arose.

At this point we selected the name Sikong Expedition. In 1932 practically none of those with whom we were dealing had ever heard of Minya Konka ("what's that?"); but all were familiar with Sikong, the Chinese Government's new name for its province in the far southwest where our mountain was located.

At last, great day! Jack Young and I (Burdsall and Emmons being still in Peking) were invited to have tea with His Excellency Dr. Lo Wen-kan, China's Minister of Foreign Affairs, at his office in Nanking to receive our long-sought official travel documents. In today's current phrase I could say: "Happiness is an official permission from the Chinese Government to travel across China at will to the Tibetan border and up onto the plateau, taking pictures freely and talking to the inhabitants in Mandarin Chinese." And so, the following month we set forth.

FOREWORD

TIBET, the forbidding and forbidden, the land of vast sweeping plateaus and giant ranges crowned with eternal snow, the land of a strange and colorful people, has a lure that cannot be denied. From the time of Marco Polo it has drawn men of the Western Hemisphere to probe its mysteries.

Yet to this day Tibet remains one of the last strongholds of the Unknown, a haven of refuge for those restless souls to whom the horizon is always beckoning. The Poles and deepest Africa, the jungles and ranges of South America, have all felt the tread of explorers' feet or heard the throbbing roar of their motors overhead. And for Tibet the years of seclusion are numbered. Expedition after expedition is penetrating its borders, filling, little by little, the blank spaces on its maps, scaling its peaks, and tightening the grip of the Known about the Unknown.

We of the Sikong Expedition feel it a privilege to have been able to add in a small way something to the world's knowledge of this austere yet fascinating country. We hope that we may have contributed to a more sympathetic understanding of the beauty of the Far-Eastern lands and the integrity of their peoples.

When this book was first contemplated we planned to write it in four parts. Burdsall was to describe the journey to the mountain and the surveying work, Emmons the reconnaissance, Moore the climbing operations, and Young the big-game collecting. Work for a Ph.D. degree prevented Moore from assuming the rôle of author, so Emmons has added this section to his own, using an account by Moore for one chapter. Because the subject of Young's narrative was not so closely connected with the main story, it appears as an appendix. To many, however, this may be the most interesting section of the book.

That the Sikong Expedition was able to carry out its program is due in no small part to the kindness and help rendered by its many friends both in this country and abroad.

We wish to thank Dr. Isaiah Bowman, director of the American Geographical Society of New York, and members of his staff, especially Mr. O. M. Miller, for assistance both before our departure and after our return; also for the loan of instruments. Two maps and part of the text of Appendix B appeared in *The Geographical Review*.

Dr. William S. Ladd, at that time President of the American Alpine Club, and the late Allen Carpe showed a keen and helpful interest in the mountaineering affairs of the expedition and gave us much good counsel.

Col. Theodore Roosevelt, then Governor-General of the Philippine Islands, showed great interest in our project and did all in his power to smooth the way for the expedition.

To Hon. Nelson T. Johnson, Minister, Willis R.

Peck, Consul-General at Nanking, and other representatives of the United States Government, we are indebted for presenting our plans to the Chinese Government and obtaining the necessary permission for our work.

We wish to convey our very sincere appreciation to the representatives of the Government of China who were instrumental in procuring for us passports and permission to carry on the work of the expedition in China and eastern Tibet, among whom were His Excellency Dr. Lo Wen-Kan, Minister of Foreign Affairs, and Mr. Chu Shih-Chien of the Department of European and American Affairs. Dr. Y. P. Tsai, President of the Academia Sinica, and Dr. T. H. Chien, Director of the Metropolitan Museum in Nanking, did all they could to aid us.

The kindness and helpfulness of the missionaries whom we met along the way will be evident. They and other friends of the expedition, whom space does not permit us to mention here, must know of our appreciation.

Finally we record here our regret that Lewis Thorne, originally a member of the expedition, had to return to America and could not take part in the field work. His thought, energy, and enthusiasm had gone with ours into the plans and preparations, and although we parted before the expedition left for the interior, we feel that he had a real share in our undertaking and that he was one of us.

R. L. B.
A. B. E.

Part One

By

RICHARD L. BURDSALL

"I am a part of all that I have met;
Yet all experience is an arch wherethro'
Gleams that untravell'd world whose margin fades
For ever and for ever when I move."

—TENNYSON

Chapter I

PLANS

A SULTRY June evening at Shanghai found the Sikong Expedition assembled around one of the two tables in the little dining-salon of the Yangtze River motor-vessel *Ichang*.

There were four of us—Arthur B. Emmons, 3rd, Terris Moore, Jack Theodore Young, and myself. Emmons and I were leaving at once for the interior, so this was a farewell dinner and there was much discussion afterward, for our next meeting was to be a long time hence and far away among the little-known mountains of the Chinese-Tibetan borderland.

There, between the great red basin of Szechwan and the high Tibetan grasslands, stands a range of gigantic, snow-clad mountains whose highest peak is Minya Konka.* This was our "promised land" and we had read and studied everything we could find about it.

Minya Konka stands about thirty miles south of Tatsienlu, at some distance from the main routes of travel, which lie for the most part in deep valleys and afford a view of the mountain only when they climb up to cross a pass. Then, in clear weather, the traveler beholds a prospect of surpassing grandeur.[1] More

---

* Pronounced somewhere between Gongka and Gungka.
[1] These numbers refer to photographs.

often clouds intervene, and these veils of mist have no doubt contributed to the fascinating mystery which has surrounded Minya Konka until recent years. The first scientific observation of the mountain was made in 1879 by the expedition of Count Bela Szechenyi. He referred to it as Bo Kunka, and on the basis of a long sight taken from Dsongo or Yin Kwan Chai, thirty-five miles to the northwest, he reported its altitude to be 7,600 meters (24,936 feet). Though this information raised somewhat the veil of mystery, it did not prevent it from descending again, and we found recent maps of the region omitting the mountain entirely, or showing it in the wrong location with no altitude given. Although Minya Konka was seen many times by missionaries and was reported by other travelers, exactly half a century passed by before a white man actually went to its base. This journey was made in 1929 by Joseph Rock, who visited the Tibetan monastery at the foot of the mountain and brought back some magnificent photographs.* The altitude of the mountain based upon his observations was computed to be 25,600 feet. In 1926 some members of the staff of the West China Union University in Chengtu had attempted a measurement of the mountain from a little distance, but their result was never published.

Even as late as 1930 there was so much speculation as to its altitude that on the map in their book, *Trailing the Giant Panda,* Theodore and Kermit Roosevelt gave expression to it by the stimulating figure of 30,000

* "The Glories of the Minya Konka," *National Geographic Magazine,* vol. 58, 1930, p. 385.

feet, followed by a question mark. Herbert Stevens of their expedition published some striking sketches of the peak. In 1930 an expedition from Sun Yat Sen University in Canton, led by Dr. Arnold Heim, made a geological study of the region and a survey was carried out by Professor Imhof. Bad weather interfered with the work, but in his splendid book *Minya Gongkar*, which appeared in 1933, Heim gives the altitude determined by this survey as 7,700 meters (25,262 feet), stating, however, that this figure is subject to revision.

In 1931 Brooke Dolan and Gordon Bowles spent several months in the region, the former as leader of a zoölogical expedition, the latter as an ethnologist. We had met them upon our arrival in Shanghai, and later, in Peiping, Bowles had given us much valuable information and had told us of his visit to the Tibetan lamasery at the base of Minya Konka. The more we learned the higher rose our enthusiasm to know this mountain at first hand, to measure its altitude, to explore its glaciers, and if possible to reach its lofty summit. There would also be an opportunity for some collecting, and whatever we could bring back from this remote region promised to be of interest.

These, then, were the three objectives of the Sikong Expedition of 1932: first, to make an accurate measurement of the altitude of Minya Konka and its neighboring peaks; second, to reconnoiter the mountain for a climbing route and make its first ascent if possible; third, to obtain small collections of the plant and animal life of the region, with special attention to birds and big game.

Each of us could contribute from our past experience certain qualifications for carrying out this program. Emmons was an engineering student at Harvard, who had climbed in the Dolomites and Alps, in the Cascades, the Canadian Rockies, and in Alaska. His record included a first ascent of the northeast face of Mount Hood. Moore was a student at the Harvard School of Business Administration. His mountaineering record included, in Ecuador, the first ascent of Sangay and the second ascent of Chimborazo; in Alaska, the first ascent of Mount Bona and the first ascent of Mount Fairweather. Jack Young was a student of journalism at New York University. His family is from Canton, but he was born in Hawaii. He had been with the Roosevelts on their expedition after the Giant Panda and was to have charge of our big-game collecting. I was a mechanical engineer, a graduate of Swarthmore College, and had climbed in the Alps and in the Rockies. As an amateur ornithologist I was prepared to collect birds.

The surveying was to be done by Emmons and myself. Before leaving America we had talked with Dr. Isaiah Bowman, director of the American Geographical Society in New York, and had received some intensive instruction in the latest methods of carrying out such work from Mr. O. M. Miller of the staff of the society.

We had no leader. At first thought this might appear a weakness, but with our small and congenial group we found it a decided advantage. We were keen to accomplish all that we had set out to do, and with such a limited personnel this required that each give of his best at all times. In some instances decisions had to be made by the one or two who happened to be on hand, and were later ratified by the others. Important matters, however, were decided only after full discussion, with due consideration for the specialized knowledge of each member.

The last few weeks had been busy ones, but much still remained to be done. However, the summer rains were due to begin in the vicinity of Tatsienlu about the middle of August, and our survey must be completed before then. It was, therefore, decided that Emmons and I should start at once, leaving the others to make some final arrangements and procure additional items of equipment. Our little vessel would carry us for fifteen hundred miles up the Yangtze to Chungking. From there we would continue, perhaps directly overland, perhaps by boat for part of the way; this could be decided best after our arrival at Chungking. By one means or another we would go on westward across the great red basin of Szechwan to Yachow, then over the mountain passes to Tatsienlu, and southward to our mountain. About two months hence, if all went well, we would meet again somewhere in that far-off region.

It was late and the time for parting had come. We saw Moore and Young ashore, and returned to our stateroom, jammed with trunks, boxes, and instruments, appreciating the willingness of our companions to remain in Shanghai and finish the preparations necessary for our later plans.

Chapter II

UP THE GREAT RIVER

A T 4:10 the next morning, June 16th, I was awakened by the sounds the *Ichang* made as she cast off, and went on deck to watch our small vessel start down the Whangpoo, past the sampans, lighters, junks, steamers, and warships which crowd the waterway of the greatest port in the Far East. A Japanese gunboat flashed her searchlights on us as we passed, a reminder of the bitter fighting we had witnessed at Shanghai four months earlier. I turned in again, and when we arose for breakfast we had rounded the point at Woosung, with its battered forts, and were in the broad muddy Yangtze, headed westward toward our distant goal.

This lower reach of the river, which resembles an arm of the sea, is the only portion known to the Chinese as the Yangtze Kiang (Djiang). This means "Son of Yang River," Yang being an ancient province whose name is perpetuated by the city of Yangchow. Different names have been given to sections of the river in its length of over three thousand miles. Where it enters China proper from Tibet, for example, it is called the Kinsha Kiang or "River of Golden Sand"; but the Chinese name for the river as a whole is the Ta Kiang or "Great River." It well deserves the name, for half

8

of the commerce of China is collected and distributed by this waterway.

The next morning we passed Nanking, the capital of China now, as it was in the days of the Ming emperors.* We had all visited Nanking by rail ten days before, and had been graciously entertained at a dinner given by Dr. T. H. Chien, director of the Metropolitan Museum of the Academia Sinica. We had been in China just long enough to become somewhat proud of our proficiency in the use of chopsticks, and had done ample justice to the bamboo shoots, lotus root, roast duck, bean sprouts, soup, mandarin fish, sweetened rice, and the long series of other delicious dishes provided by our host.

Scientific expeditions in China must apply to the Government for permission to carry on their work. We had done this through the good offices of the American Legation, and the necessary permits had been promptly granted. As a token of its interest and coöperation the Academia Sinica had supplied us with some of our collecting equipment. Under our agreement it was to receive one specimen of each species collected.

At Nanking the *Ichang* took on two passengers, making eleven in all. The trip up the Yangtze to Chungking is quite popular with tourists, the chief attraction being the famous gorges above Ichang. Then there is the novelty offered by travel in an armored vessel. For all of these boats are protected against the pot shots which they sometimes draw from the banks. Disbanded soldiers

*The name Nanking means "Southern Capital," just as Peking meant "Northern Capital."

and "bandits" are said to take great delight in this amusement. As in the case of other sports, mercenary motives may creep in, for the boats sometimes carry large shipments of silver dollars, which would make a handsome prize. The ship's bridge, which is regarded as the "bull's-eye," is provided with steel plates which can be lowered over the windows, and there are other plates along the rail for passengers to stand behind in case of firing. On our trip, however, we did not have occasion to try them. At Kukiang we saw three gunboats, one of which flew the flag of Chiang Kai-Shek, China's commander-in-chief, who was holding a conference there on bandit suppression.

The banks were low and we saw coolies building dikes, designed to prevent the rising river from repeating the disastrous floods which had occurred the year before. These had brought death to tens of thousands of people; yet the Yangtze is not as destructive as is the Yellow River, "China's Sorrow." The dikes there are but a temporary cure, for they result in the river slowly building up its bed above the level of the country through which it flows. Finally a break occurs, bringing disaster and the formation of a new channel.

We saw many fishermen along the banks. Each sat under a little shelter to protect him from the sun, and at intervals pulled down on a rope which, by means of a bamboo frame lever, raised an enormous dip net, occasionally with a catch of fish.

On the third morning we reached Hankow with its sister cities, Hanyang and Wuchang. It has been called the "Chicago of China" and marks the head of navigation for ocean steamers. Above this point we found the river about half a mile wide and muddier than ever, with a strong current which we avoided as much as possible by keeping near one shore or the other. The course of the river was very crooked and that evening we sat on deck watching the sun set over our stern, though we were supposed to be traveling westward!

We were now passing what our Captain Miclo called the "Soviet Republic of Western Hupeh," and next morning saw some large signs on the north bank. One of the Chinese passengers, a young man who was traveling for the China Christian Council, translated them for us: "We oppose the partition of China by foreign imperialists." Another read: "Down with the Kuomintang, which has surrendered to the foreign imperialists. Join the red army and divide the land."

It was land well worth owning—beautiful farming country in which the chief crop appeared to be maize. This was introduced from America and is now an important grain crop in China, ranking next to rice and wheat. We saw a few soldiers at most of the towns. They wore the customary gray uniform, but very few carried guns. Junks were not so numerous as on the lower river.

Late on the fifth day we reached Ichang, where we dropped anchor, for the difficulties of navigation prevent night-running above this point. We seized the opportunity to go ashore. Though the waterfront was dark, we found the little stores on the main street open, some of them lighted by electricity. It was very hot and from the ceilings of some shops hung punkas, or big fans, swung back and forth by boys pulling on cords. A specialty at Ichang is the manufacture of model junks, samples of which we purchased on our return journey. The city used to have great importance as a trans-shipping point for the upper river, but now many boats run clear through, except in winter, when the water is so low that only very small vessels can reach Chungking. This city is about four hundred miles above Ichang, and the climb is over four hundred feet.

We were off at five the next morning. The two sampans which we carried as lifeboats were swung out on the davits and we soon entered the Ichang Gorge amid swirling mists. This is twelve miles long, with sides a thousand feet high, rising steeply and in some places precipitously from the dark river, which narrows abruptly at some points to a width of but two hundred yards. The muffled sound of the exhaust from our laboring engines reverberated from cliff to cliff.

On the north bank near the entrance stands a monument erected to the memory of Captain Plant, who took the first commercial steamer to Chungking in 1900. It was a side-wheeler, appropriately named the *Pioneer*. Others followed, for though wrecks were frequent, profits were great, and a few trips paid for a boat. Steamers have put most of the junks out of business. One still sees many of them, however, and we observed the tremendous labor involved in getting them upstream. They are smaller than the lower-river junks and have only one sail, which is hoisted to take advantage of every favorable puff of wind.[2] This is not of much help

in going up the river, however, and they have to be
towed practically all the way by trackers.

Each junk has a long towrope, woven of split bamboo,
at the end of which we saw gangs of coolies straining
in their harness, naked except for wide straw hats. In
places the towpath is a groove cut in the solid rock,
high above the water; in others it clambers among huge
boulders on the shore and great care has to be taken
to keep the rope from catching. We saw one junk get
out of control, turning sideways to the current, so that
the trackers had to let go the rope. Fortunately, the men
on board were able to row it in to a rocky point and
hold it there until the rope could be retrieved. The
wash from steamers adds to the difficulties of the
heavily-laden junks. Usually they reduce speed in passing, but when running rapids this is not safe, for they
must maintain steerageway at all costs.

That afternoon we passed through the twenty-mile
Wushan Gorge anchoring at its head for the night,[3] and
early the next morning went through the Windbox
Gorge, only four miles long but very precipitous. The
grandeur of these gorges has often been described, and
some idea of it may be had from photographs. One
feature, however, which these cannot show is the rush
and swirl of the imprisoned river. All of the water
poured into the Yangtze by its great upper tributaries
must pass through the narrow confines of these gorges.
Hence it piles up to great depths. In places scales of
feet have been painted on the cliffs, the zero mark
being placed at the low, or winter, level of the river. At
the head of the Wushan Gorge we noted the water lap-

ping the 105-foot mark, and it is said at times to pile up over two hundred feet above the winter level.

It has been pointed out that the rise of the Yangtze is caused by heavy rains in its upper basin, not by the melting of snow in Tibet. In fact there is little snow to melt, for the winter precipitation in eastern Tibet is very light.

As the river rises, some rapids are covered and smoothed out, but others appear, so that each level presents its own difficulties. All ships carry native pilots who have learned the river from years of experience on junks.

There is tense excitement in fighting up a rapid slowly, foot by foot, amid the wild roar of the rushing water. Sometimes boats must put a cable ashore and work their way up by its help. It has taken as much as two and a half hours to heave a ship a distance of seventy feet in this way. Our engines proved just powerful enough to get us up all of the rapids without recourse to a "wire," but sometimes the issue appeared doubtful.

It is in going downstream that most wrecks occur. In order to maintain adequate steerageway through the rapids the boats have to keep their engines going full speed ahead, and the resulting speed through the water, added to the velocity of the current, carries them along like express trains. In spite of the great skill of the pilots the river sometimes gets the upper hand. We passed by, or over, the spot where our sister ship had sunk a short time before, with a loss of twenty lives. She was going downstream, struck a rock, and sank in two minutes in deep water so that no trace of her could be seen. Below Chungking we saw the funnel, mast, and bridge roof of the *Wan Loo*, sticking up in midstream. She had been wrecked about a month before, without loss of life. Another boat going to her assistance had attracted bullets from the shore, but it was afterward explained that this firing had taken place by mistake!

Work is being done to lessen the dangers of navigation on the Yangtze and an important improvement has been made since our return. Thirty-three miles west of Ichang, at the rapid known as K'ung Ling T'an, the river is divided into a north and a south channel by a great rock called Ta Chu. The north channel was dangerous and the south channel impossible at low water because of two rocks which projected from its center. After a careful survey and an investigation to make sure that the walls of the gorge would not be brought down by the explosion, it was decided to remove these two rocks by mass blasting. The drilling was done during the winter of 1932, the workmen living in huts on Ta Chu. A bridge of sampans was constructed in the seven-knot current and concrete "ships" erected to protect the mine shafts. On March 22nd, the local inhabitants having been removed to a distance of two miles, the charges, consisting of more than eight tons of high explosive, were fired simultaneously. Ten thousand tons of rock were scattered completely, some of the pieces flying over half a mile. In spite of the great difficulties under which the work was carried out, not a man was injured. The result was a channel two hundred feet wide, with a minimum depth of eighteen feet at low water, truly a fine piece of engineering.*

Even in the gorges people were succeeding in their struggle to make a living. In the Wushan Gorge little coal-mines were being worked. Wherever the banks were not precipitous, cultivation was in evidence far up their sides. Some patches of maize were no larger than a card-table, and it looked as though a single false step would send the farmer hurtling to the river hundreds of feet below. Other people were farming land right down to the water's edge, but theirs was also a hazardous business, for there was every possibility that before the crop could mature it would be covered and swept away by the rising river.

At several places we saw lone fishermen standing on rocky points, tiny figures amid stupendous surroundings. They were using hand dip nets, thrusting them into the water upstream, bringing them down with the current, and lifting them out, over and over again, always empty.

Our first stop above the gorges was at Wanhsien, which is one of the two treaty ports of Szechwan, Chungking being the other. Customs officials came on board, but did not trouble us. Six hours after leaving Wanhsien we passed Fengchow, "the capital of the dead," where we were told the head of one of Buddha's disciples is preserved. The next evening at dusk we reached Chungking, nine days and sixteen hours after leaving Shanghai, a record for the run.

* See "Mass Blasting on the Upper Yangtze," by H. R. Dixon, M.C., B.S.C., *The China Journal,* May, 1933, vol. xviii, p. 281.

Chungking with a population of over 600,000 is the largest city in western China.[4] It has an imposing location on the north bank of the Yangtze, spreading over a high bluff at the junction of the Kialing, or "Little River," as it is called locally. In the upper part of the city there were rickshas and even a few automobiles, but in the lower part sedan chairs have to be used instead, as the streets are narrow and ascend in steps. We found them crowded with all sorts of traffic—chairs, pedestrians, and coolies carrying water or other loads; we saw men driving pigs along the street, and a couple of coolies carrying a squealing hog slung on a pole between them. The shops offer a great variety of wares, notably silks, for which the province of Szechwan is noted.

The sedan chairs are supported between two bamboo poles which are carried on the shoulders of the bearers, one in front and one behind. I well remember one of my first rides on such a conveyance. It was at night and ended with the descent of a long, dark flight of wet, stone steps. Looking down over the shoulders of my leading bearer, I could not see the bottom, but knew they went down to the river.

The Yangtze at Chungking, fifteen hundred miles from the sea, is still a mighty river with a strong current. When we took our first trip across it in a sampan, our boatmen made use of a long bamboo pole with an iron hook in its end. With this they clawed their way upstream by hooking into the sides of the junks moored along the shore. Then they launched out, rowing with all their might, and after reaching the other side at a point far below, poled upstream to our destination.

We arranged to stay on board the *Ichang* while preparing for the next stage of our journey. On the second morning we were awakened by the steward, who told us that there was an American to see us. It proved to be Floyd Tangier Smith, who, with a corps of thirteen Chinese assistants scattered over the country, was engaged in collecting vertebrates for the Field Museum of Chicago. He was sending one of his assistants back to Shanghai on the *Ichang*, with some live specimens, including pheasants, doves, owls, and two baby wildcats. As his work now called him to Chengtu, we were glad to join forces with him, and engaged deck passage on a little Chinese steamer for Kiating (Jäding).

As the *Ichang* was due to leave for Shanghai very early on the morning of our last day at Chungking, we moved to the Chinese hotel where Smith was staying. A game of mah jong was in full swing most of the night, and the sound of tiles on the hard table, resounding through all of the rooms, was not conducive to rest. Next day we got our baggage onto the little Chinese steamer *Yuen Tung* and, after having tea at the Canadian Mission, went on board for the night. The four tiny staterooms had already been engaged, so we made use of some of the open wooden bunks which had been temporarily erected in tiers on the after deck. Smith said he usually found deck passage on these boats preferable to a stateroom.

We left early next morning in the rain. Szechwan has so much rainy and cloudy weather that the province bordering it on the south is named Yunnan, which means "South of the Clouds."

On the *Yuen Tung* every foot of deck space not occupied by the bunks was covered with baggage, cots, and mats, with people lying upon them. There were about thirty passengers, all Chinese except our party. One attractive family consisted of a man and wife with two little boys, aged about two months and two years, respectively. It was interesting to watch them feed the latter by means of chopsticks; also to watch a slightly older boy deftly using his own sticks in a manner we could never hope to equal.

The meals served on the boat were one degree better than coolie food. The rice and tea were good, but the few vegetables were so highly seasoned with pepper that they tasted more like fire than anything else. When we stopped at night, however, we were able to supplement them with purchases, from the shore, of oranges, eggs, chickens, and rice cakes. These were bought for us by Smith's boy, Pem.

Pem was an individual of remarkable appearance. He was of short and stocky build, with a broad face and very large mouth. Viewed in profile, his head was the shape of a triangle, flat on top, with a line sloping straight from the back of his crown to his chin. The calf of his right leg was much larger than that of the left. This was probably due to using it in lifting his load up steps, one at a time, while engaged in his former occupation as a chair coolie in Chungking. Though he could speak no English, he was a perfect servant, anticipating most of our needs. His keenness and quickness to learn were remarkable, considering his origin. He had become proficient in the preparation of specimens, and could write just well enough to keep track of the number of coppers which he spent for different items.

We were now beyond the territory of paper money and had to carry the large silver Mexican dollars. Their name is derived from the fact that the first ones used were introduced from Mexico. They are now coined in China. Only certain varieties of them were acceptable in Szechwan, and of these there were many counterfeits. With the silver dollars you buy coppers, from seventy-five to ninety for a dollar, the rate and variety changing from place to place. Each copper is worth two hundred cash, the cash being the old coin with the square hole in it. These used to be carried on strings, but are not often seen now. Bargaining, however, is still done in terms of cash, and the prices therefore sound high. When you pay a chair coolie or a ricksha boy three or four thousand cash it seems like a lot of money, but was then equivalent to about four American cents.

When we stopped at a city, soldiers came on board as customs officers, but our papers exempted us from paying duty. They were soldiers belonging to Liu Hsiang, the military governor at Chungking, and were making sure that no arms or munitions could reach his uncle, Liu Wen Whei, at Chengtu, who was at that time the governor of Szechwan. Open hostilities were expected to break out between them at any moment. The soldiers always admired Emmons' rifle and often took it ashore to show to their officers, Pem going along with them to bring it back.

Fighting the swift current from dawn till dark and

anchoring each night, four days were required to cover the two hundred miles to Suifu, which we reached on the 4th of July. Smith and I paid a visit to Dr. and Mrs. Thompson of the American Baptist Mission, which has a fine hospital here. Upon our return to the ship we found that all of the wooden tiers of bunks had been removed, ostensibly to save weight and reduce our draught, though the change could hardly have been appreciable. The deck was now more crowded than ever, but we managed to get space enough for our folding-cots.

Leaving Suifu, we turned northward up the Min or "Clear River," which is navigable by steamers only at high water. It is, however, of greater commercial importance than the Yangtze beyond Suifu and is regarded by the Chinese as the main river. The Min can be ascended by junks for two hundred and sixty miles to Chengtu, whereas the Yangtze is navigable only as far as Pingshan, forty miles above Suifu.

The current in the Min River was very swift, and sometimes our little steamer would be held motionless, or even forced backward, until we moved over to a more favorable part of the channel. Cross currents below the surface often seized the keel and tipped our vessel suddenly to one side or the other in an alarming manner. When passing over shoals, a man in the bow took soundings with a painted bamboo pole. He was skillful in this operation, turning the pole over and over, sounding first with one end and then with the other. Speed was important, and this was much quicker than the usual method of sounding with a lead and line. In some places there was little water to spare and twice we scraped bottom.

One afternoon we tied up at the bank in the open country. Asking the reason for the delay, we were told that the engineer had gone ashore to buy some coal. Coaling ship is usually associated with the thought of a port, and seemed quite novel in our rural surroundings. The country we were passing through was fresh and green, brightened by patches of red soil and brilliant red cliffs. Some thirty miles away to the west were the blue hills on the outskirts of "Lolo Land."

The Lolos are a great aboriginal tribe which has never been conquered by the Chinese. The men are tall, many of them over six feet, with high cheek bones. They permit only a few Chinese traders to enter their domain.

We saw beautiful bamboo trees, growing in clusters like tufts of gigantic grass; in fact, that is what bamboo really is. It is difficult to imagine what China would do without this, her most useful tree. It furnishes food in the form of delicious young shoots, and chopsticks with which to eat them, ropes, rafts, ladders, irrigation pipes, carrying-poles, paper, ornamental carvings, and a thousand other articles.

There were many white egrets and a few large gray herons. The three-syllable whistle of a cuckoo sounded from the shore. Great spotted kingfishers and beautiful golden-rumped swallows were seen, and the black-eared kite, the common hawk of the Far East, was numerous all the way up the river. In the vicinity of Chungking a pretty little white tern was in evidence.

In many places on our journey up the river we saw figures of the Buddha of various sizes, cut in niches in the rock. The large gilded one on the south shore just below Chungking is famous. Several monasteries were also seen, groups of white buildings in picturesque locations, and many pagodas on commanding sites. The pagoda was introduced with Buddhism from India and stands out as a characteristic and attractive feature of the Chinese landscape. At first they were built as repositories for religious relics or images. Those erected at a later period, during the Ming and Manchu Dynasties, which are the pagodas seen today, were often partly Taoist, built "to ward off the evil influences of wind and water."*

On the seventh day after leaving Chungking we arrived at Kiating. Just below the city, on the east side of the river, we passed some high cliffs in one of which is carved a gigantic, seated figure of the Buddha, the largest in China.[5] It extends the full height of the cliff. The left arm and hand were almost covered by vegetation, but the right hand was conspicuous, resting upon the right knee, with its long fingers pointing downward. Rev. L. A. Lovegren of the American Baptist Mission in Kiating has recently made some measurements of the figure and found it to be 196 feet high from bottom of toe to top of head. The nose, measured from the center line of the eye pupils is eight feet long, and the length of the middle finger of the right hand, from the top of the knuckle, is thirty-seven feet. The colossus is said to have been made about 700 A.D. and

* *The Pilgrimage of Buddhism,* by James B. Pratt, p. 315.

has been gazing across the river toward Mount Omei with the same benign expression for the past twelve hundred years.

Mount Omei stands about twenty-five miles west of Kiating. Its altitude is usually given as 11,000 feet. It is one of the three most sacred mountains of Chinese Buddhists and its temples are visited by many pilgrims. We were told that a phenomenon similar to the so-called "Specter of the Brocken" occurs there, known as "Buddha's Glory." In looking from the summit down the precipitous eastern face, under certain conditions, one's shadow is projected upon the mists below. In times past, pilgrims, seeing their magnified shadow, have believed it to be the Buddha himself and have cast themselves over the cliff into his arms! In summer many of the foreign missionaries of Szechwan take refuge at Omei from the oppressive heat of the plain.

Kiating is located on a point formed by the junction of the Min River flowing down from the north and the Tung which comes rushing in from the west. The Ya River joins the Tung about half a mile from its mouth, so Kiating is practically at the confluence of three streams. I shall never forget the spectacle presented by a dozen coolies on the boulder-strewn shore of the Tung opposite the city, harnessed to a bamboo rope towing a junk against the current. At first it looked as if they were creeping on hands and knees, but closer inspection showed that only their feet touched the ground. They were leaning forward in their harness until their heads were close to the stones, exerting all their strength and progressing inch by inch.

We spent two days with Rev. L. A. Lovegren, re-packing all of our equipment and weighing it off on a Chinese beam scale in loads of the proper size. We then sent it by thirteen porters with a small military escort for a three-day journey by road to Yachow (Yäjo), where we would pick it up after attending to some affairs at Chengtu. Emmons and I regretted that we could not visit sacred Mount Omei, but time was pressing and the next morning we left with Smith and the faithful Pem by bus for the capital city.

Chapter III

THE RED BASIN AND THE TEA ROAD

NO TIME-TABLE is required for bus travel in Szechwan. The only rule is an early start, soon after six o'clock. There are several cars, and each departs as soon as there are enough passengers to fill it. As the later busses are apt to be delayed by breakdowns of those preceding, everybody wants to get into the first one. If the morning is rainy the cars are late in leaving because the passengers do not arrive so early, and in case of heavy rains the roads will not permit them to run at all.

We had spent the last night at an inn on the outskirts of town near the bus terminus, in order to be on hand early, and were able to get good seats, well forward in the first bus. However, when nearly all of the passengers were in, it was decided to abandon this bus and use another. Of course this resulted in our being left with the roughest seats, directly over the rear wheels.

The bus was a little Chevrolet on which a big wooden body had been placed, with bare seats running all the way across. Twenty-one passengers with their baggage crowded into it, but in spite of this load some soldiers along the road held us up so that they could ride on the running-boards. Our driver stopped frequently at little streams to refill the leaky radiator. Remarking on the narrowness of the bridges, which were barely wide enough to accommodate the wheels of the bus, we were told that originally they had been wider, but that the farmers had considered this a great waste of material and had sawed off the ends of the boards for firewood.

The day was clear and, looking back, we could see Mount Omei with the great precipices on its eastern face. We were in the heart of Szechwan, the largest province of China, a great inland empire with a population of fifty-five million people. The name means "Four Rivers" and refers to the Min, To, Fu, and Kialing, all of which drain into the Yangtze. There is a "Big North Road" overland from Peiping, and a "Little North Road" from Wanhsien, but, practically speaking, the only outlet for the products of the rich province of Szechwan is down through the gorges of the Yangtze.

We saw fields of corn and sugar cane, but most of the land was in rice, and the white cattle-egrets and pond herons showed beautifully against the green paddy.

What a rough road it was! Our chief concern was for the delicate barometer which had been loaned to us by the American Geographical Society. It looked substantial enough in its leather case, and most people took it for some kind of gun; but it contained a glass tube over thirty inches long, filled with mercury. I had to hold it vertically in my hands so that it would be eased gently over the little jolts and yet not strike the floor or roof when we hit a big bump. It was not a light instrument when we started, but easily doubled in weight during the day! With a sigh of relief I descended with it unbroken at Chengtu, late in the afternoon.

Chengtu, the capital of Szechwan, is a fine city of 400,000, which reminded us somewhat of Peiping. Marco Polo described it under the name "Sindafu." We spent the night at the West China Union University, built and supported by five denominations engaged in missionary work. It has a large campus and a group of fine buildings of Chinese architecture. We met Dr. Beach, the chancellor, Mr. Small and a few other members of the staff, but the university was not in session and most of the faculty were away. Smith found a flock of blue eared-pheasants which had been secured for him and decided to return with them next day by boat to Kiating.

Up to this time, thanks to our English-speaking friends, we had not come really face to face with the language problem. Fortunately for us, the speech of Szechwan, though it has many words and expressions of its own, is very similar to the Mandarin spoken in Peiping and northern China. We had studied this, but realized that we did not know it well enough to undertake the trip to Tatsienlu without an interpreter, so engaged an English-speaking student from the university for this purpose. Yang proved a pleasant traveling companion and by his explanations added much to the interest of our trip.

We planned to leave Chengtu the next morning, July 13th, and Yang agreed to meet us at the bus terminus. Emmons and I arrived early and got good seats. The bus soon filled with passengers, but still no Yang. It had rained during the night and we were afraid he had assumed that the bus would not run. Finally Yang arrived, as complacent as a commuter a minute ahead of train time.

At Shintsin we had to change busses in order to cross the Min. The porters here were women, and some, in spite of their gray hair, clamored for enormous loads, which they carried in baskets on their heads. One of them took a bag and two heavy suitcases. There were four channels of the river to cross, and we traversed each in a large sampan tied to a long rope anchored upstream. The boat was steered at an angle to the current, which, pressing against the side, carried it across. The second bus took us over a terrible road to Kiungchow and again we feared for our barometer. Our automobile travel ended here, however, for the road beyond was so muddy that busses had not been over it to Yachow for a fortnight.

We engaged three rickshas for ourselves and a fourth for luggage and continued all afternoon and the next day, walking a good deal of the way because of hard pulling through the mud. At one place we heard a perfect bedlam of voices coming from a small building, which proved to be a school; the children were reading their lessons aloud, and as each one was apparently at a different point in the lesson, or else reciting a different subject, the resulting din may be imagined. Those pupils will be able to concentrate on their work in any surroundings!

On the second afternoon we had several hills to climb, and at length crossed a divide from which we looked down into the Ya Valley. Our men started down-hill on the run. Emmons' ricksha was in the lead when, sweeping around a bend, he was confronted by a land-slide nearly blocking the road. The coolie was going too fast to stop and there was barely room for the rick-sha to pass by on the outside, bumping over the loose stones, in grave danger of careening off the edge of the road and hurtling down the slope. Our rickshas following managed to stop in time.

Having circumvented the slide, we descended into the valley and followed up the river for a few miles to the crossing, where we were ferried over to Yachow, rickshas and all, in a large sampan. A few minutes later we reached the American Baptist Mission, where we were cordially received by Dr. and Mrs. R. L. Crook. We were glad to find that all of our baggage sent from Kiating had arrived safely, having been carried up the river road in three days.

Yachow is a city of about 30,000 inhabitants, beauti-fully situated in the Ya Valley, surrounded by foothills of the Tibetan front ranges. It is at the head of raft navigation on the Ya River, a form of transportation which we decided to use on our return journey.

A day was spent in repacking our loads to make them a little lighter for the mountain road to Tatsienlu. The best method of carrying is by "tiaoing." The porter carries a pole on one shoulder, from each end of which, front and back, is suspended a load of fifty pounds. The pole springs slightly with each step, and by main-taining the proper rhythm he can make excellent time on level ground.[6] When "bai-ing," with loads strapped directly on their backs, porters cannot travel so fast, except when climbing hills, but can take heavier burdens. Articles of over fifty pounds have to be carried in this way, or else included in a two-man load of 160 pounds. This is lashed to the middle of a pair of bamboo poles and carried by a man in front and one behind, like a chair or "whakan." We had nearly fourteen hundred pounds of baggage, which required fifteen porters. In addition there were the two chair men for Yang, and a futow, or head man, who carried nothing.

With this considerable caravan we set out next morning on our eight-day walk to Tatsienlu, a distance of 530 li, or about 140 miles. The Chinese li is supposed to be roughly equivalent to one-third of a mile. In popular usage, however, it is not an exact distance, the time and effort required to make the journey being taken into consideration, so that a li on a good level road is longer than one on a rough ascent. In this part of China a li seemed to average only a little over a quarter of a mile.

While we were eating breakfast with the Crooks, eight soldiers appeared to go with us. Soldiers perform the function of police in this part of China, and General Wu, the city magistrate, had sent these to safeguard our baggage for the first stage of the trip. On the second stage we were given ten, probably because we had been a little generous in rewarding the first eight. During the remainder of the trip our escort varied in size according to the number of idle soldiers available.

Our soldiers carried not only guns, but umbrellas as well! The protection afforded could not have been very effective against robbers, for the caravan strung out a mile or two in length. After trying in vain to keep the men together, we attempted to spread the soldiers along to cover them. This did not work, however, as they preferred to visit together as they traveled. The soldiers undoubtedly added some prestige to our caravan, and they looked quite picturesque walking along in straw sandals, with trousers rolled up above their knees, and umbrellas raised to keep off the sun.

As may be seen from the map (page 336) there are three roads from Yachow to Tatsienlu. The northern or "small road," as it is called, is the shortest and the poorest, although it does pass through Tienchuan, whose name means "Complete Heaven." The Roosevelts, however, who passed through it on their hunting trip, wrote that "to Occidental eyes, at any rate, there was much to belie the name." The small road is difficult and not suited for pack animals or for chairs. Its length is from five to eight stages, according to the weather, loads, and men, and there is one high pass near Lutingchiao.

The "New Road" is a short cut from near Jungking* to Hualinpin. It is not suitable for pack animals but is better than the small road, and chairs can be accommodated. There is one pass near the western end. Here the road forks, one branch going to Hualinpin and the other to Lungpapu. The latter is said to be poorer, but is shorter and therefore more traveled. The new road and the small road are used chiefly by tea-carriers. The new road saves one day over the big road

* Do not confuse with Chungking.

and was used by Moore and Young on their way in to join us.

The "Big Road" via Tsingkihsien takes most of the traffic and, because of its better accommodations and easier going for our men, Emmons and I decided to follow it. Even this road is too rough for a wheeled vehicle. [7] It is true we saw, on our way out, a couple of field-guns being transported over it, but they were in sections on the backs of animals. One mule carried the barrel, followed by a second with a wheel strapped on each side, and a third with the mounting. We passed a few pack trains of mules or diminutive horses, but nearly all goods are carried by porters.

Westward bound were loads of tea, salt (looking like big chunks of black stone), cotton cloth, rice, and straw sandals. These sandals are worn by all porters on this road, as they are very cheap, last several days, and do not slip on the smooth, rounded steps by which the road climbs up over the passes. Conspicuous among the articles eastward bound were big loads of medicinal bark. For the first two days there was a good deal of coal from mines near Jungking. One amusing load which we saw was a live pig strapped on the back of a porter, climbing up to the Tashangling Pass. Another porter was carrying a man on his back up this weary climb. The chief article of commerce, however, is tea for Tibet, and as there is such a vast quantity of it, and no corresponding weight of goods coming out, many of the porters return without loads.

The tea is grown in the vicinity of Yachow, dried, and pressed into bricks measuring eleven inches long and weighing six pounds. Four of these are placed end to end and enclosed in a case of plaited reed or bamboo. The resulting faggot, or "pao," as it is called, weighs eighteen catties, or twenty-four pounds. The porters are paid by weight and so carry as many of these as they are able. Ordinary loads vary from seven to eleven pao, but we saw a few men carrying fifteen, which means 360 pounds.[8] Each carrier has a stout, tee-headed stick, with an iron point, on which he can rest his burden. And so he goes, staggering along for a few hundred yards, and then resting. We were told that it takes these men twenty-four days to reach Tatsienlu, and that they make by their terrific toil about one Mex. dollar per day.

We saw many tea trees or bushes near Yachow. Yang told us that the best tea is made from leaves picked in the spring. In the days of the Empire, the tea grown at Yachow was considered to be the finest in China, and each spring some of the first picking was sent by special courier to the Empress Dowager. Later pickings yield tea of inferior quality. The leaves are boiled in water for fifteen minutes, then put on big straw mats to dry in the sun, after which they are ready for use.

We stopped frequently at the little tea-houses along the way for two or three cups, which we found quite refreshing after a hot walk. It is green tea and is taken without sugar. The leaves are placed in your cup and boiling water is poured over them. Food-shops were indicated by a table placed outside the door, with a small mound of white rice on the end of it. Vegetables were also displayed in little bowls. One of the commonest articles was bean curd, like white gelatin, its top neatly formed into a low pyramid. The common meat was pork, and as we ate the little pieces with our rice we could often see the source of a vast future supply walking around the room with contented grunts. Eggs were plentiful, as they are everywhere in China with its estimated 350 million hens.

On the streets of every little hamlet were chickens, hogs, and mongrel dogs. These gave us little trouble, but barked ferociously at all Chinese beggars. Our theory for this is that beggars are given food which would otherwise go to the dogs. There were apples, plums, and apricots, but most of this fruit was picked too green. On our return journey in November there were delicious persimmons and small, sweet oranges, with loose skins like tangerines. Peanuts were laid out on tables in flat, round groups the size of a plate, at one copper a group. In places where the crop had been unusually good the groups were quite large. It is interesting to note that the peanut, now so extensively grown in western China, came originally from South America.

The roadside tea-shops and eating-places were open to the street, and whenever we stopped at them we became the objects of much attention. The people gathered closely around our table, row after row, fifty or so by actual count, watching us with calm, expressionless faces.[9] It was quite disconcerting at first, but we became accustomed to it.

Another performance which never failed to arouse interest was writing in our diaries or writing letters.

Boys standing by our sides would sometimes lean over to watch the points of our pens, their faces within six inches of the paper. They must have considered our barbarian scrawls far less attractive than their artistic characters. We did not mind their close examination, for of course they could not read what we were writing, and when they crowded too much Yang would shoo them all away.

We had folding-cots to sleep on, and found mosquito netting a necessity. Our first night on the road was spent at Malichang, the second at Huangnipu, where we had a fine bath in a clear cold pool in the stream above the town. On the third day we made the long climb up to the Tashangling Pass. A clear mountain torrent added to the beauty of the road, and just before reaching the pass we had an extensive view down the valley behind us. From the pass we looked out to the west,[1] but the weather was not clear enough to give a view of the snow mountains and we paused only long enough to set up the barometer and take two readings a few minutes apart. These gave an altitude of 9,660 feet, which, because of a large temperature correction, appears to be a little high. A steep zigzag descent brought us onto a little plateau and into the town of Tsingkihsien. It is surrounded by cornfields, and beyond them, at the edge of the plateau, is the city wall.

Next morning we dropped down, crossed the west stream, and then climbed up around a range of reddish hills, the southernmost bend of our road. That afternoon, at a place called Iwanshue, we found a big landslide of broken rocks across the road. It had occurred during a thunder storm six nights before, completely destroying one house and badly injuring some of the occupants, who were extremely fortunate to have escaped with their lives.

Some of them wanted to know if there were any dragons in the ground. According to Yang, a belief commonly held by natives in this region is that white men have the power of looking into the earth. These particular people thought that the recent landslide might have been caused by enormous dragons, and they wanted to know whether there was any evidence to support their theory.

In the country through which we passed the hillsides were generally planted with corn, and the valley floors with rice. This, of course, stood in water, and the little earthen retaining banks which held the water in had beans growing upon them. The weather was hot and it was a refreshing sight to look down upon the green rice rippling in the breeze. Surely there is no green so delicate as that of young rice plants.

Accompanying our caravan part of the time was an attractive little boy of thirteen, who had walked all of the way from Yachow, while his mother and little brother rode in a chair. They had come to visit his elder brother, who had a position in the telegraph office at Nitow, where we stopped for the night.

Next morning Yang brought word that the men wanted to wait over for a day on account of threatened rain; but we were determined to push on. The showers made walking cooler, but the clouds must have concealed some magnificent views, and the trail up to the Feiyuehlin Pass was wet and slippery. The pass is on a steep knife ridge, over which the road climbs with many zigzags. The hills on each side are wooded, offering excellent cover for bandits, to which the clouds contributed, so our four soldiers prepared for trouble, advancing with guns in readiness. The only resistance encountered, however, was that of the climb itself.

On the summit of the pass were the ruins of a house destroyed by robbers, and we were told that thirteen had been captured here earlier in the spring and beheaded. We decided to wait with the soldiers until all of our loads were safely over. Setting up the barometer, we took two readings, which gave an altitude of 9,330 feet. There were a few wild strawberries with which we refreshed ourselves, but a cold mist was sweeping through the pass, and most of our energy was devoted to keeping warm while we waited for over an hour. Finally the last load came up, being carried by the futow. The poor coolie had not been able to make the grade with it. Our contract with the futow for transporting the baggage to Tatsienlu called for an extra payment of half a catty of pork* to each of the porters for crossing the two high passes. We made it a half a catty for each pass, and felt that a whole hog apiece would be only fair recompense for such toil.

Feiyuehlin Pass marks the boundary between Szechwan and Sikong. We descended into the new province, a steep crooked road bringing us down to Hualinpin, where we stopped for the night.

* One catty equals 1 1/3 pounds.

On the way down we passed a few poppy-fields, with some of the flowers in bloom, white, purple, and red. These were the only poppies we saw growing, as it was not their season. A great quantity of opium, however, is produced in Szechwan, and a large percentage of the people smoke it. This is especially true of the porters on the road from Yachow to Tatsienlu. Opium shops are spaced at intervals along the way, and our men all smoked three times a day, spending one-fifth of their wages for the little black pellets. The hard, weary lives which these men lead, especially the tea-carriers, seem to be focused entirely upon opium, which they must have even if they cannot buy food. Yang told us that most of them have no homes, and if they become ill they must resort to begging.

When we passed through Yachow there were three patients in Dr. Crook's hospital taking the opium cure. They remain four weeks for this treatment, and are then completely cured. Dr. Crook told us that many start to use it again if they are ill, or are tempted too strongly by their friends. Some take the treatment because they cannot afford the increasing quantities of opium necessary to satisfy them; after treatment they can start again with small amounts.

On a slippery road such as that leading down from the pass to Hualinpin, we had to take special care not to fall with the precious barometer, which Emmons and I took turns in carrying. We called this instrument the "expedition baby" and never trusted it to the care of anyone else.

Next morning we continued the descent. A fine snow

mountain, probably one of the Tatsienlu peaks, appeared ahead of us, but was soon covered by clouds. While taking tea at Lungpapu (Dragon Place Shop) we noticed that some of the dwellings had wooden signs over the doorway. Yang said it was quite customary for friends to present the owner with one of these, and translated some of them for us. One sign said that the house was then occupied by five generations of one family! Another, saying, "Old age, good character," had been presented to a man who had passed his eightieth year.

We were now in the deep valley of the Tung,[5] whose mouth we had seen at Kiating. It is a broad, swift river, with many patches of white water, and our road ran along a ledge high above it. At one point we passed a little wayside temple known as "Buddha's Ear," where some of our men stopped to burn joss sticks. How it got its name I do not know unless it was suggested by the shape of the cliff. It is of interest because it marks the halfway point on the old courier road between Peking and Lhasa.

In the days when China had official representatives in Lhasa, a very efficient messenger service was maintained between the two "Forbidden Cities," and it is said that a dispatch could reach either capital in nineteen days from this halfway point. J. Huston Edgar estimates that 480 men and 660 animals were employed on the Tibetan section of this service between Tatsienlu and Lhasa.* Urgent messages traveled day and night and could cover the twelve hundred mile journey in fifteen

* *Journal of the West China Border Research Society*, vol. iv, 1930-31.

days. A consideration of the difficulties encountered in this work inspires the greatest respect and admiration for the men who took part in it. Summer heat and winter cold, deep gorges and 15,000-foot passes, rain, hail, wind, and snow, and the danger from robbers in waste places, all were faced as a matter of course by these hardy inland couriers. After successful operation for over two hundred years the service was discontinued in 1911, with the founding of the Chinese Republic and the withdrawal of the Ambans from Lhasa.

We stopped for the night at Lutingchiao, and next morning crossed the famous iron-chain bridge to the west bank of the Tung. There are two chains of seven-eighths-inch iron on each side, one above the other, which serve as railings, and the wooden floor boards, running crossways, rest on nine chains of three-quarters-inch iron. The bridge is about ten feet wide and I paced its length at 112 yards. There is no support in the middle and the sag is slight for so long a span. W. W. Rockhill crossed this bridge on July 11, 1889, and his description in *The Land of the Lamas* shows that it was the same then as now. He says it was built in 1701.

At Ta P'em Pa (Big Cook Place) there was a government school in session. All of the thirty-six children were reading aloud as in the school near Yachow, but in this case they were all reading the same lesson in chorus, a considerable improvement. We stopped to eat lunch beside a clear stream which came tumbling down a little valley, then over a waterfall below us, and through a narrow canyon to join the Tung. The afternoon march to Waszekow took us along the side of a mountain rising steeply on our left, and falling away even more steeply on the right to the river, hundreds of feet below. We were told that a number of people are killed on this stretch of road every year by rocks falling upon it. We passed the coffin of a victim killed a month before. It had been placed high up in a niche in the cliff, thirty feet above the road, the very spot from which the fatal rocks had fallen upon him. It looked almost as if he expected to wreak his vengeance on some future traveler, by dropping upon him in the heavy wooden coffin!

We stopped to photograph a high, snow-capped peak, partly concealed by clouds. Hoping it would clear, we let our caravan pass by and waited. A portion of the mountain, however, was always hidden by the shifting clouds, and in trying to get it all we missed our best chance and in the end got nothing.

While we were waiting, a native hunter, with three dogs, stopped to chat with us. He said there were "Yeh Gnu" (takin) on the snow mountain, also that there were black bears in the neighborhood, and two brown bears far up the valley of the stream where we had eaten lunch.

Proceeding on our way, we rounded a point, turning westward away from the Tung, and descended abruptly into Waszekow.[10] While we were eating dinner at a little inn there, the head man of the town called. Up to this point we had been given an escort of soldiers for each stage. This magistrate apologized profusely because he had none to send with us. He could indeed give us two soldiers, but they had no guns. As he re-

ported the road peaceful, we told him we would not
need their services.

Next morning we set out on the eighth and last stage
of our journey, traveling westward up the gorge of the
Tatsienlu River. Day by day the scenery had increased
in grandeur, but this surpassed it all. In the fifteen miles
to Tatsienlu, the road climbs over three thousand feet
along the side of the river, which comes roaring down
over boulders as big as houses in a grand series of
rapids and cascades. In some places the sides of the
gorge are almost perpendicular and at one point we
could see, far ahead, one of the snow-capped Tatsienlu
Peaks. Several picturesque bridges carried the road
across tributaries, but it did not cross the river itself.
The latter was spanned at several points by bridges consisting of a single bamboo rope about three inches in
diameter. Over this slid a hollow wooden sleeve, some
eight inches long, to which the load was hung and pulled
across by a small line, supported by little hoops. I
watched a basket of potatoes being hauled over. People
also use these bridges, and it is exciting to watch a
person hanging from the sleeve in midstream, the sag-
ging rope barely holding him clear of the rapids.

Pressing on ahead of the caravan, we reached Tatsienlu late in the afternoon, and were met just inside
the East Gate[11] by Rev. R. L. Cunningham and Dr.
John Lenox, who had been informed by letter of our
coming. After arranging for our loads to be passed
through the customs, they conducted us to the large
compound and building of the China Inland Mission,
where we arrived in time for tea, served by Mrs. Cun-

ningham. There were also delicious biscuits with yak butter. The latter has a rather pleasing taste, peculiar to itself, but yak meat, to which we were introduced at dinner, is scarcely distinguishable from good beef. Following the luxury of baths, Emmons and I did ample justice to the excellent meal, after our eight days of Chinese fare at the roadside inns.

Chapter IV

THE GATEWAY TO TIBET

TATSIENLU, the "gateway of Tibet," lies at an elevation of 8,500 feet in a narrow valley with mountains rising thousands of feet on each side.* The name is pronounced Da Chien Lu, and comes from the Tibetan Da r'Tse m'Do. "Do" which appears as an ending to the names of many Tibetan towns, such as Jyekundo and Chamdo, means the confluence of two streams. In this case it signifies the junction of the rivers Da and r'Tse. The latter, coming from the south, flows through the middle of the town, being spanned by several bridges. The Da, from the northwest, joins it within the limits of the town, and the united river flows eastward, tumbling down the fifteen-mile gorge to join the Tung at Waszekow. The natural approach offered by this gorge is probably responsible for the location and importance of Tatsienlu.

That the town is progressive was shown by the recent installation of a hydro-electric lighting plant. To be sure, the capacity of the single generator was only twenty-four kilowatts, and the system was so overloaded with lamps that they were able to emit only a

* The new official name of the city is Kang Ting, which means the "Pacification of Kham" or eastern Tibet, but we heard no one use it.

dull red glow. The military officials required that the
company, a private venture, supply them with lights
free of charge, claiming that the water being used was
theirs! Nevertheless, the installation was considered a
great success, and plans were under way for the addition of a second unit. The water power going to waste
in the center of the city is ample for a really good plant,
but it must be remembered that all machinery has to be
carried in from Yachow on the backs of men or animals.

Situated at the same latitude as New Orleans, Jack-
sonville Florida, and Cairo Egypt, Tatsienlu has a
mild climate in spite of its high altitude. According to
Heim, the observations of Bishop Valentine show as
average temperatures, a summer maximum of 86 and a
winter minimum of 14 degrees Fahrenheit. Snow falls
occasionally, but does not last long. Vegetables of good
quality and great variety are raised: beans, cabbage, let-
tuce, spinach, eggplant, peas, potatoes, pumpkins, tur-
nips, onions, cucumbers, etc.   Barley, wheat, maize,
buckwheat, and oats are grown locally, but rice is ex-
pensive, as it has to be imported from the lower valleys.
This also applies to fruits such as oranges, persimmons,
apricots, peaches, pears, plums, and prickly pears. Eggs
are plentiful, and available meats include chicken, pork,
mutton, and yak beef. Yaks also supply milk, butter,
and cheese.

Tatsienlu is on the geographical and ethnological
border between China and Tibet. The political boundary, beyond which lies autonomous Tibet, forbidden
to travelers, is over 150 miles farther west, beyond
Batang and the Yangtze. The intervening territory

is under Chinese administration, but the culture is Tibetan and the people are Tibetans or of related stock. We found the rice and water buffaloes of China replaced by barley and yaks; the temples, pagodas, and wayside shrines, by lamaseries, mani piles, and prayer flags.

Tatsienlu itself seemed more Chinese than Tibetan. There were few pretentious buildings, the little shops which lined its narrow streets having been erected with an eye to utility rather than architecture. The Catholic Church and the buildings of the China Inland Mission and of the Seventh Day Adventists stood out above the general mediocrity.

Perhaps ten thousand is a fair average for the fluctuating population. What a variety of types there were! Chinese officials, soldiers, and traders from many provinces; Tibetan lamas, nomads, and caravan-drivers, half castes of every degree; and tribesmen, belonging to the several one-time independent little states and kingdoms of the Tibetan marches or borderland.

Five main trade routes meet at Tatsienlu.*

* First the tea roads from Szechwan, which unite and ascend the gorge from Waszekow; second, the old official road to Lhasa, leading west through Hokow, Litang, Batang, and Chamdo, a difficult road because of the many high passes; third, the northwest road which is nowadays the most frequented route to Tibet. It passes through Dawo, Kanze, and Jyekundo, where it meets the road from Kokonor. An alternative route connects Kanze with Chamdo via Derge, noted for its metalwork. This northwest road is traveled by enormous caravans, some with as many as three thousand animals. A fourth road from Tatsienlu leads north to Tsungwha and Hsuching, via Tanpa, where it meets a road coming from Kwanhsien, and so offers a northern but rather difficult route to Chengtu. Some twenty-five miles from Tatsienlu, just below the Haitze Shan, this north road connects with a bifurcation of the northwest road from Kanze. The fifth important road leads southward to Yunnan and Burma.

The city was the capital of Mi-nyag, a province of Kham, and also of the small kingdom of Chiala. Now it is the capital of Sikong, a province which extends roughly from the Tung River on the east to the Yangtze on the west; from the Ngolok country in Chinghai on the north to the land of the Lolos and Yunnan on the south. This territory is sometimes called Chinese Tibet, and together with the adjoining portion of independent Tibet, is one of the least known of all the inhabited areas on the earth's surface.

This "Land of the Great Corrosions" is a rough country with high mountain ranges running north and south, separated by deep gorges. Here three of the world's great rivers flow southward in parallel courses; for a distance of 130 miles all three are within a strip fifty miles wide. The Salween continues southward, passing by Moulmein in Burma, the Mekong southeastward to Saigon in French Indo-China, while the Yangtze swings eastward across the Chinese plain to the Pacific. Its mouth near Shanghai is over two thousand miles from that of the Salween, from which it was separated at one point by only forty-two miles, with the Mekong lying between.

A short distance to the west of these three rivers is the Brahmaputra, also following a parallel course before curving off to India; to the east of them are the Yalung and the Tung, large tributaries of the Yangtze, and there are other lesser streams, all flowing in the same southerly direction. A traveler on the old official road west from Tatsienlu must cross at right angles no less than thirteen rivers and their separating ranges of mountains, many of the passes being over 15,000 feet high.*

Sikong has a rich flora and fauna, especially the former. The cold mountain barriers separating hot valleys are unfavorable to the spread of species and favor the persistence of local forms. The range of climatic conditions offers opportunity for the survival of these and encourages fresh variation, so that naturalists can expect to find type specimens here for many years to come. Western China has the richest flora of any tem-

* There seems to be no general name for these mountains, which are sometimes referred to as the "Alps of Chinese Tibet." According to Gregory (*To the Alps of Chinese Tibet,* by J. W. Gregory and C. J. Gregory) they are comparatively young, geologically speaking, having been formed about the same time as the Alpine-Himalayan system, in which a continuity has been traced from western Spain to eastern India. Here the folds butted against the older Indo-Himalayan Mountains, and, according to one view, were bent back around Assam and southward through western Burma as the "Burmese Arc," continuing through Sumatra and Java as the "Malay Arc." Gregory, however, found evidence that the Alpine-Himalayan movement was not entirely stopped by the older mountains, but extended beyond them, eastward into China, as the Nan Shan Mountains south of the Yangtze.

The "Chinese Alps" are young, and it is thought by some that the forces which built them are still at work. Their steep slopes are being continually worn down by landslides. Earthquake shocks are felt every few years, and a particularly severe one occurred in 1926, leaving spectacular cracks in the vicinity of Kanze. Some of the cracks in the walls of houses in Tatsienlu were probably caused by this earthquake.

According to Heim, Minya Konka itself is a batholite, perhaps the largest on earth, a great mass of granite which was consolidated far below the earth's surface and later pushed up through it. The vertical movement must have been more than four miles, and probably exceeded six. This upward movement was probably caused by lateral compression during and shortly after consolidation. The effects of *contact-meta-morphosis* on both sides and the relation with folding shows that the chief mountain-making is relatively young, probably alpine. "Being one of the highest granite peaks of our planet, around which the erosion is in course of intensive work, we even must consider that the epeirogenetic movement has continued into Quaternary time and possibly is still at work" ("The Structure of Minya Gongkar," by Arnold Heim, *Bulletin of the Geological Society of China,* vol. xi, no. 1).

perate climate in the world, and it has been estimated that "there are between six and seven times as many kinds of plants in this region as there are in all of Europe."* It is a curious fact that this flora has much more in common with that of the eastern United States than with that of western America.

Sikong offers an attractive field for the ethnologist in studying and tracing the history of the border tribes. It also invites the archeologist. J. Huston Edgar, of the China Inland Mission in Tatsienlu, showed us some of his specimens, chiefly artifacts of black stone which he had been collecting since 1914. In 1931 he and Gordon Bowles made a large collection of these chipped-stone implements, and of primitive pottery, found in loess pockets northwest of Tatsienlu, some at altitudes of 15,000 feet.

We rented two rooms in a Tibetan house next door to the mission as expedition headquarters, and spent four busy days in repacking equipment and making preparations for our journey south. Light straw cases, which had served admirably for porter transport, were not adapted for use on the backs of less considerate yaks. These sturdy animals, we were told (and later found it true), have an unfortunate habit of brushing past each other, or past rocks, without making allowance for the loads strapped to their sides. Breakable loads are apt to be smashed; others scraped off. So we procured wooden cases, and had fresh hide sewed over them, with the hair side next the wood. In one day this had shrunk in the sun until it became almost as hard

* *Journal of the West China Border Research Society*, vol. iv, p. 108.

as sheet steel, and the cases thus reinforced served us well.

In the courtyard of our house Tibetans were similarly engaged in repacking tea. The bricks were taken out of the woven containers in which they had been carried from Yachow, and were sewed up in raw yak hides with the hair side in. Six bricks were enclosed in each skin, making a seventy-two-pound bundle, which appeared unbreakable and well able to withstand its long, rough journey to the interior of Tibet. Two of these bundles make a load for a yak.[12] Some of the Yachow-Tatsienlu porters, as we have seen, carry over twice as much.

At night as we lay on our camp beds in this house, we listened to the distant beating of Tibetan drums and the low chanting of prayers. At times perhaps our thoughts wandered back to the other side of the world as we were lulled to sleep by these strange, oriental sounds of innermost Asia.

We took our meals with the Cunninghams, and were at dinner one evening when, looking over to our house, we saw a fire in it. We jumped up in horror—all of our equipment, impossible to replace, would be lost unless we could rescue it. Rushing around through the little alley, we found, to our amazement and relief, that the fire had been merely the glow from a lantern flickering on a paper window.

Our passports from Nanking (they were large, impressive folders measuring nine by twelve inches and bearing the seal of the Chinese Republic), supplemented by papers from General Liu Wen Whei in Chengtu, the Governor of Szechwan, enabled us to use

"Ullah" transport. Under this ancient system, certain Tibetans furnish animals and men to drive them for government officials or others holding the necessary papers, as one form of taxation. In former times they had to do this without any charge, but now they receive pay at one-half the regular rate. As the regular rate was one rupee per day for an animal with driver, equivalent at that time to seven cents in American money, we did not consider half of this sum an exorbitant charge.

In spite of our papers, however, transport was difficult to obtain. Some fifteen thousand Chinese troops were on the border, engaged in fighting with Tibetans to the northwest, and they had of course taken many animals. They were enlisting local Tibetans to fight for them, and those speaking Chinese were in great demand as interpreters. Such an individual was an absolute necessity for us.

Mr. Edgar and Dr. Cunningham gave us much information about the country—routes to the south, passes, and points from which Minya Konka could probably be observed to advantage. Two young missionaries from Chengtu, Dr. and Mrs. John Lenox, who had come to Tatsienlu for a vacation, decided to go with us.

On the fourth day, July 27th, most of our animals arrived and were assembled in the mission compound late in the afternoon. In due time, which means a considerable time, they were loaded and we were ready. A few additional animals with the rest of our cases were to follow later. We did not leave the compound until nearly six o'clock, but were glad to be on our way, and would make a few li before dark.

Dr. Cunningham walked with us through the narrow streets out of the south gate, and for some distance down the road before turning back. We had hoped to reach the warm sulphur spring at Yulongkung, but our start was too late for this. Soon after dark we camped in a rough field, without setting up tents, as the night was clear.

Early next morning the rest of our equipment arrived on two yaks, in charge of Gaomo, a Chinese-speaking Tibetan, whom Dr. Cunningham had finally secured for us. Gaomo was on horseback and with him came four Tibetan animal-drivers on foot, their belongings on a cow! Our caravan of sixteen animals and eleven persons soon got under way. It consisted of eight pack horses and two yaks for our equipment, six drivers on foot, with a horse and cow for their baggage, Gaomo on a horse, Dr. and Mrs. Lenox on horses, and Emmons and myself, who took turns riding, one of us having to walk with the barometer.

We had not seen Gaomo[13] before, and were naturally interested in him, for he was to be our cook, interpreter, and general handy man while in the field, though he had never been with foreigners. His countenance was pleasant, indicating a good disposition. He wore a rough wool cloak, three-cornered black hat, and the typical Tibetan boots of cloth, with round leather soles turned up in points at the toes. His most prominent article, as he rode ahead of us, was a cheap, black umbrella, slung across his back. It was odd to see this rough, hardy fellow carrying his precious umbrella. To be sure, he seldom used it; never for rain, but only when seated on the ground, to keep off the sun!

When we stopped for lunch we made our first trial of the staple Tibetan diet: tsamba, in buttered and salted tea. The tea is of rather coarse quality and quite strong. The sticks are thrown into the water after it has come to a boil, and when the desired strength appears, it is ladled out into a small wooden churn. Yak butter and salt are added and mixed in thoroughly with the dasher. Then it is drunk from round wooden bowls, five inches in diameter and two inches deep. It does not taste bad if one is hungry and imagines that he is drinking soup instead of tea.

Tsamba is barley which has been roasted and then ground into a fine, whitish flour. It is added to the tea, absorbing much of it, and is kneaded with the thumb into a dry, pasty lump, the bowl being revolved in the process. It is then eaten with the fingers—good nourishing food, and easily prepared, but rather tasteless. We often cooked it in the mornings for breakfast like ordinary cereal. Tea and tsamba form the regular diet of the people throughout Tibet, with occasionally some meat. With his leather bag of tsamba, some lumps of butter, and a little tea and salt, a Tibetan is provisioned for a long journey. There is no danger of a general famine in Tibet, for great quantities of tsamba are kept in storehouses, and in the dry climate it is said that it will keep for a hundred years. Even meat is said to keep for several years.

At every halt the loads were removed, but the wooden

pack saddles were allowed to remain on the animals. The Tibetans have a quick and easy method of fastening loads, which are placed one on each side of the animal, not on top of his back. The man (or woman) picks up a case and holds it against the side of the yak. A leather strap, tied to the front of the saddle, is brought around the side of the case and fastened to the back of the saddle. Then another strap, from the center, is passed under the case, and its end tied, on the outside, to the middle of the first strap. Often a third hand is required in the process, and for this purpose the Tibetan uses his teeth, holding the end of one strap tight with them while taking up on another.

We continued southward up the narrow, wooded valley of the Tse River,[16] bending eastward in the afternoon. A rock pinnacle, on which we had been taking bearings since leaving Tatsienlu, finally disappeared behind a shoulder of the mountain of which it formed a part. As we ascended the valley, the trees gave way to lower growths, and finally to bushes and grass. There were wild flowers in great profusion—asters, buttercups, dandelions, ladies'-tresses, paint-brush, yarrow, a gray-blue, bell-shaped flower with a disagreeable odor, rock pink, forget-me-nots, and countless others, conspicuous more because of their variety than because of their individual showiness.

Behind us we had a fine view of Yachiagan with its two snow-covered summits. Late in the afternoon it began to rain, and we camped about a li before reaching a point where the trail turned to the right and climbed steeply out of the valley. A barometric observation

showed our altitude to be 12,835 feet. The rain stopped
before dark and we saw the tip of a sharp white peak
rising beyond the mountains which hemmed us in. It
proved to be Chiburongi Konka, the first of Minya
Konka's neighbors to greet us.

We got an early start next morning and made the
steep climb up to the Djezi La.* At times we caught
glimpses of Chiburongi Konka[17] through the clouds, but
the other peaks were hidden. This was a disappointment, as the top of Minya Konka is said to be visible
from the pass, and we had hoped to see it. Like all
Tibetan passes, the Djezi La has a cairn of stones upon
it, supporting some sticks with tattered prayer flags. We
set up the barometer and made four observations over
a period of three hours, which gave an altitude for the
pass of 15,685 feet.[18] While I was thus engaged, Emmons climbed a summit northwest of the pass and built
a seven-foot stone beacon upon it for surveying purposes. We called this Station A. It was foggy and cold
on the pass, with rain and hail part of the time, so
we were glad to leave and descend into the Yulong
Valley.

We now found ourselves in the "Tibetan Grasslands," a country with a peaceful beauty all its own.
The broad valley floor was carpeted with short grass
and there were low bushes on the rounded hillsides, but
no trees, for we were above the timber line. In fact,
the elevation (over 13,000 feet) was too high for any
crops. In summer the Tibetans[19] pasture their yaks here
in the upper part of the valley, and during the after-

* La is the Tibetan word for pass.

noon we passed several herds, some with four or five hundred animals.

The yak is about the size of a domestic ox, black, with long horns and a bushy tail. Some have white faces, probably due to crossing with cattle, for the color of the wild yak, still to be found in inner Tibet, is said to be entirely black. It is also said to exceed in size the domestic yak, which was the only kind found in our region. The old bulls which we saw were magnificent animals, with long hair reaching nearly to the ground. In spite of their formidable appearance, they do not seem to be dangerous. When we camped that night, two neighboring bulls started to snort a low "Huh-huh-huh" and to walk menacingly toward each other. Our Tibetans seemed pleased at the prospect of a fight, but by alternately advancing and retreating, the animals managed to maintain a certain dignity without coming to close quarters.

It is difficult to imagine how Tibetans could live without their yaks. They furnish excellent meat which we purchased frequently. The milk is not used directly, but is made into butter and into big lumps of hard, sour cheese. We used some of this, taking out a little of the sourness by toasting it, though it crumbled badly. The butter, however, was good, and we used a great deal of it. We bought it in cakes costing one rupee. They were four inches square and an inch and a half thick, wrapped in leaves. As there was always a considerable quantity of dirt mixed in with the butter, we melted it, skimmed off the foreign matter, and then poured the clear yellow butter into tin cans to cool. Yak hides have

many uses, and the hair is woven into tent cloth and
strong ropes. The tails are used as ornaments or as fly
whisks, and the horns as receptacles. We saw some
Tibetans carrying snuff in them. Yak dung is the only
available fuel over large areas of the country.

The camel has been called the "ship of the desert";
the yak the "ship of the high plateau." As beasts of
burden they plod phlegmatically along, the Tibetans
urging them on by whistling and yelling, or gently guid-
ing them back into the trail by hurling rocks at them, for
yaks are of an independent nature and like to make a
new trail whenever possible. For this reason roads in
Tibet usually consist of many parallel paths. Each yak
used for carrying burdens has a wooden ring in its
nose, to which are attached a few feet of yak-hair rope.
This is used to lead or tether it when necessary, and
while traveling the end is wound around its horn. They
make poor riding-animals, and we did not try them,
realizing that we would be taken not where we wanted
to go, but where the yak wanted to go. In this respect,
therefore, we failed to fit the picture drawn by a friend
of ours (now Mrs. Terris Moore) in the following
lines:

> Behold the ever-patient Yak,
> With four explorers on his back.
> He treks for miles across the snows,
> Wearing a bracelet in his nose;
> And when they stop to have a snack,
> It's slices of the useful Yak!

We pitched our camp not far from a black nomad
tent[20] inhabited by a man and his wife, an old woman,

and two children. They permitted our cook, Gaomo, to use their fire for cooking. A big, black Tibetan mastiff, tied outside the tent, barked ferociously until quieted by the boy. These dogs are powerful animals and are usually seen barking and tugging at their chains in an effort to reach one. The tent appeared to be surrounded by a small forest of tall stakes. A rope, passing over the top of each, helped to hold the walls out and brace them against the strong winds. An opening extending clear across the top of the tent let the smoke out, or rather part of it, for there was plenty inside. When I had become slightly accustomed to it, I noticed two baby yaks lying down near one side of the tent.

Upon leaving next morning, we learned how easy it is to please Tibetan children. Our cameras used film packs, and when we tore off the black paper tab, after making an exposure, they reached out eagerly for it. Though they looked in vain for their picture on it, they seemed glad to have the paper as a curiosity. Later we found them eager for discarded shotgun or rifle cartridges. When I went out to collect birds, one or two boys would often follow to retrieve the little .410 shells, and if they did not come along, I was careful to bring all the shells back in my pockets for distribution. Some of these afterward appeared as cleverly made little boxes. Empty tin cans were greatly prized by all the natives.

We continued on our way down the valley, crossing and recrossing the small river, and reached Yulonghsi about noon. Here we found three widely separated houses,[21] substantially built of stone, with roofs of long wooden shingles, held down by stones. They were two-story buildings, and in contrast to the typical, flat-roofed Tibetan houses, which are used farther west, the roofs of these had a ridge in the center high enough to give a good pitch. At each end of the ridge was a mast, and a string of prayer flags extended from one to the other. Seen from a little distance, the arrangement looked like a radio receiving-antenna. In addition to this a Tibetan house usually has a Mani pile[22] in front of it, consisting of many stones,[23] on each of which is carved the sacred formula, "Om Mani Padme Hum." We had seen several of these piles on the road from Tatsienlu, always passing to the left of them. On the return journey one also keeps to the left, and so by his trip accomplishes a circumambulation of all the Mani piles encountered. The circumambulation of a pile is said to be equivalent to repeating the prayer as many times as it is carved on the stones, but of course one must go around in the proper direction, that is, keeping the pile to one's right.

No one can travel in Tibetan country without being impressed with the important place which religion occupies in the lives of the people. We had an unusual opportunity to observe many of their practices because we were later permitted to use the Konka Gompa as a preliminary base from which to start our climbing operations.

On approaching this lamasery for the first time along a beautiful open trail through a forest of prickly oak, whose branches met above our heads, we soon became aware that we were treading on holy ground. Pieces of birch-bark with Tibetan texts printed upon them appeared on rocks along the way, being held in place by small stones. At one point in the middle of the trail was a little cairn supporting a large stone with several parallel grooves in it.[24] Gaomo with an awed expression gave us to understand that this had been hurled down from the Konka, the grooves having been formed by the fingers of the mountain god.

We found the lamasery a group of half a dozen stone buildings with shingled roofs.[25] The largest had two stories and surrounded a square open courtyard. A large room on one side was placed at our disposal, and here we stored all of our equipment not needed on the mountain. A small room on the opposite side was used for cooking our meals as well as those of the three or four lamas. The former were prepared by Gaomo, and the latter by some old women whom we were somewhat surprised to find here. It developed, however, that this lamasery belonged to a branch of the red sect and not to the reformed yellow sect whose lamas are celibate. The cooking was done in the center of the room on a square hearth on which stood a shallow iron pot. We ate seated around the hearth on low stools—the lower the better, for the upper portion of the room was filled with smoke which gradually found its way out through a couple of small openings.

Across one side of the court ran a wooden trough in which flowed a little stream of clear cold water from a spring on a hill outside. In the center of the court was a pole with a prayer flag, and beside it a post with an iron bowl on top. An offering of juniper was burned in this bowl every morning. Tsamba for the lamas was supplied by people from the valleys, but the monastery kept its own herd of six small black cows. There was also one lone white rooster of enormous size that used to waken us before dawn with its mournful crow.[26]

Soon afterward we heard the neophytes chanting their lessons. I watched one little fellow as he sat on the balcony floor, reading aloud from a book which stood on a little stand in front of him. He was putting his whole energy into the task, jerking his head emphatically with each syllable. At least one boy from each family in Tibet is dedicated to the priesthood and enters a lamasery at an early age, to commence his studies. He learns to read and write, memorizes prayers and religious texts, and later studies their meaning.

Lamaism, the religion of Tibet, is a modification of the Mahayana, or northern school of Buddhism. This "Greater Vehicle" is quite different from the Hinayana, or "Lesser Vehicle," practiced in Ceylon, Burma, Siam, and Cambodia, which does not seem to have drifted so far from the teachings of Gautama.

"Lama" was originally a title given only to the leader of a monastery, but it is now applied to all priests and monks in Tibet.

Some of the practices adopted bear a resemblance to those of the Catholic Church, and it has been suggested that Tsong-ka-pa (1356-1418), founder of the reformed or yellow sect, may have had some contact with early Christian missionaries. We saw the rosary in use at the Konka Gompa. Not far from the lamasery was a sacred stone with five little hollows worn on it, close together in the shape of a cross, made by tapping with other stones. Gaomo and another Tibetan who was with us tapped it, striking twice in the center hollow and once in each of the other four. The number of taps corresponded with the six syllables, "Om Mani Padme Hum," but as their faces were turned away I could not see whether they repeated them.

The mantra "Om Mani Padme Hum," generally translated, "Oh, the Jewel in the Lotus," is an adoration of Avalokitesvara. In its literal meaning it is not a prayer at all, but rather a hymn of praise. Simpson, in his book, *The Buddhist Praying Wheel,* says that at least five of the syllables are derived from Sanscrit, and belonged to Mahayana Buddhism before it reached Tibet. "Om" is a very sacred word among the Hindus. "Mani" means jewel or gem, "Padme" means in the lotus, and "Hum" is roughly equivalent to Amen. "Adoration to the Jewel in the Lotus. Amen." On all of the mani stones near Yulonghsi, the mystical word "Hri" was added to the formula. This did not appear on stones at Tatsienlu, and it is not an integral part of the mantra. In addition to the literal meaning, the words have a deeper significance. Each of the six syllables is said to stand for one of the six classes of Beings which, Tibetans believe, inhabit the physical and spiritual universe: Gods, Titans, Men, Beasts, Yidah or hungry ghosts, and the Inmates of Hell. Repetition of the mantra will help each to escape from the endless round of reincarnations and enter into Nirvana.

It seemed to us that the constant repetition of "Om Mani Padme Hum," in as many ways as possible, was the chief religious practice of the Tibetans. Not only is it beautifully carved on stones and printed on prayer flags, but it is also printed over and over again, as many times as possible, on pieces of paper, which are crammed into prayer wheels, or "praising wheels" as they have sometimes been called. The common form is a small metal drum on the end of a stick. A little weight, attached to one side by a short leather thong, enables one to keep the drum revolving. Care must be taken to have it turn in a clockwise direction, so that the words will pass by as if one were reading them. Some of the houses we entered had large prayer cylinders, mounted vertically on spindles, to be given a turn in passing. At the little village of Tsemei we saw a large prayer wheel driven by water power. One of the buildings at the Konka Gompa had many rows of big prayer wheels inside—185 according to Heim. Another building housed a brightly painted prayer wheel, four feet in diameter and ten feet high. An old lama turned it for us, a little bell ringing automatically at each revolution. When turning prayer wheels the Tibetans always repeated the prayer also, some muttering it audibly, others only moving their lips. It would seem that this spoken repetition would be scarcely worth while when compared with the hundreds or thousands of repetitions produced by each revolution of the wheel. They seem to believe, however, that its omission would mean the neglect of an opportunity to acquire additional merit. One feels also that the spoken words should have a higher value than those mechanically produced, but I was not able to verify this.

Tibet is ruled by the Church, and the large lamaseries, with hundreds or even thousands of monks, have great power over the people who support them. The lamas do religious work not only for themselves but for all of the people. On important occasions they are employed by wealthy families to read religious texts in their homes. At one prosperous farmhouse where I stopped I found a lama twirling his prayer wheel and repeating the usual mantra. There were many people on the farm and the lama moved from place to place, usually sitting on the ground beside the largest group. But he did not stop his work to speak, and while I watched him his lips never ceased moving in their silent repetition of "Om Mani Padme Hum," at the rate of sixty times a minute.

Chapter V

CAMP ALPINE

SOON after reaching Yulonghsi, Dr. Lenox and I rode our horses up a steep hill to the west, from which Gaomo said we could see Minya Konka rising above the ridge on the east side of the valley. A sudden rainstorm prevented a view and we went down again, to find that Emmons had arrived, having reconnoitered the eastern ridge on his way, for a base line. He reported possibilities, but nothing definite, so we decided to keep our caravan until the next day. Dr. and Mrs. Lenox arranged to spend the night in the house of Jumeh, head man of Yulonghsi, while Emmons and I crossed the valley and climbed the eastern ridge on foot, packing a little tent, sleeping-bags, primus stove, and some food. Darkness forced us to camp before reaching the crest of the ridge.

Next morning we set out early and soon reached the top, only to find everything enveloped in mist. We explored the ridge northward, groping our way through the fog, until we reached a little peak which Emmons had seen the day before. Nowhere was there ground suitable for the measurement of a base line, but we did discover a nice camp site by a tiny lake, lying on a step on the eastern slope of the ridge, just below the top. The location is shown at "G" on the map, the lake being too small to appear. On summits of the ridge we erected two stone beacons, stations "B" and "C," hoping they would prove suitable points from which to sight our instrument on Minya Konka, which we were quite certain stood before us, beyond the clouds.

After descending to Yulonghsi, we started with the caravan early in the afternoon, and finally got all of the animals up over a little pass on the ridge and down to our camp site. When Gaomo saw the spot we had selected, he put in a protest through Dr. Lenox. He said it was very bad to camp so close to water because of the danger from spirits. We let him know that if he were afraid he might pitch his tent beyond a knoll, a short distance away. When he saw, however, that we were going to camp boldly right beside the lake, he evidently decided that it was his duty to protect us, or more probably that our presence would protect him, and he quietly set up his tent near by.

We now put up our ten-by-twelve-foot wall tent for the first time. This had already seen service in Mongolia, having been used by members of the Sino-Swedish Expedition under the leadership of Sven Hedin. We had purchased it from them in Peiping. It was a luxurious affair with a fly which extended beyond the front of the tent, forming an awning. It had been quite a heavy load to bring along, but when we had it erected, with our folding-cots set up inside, and saw how comfortable we were going to be while engaged in our survey, we decided that the extra effort had been well worth while. The Lenoxs' tent was set up close by,[28] and then we bade farewell to our Tibetan drivers, who went off with their animals.

Next morning the clouds still hung heavy in front (we hoped) of our elusive mountain. However, it was the first day of August, and as we were expecting the rains to commence about the 20th we could afford no delay. I went southward along the ridge for a couple of miles and climbed the highest summit, where I built a stone beacon, seven feet high. On the way I saw a small brown snake, but it escaped before I could capture it. I believe it was a small viper, the same species as a specimen which we later secured near Tsemei.

Meanwhile Emmons, who had started down to Yulonghsi, to locate a suitable place in the valley for our base line, had met with the first accident of our expedition. When mounting his horse, which was blind in one eye, the animal jumped and went plunging and tumbling down a thirty foot bank, giving Emmons a bad fall which wrenched his back. Upon my return to camp I found him resting, having received treatment from Dr. Lenox. With the help of the latter I then commenced the work of putting our transit in adjustment.

Late in the afternoon the clouds broke away for a few moments and gave us our first view of Minya Konka, towering across the valley, a stern and imposing sight. A few of the other peaks were also revealed, and then the curtain closed once more; but we had seen enough to satisfy us that here was one of the greatest mountain giants of our planet. No wonder its call had been powerful enough to summon us from so far. Emmons was feeling better, and after supper and some discussion of plans, we turned in, filled with renewed enthusiasm for the work ahead.

Next morning I raised my head from my sleeping-bag, gave one glance, and called, "Art, look outside!" It was perfectly clear, and the whole range stood out sharp and gray in the early morning light. Looking down on our little lake, we saw them again, the great, gray mountains, reflected clearly by its smooth surface. As the sun rose the gray was changed to dazzling white, except in places where the rocks were too steep to hold the snow. The mountains rose seven miles away across the deep Büchu Valley, while beyond a second little valley stood Minya Konka. Gordon Bowles had said, "It sticks right up," and indeed it did, towering far above its huge neighbors in matchless supremacy.[29]

Most conspicuous was the white, northwest ridge, rising steeply to the summit. Beyond it we looked across the north face to a similar ridge, rising from the northeast. In front of us the gray, western face dropped almost sheer into a big snowfield with a high spur at the right. From the summit southward the skyline descended to a big shoulder, and from that dropped nearly straight down, the lower part of the precipice concealed by intervening mountains. Hiding the bottom of the northwest ridge was a sharp symmetrical peak, nearer than the others, from which a ridge ran to the south. The valley of the Konka Gompa, we rightly surmised, lay beyond this ridge.

Could Minya Konka be climbed? From our position, the northwest ridge looked impossibly steep; the

north and west faces were out of the question; but what
about that southern shoulder? If it could be attained,
the route from there to the summit offered some hope.
So far as we could see, however, the shoulder was absolutely inaccessible, unless it could be reached from the
other side. However this must wait. For the present
we had work to do.

How high was that white summit which rose so far
up in the blue? This was the first question we had come
so far to answer. As we watched, clouds began to form
on the mountain-sides, and before long they were obscured. It was evident that the uncertainty of the
weather threatened the successful accomplishment of
our task, and the need for haste was apparent.

Emmons had sufficiently recovered from his fall to
ride again, so we went down into the Yulong Valley,
and spent all of that day in the selection of a base line.
Each tentative choice was roughly paced for length, and
at each end the angles were measured by a pocket compass to the cairns at "B" and "D." We had been
pleased to find that these stations, though established
before we had seen the mountain, turned out to be
well located with respect to it. It would not be necessary to use station "C," located between the others.
Finally a suitable base line was decided upon. (V-W
on map, located on valley floor at right of photograph.[32]) A Mani pile, capped by a stone of white
quartz, served to mark the north end, and a stone
beacon was erected at the other. I climbed high up on
the western side of the valley to see whether station
"A," near the Djezi La, was visible. An intervening

mountain hid it from that point, but it could be seen from both "B" and "D." Looking eastward, I had a magnificent view of Minya Konka and the whole snowy range rising beyond the ridge on which our camp was located. With this foreground the snowy summits looked even higher than they had in the morning. It was interesting to note that all of the drainage from the Minya Konka range passes into the Tung, while the ridge upon which we were camped, though a mile lower in altitude, forms the divide between the Tung and the Yalung rivers.

It had been a long day, and we did not start back until eight o'clock. The night was dark, but, fortunately, not foggy; after a long climb we managed to strike our little pass and reach camp about ten-thirty. In slipping the saddle off our horse, already notorious for his skittishness, we neglected to untie from it the lead rope, whose other end was fast to the halter. The saddle slid off, but not free, and our noble steed dashed madly about camp in the darkness, dragging the saddle with him, until something gave way. Fortunately, he missed the tents and no damage was done, but the row had served to awaken our sleeping campmates.

I spent most of the next day in adjusting the transit, with the assistance of Dr. Lenox, while Emmons went down into the valley once more to change the monument at the south end of the base line. It had been located too close to the foot of the hill on which station "D" stood, to be seen from that point. Late in the afternoon we climbed up to station "C" and got our first glimpse of the Jara, fifty miles away to the north. The measurements of the Szechenyi Expedition gave a higher altitude for the Jara than for Minya Konka, and some of the Tibetans believe that it is higher, probably because of its solitary location. Heim, however, reported it to be considerably lower, and we were glad to find that we would be able to make a measurement of it from our survey stations already established.

One more day was spent in adjusting the transit, until all tests showed it to be correct. The following morning we took it up to station "B," about half an hour's climb from camp, but clouds prevented any observations of the mountains. Upon returning to camp we found a new arrival. Mrs. Peterson, a missionary from Chengtu, who had come to Tatsienlu for a vacation, had decided to pay us a visit and get a close view of the mountains. She arrived with a cook, two Tibetan drivers, and five yaks, one of which she had used as a riding-animal! Camp Alpine was now quite a little community with its four tents.

That evening our guests made plans for a trip to the Konka Gompa, which was undertaken the next day, while Emmons and I continued our work. They went down into the Büchu Valley on foot, the descent being too steep for animals, and made their way for some distance down the river. Unfortunately, they found the trip too long to complete in a day, and were forced to turn back, reaching camp just before the evening mist rolled in.

It was interesting to note that the cloud banks which frequently lay across the Büchu Valley stopped at the crest of the ridge above Camp Alpine, leaving the

Yulong Valley entirely clear. Later we also observed this plainly when we were high on Minya Konka.

August 7th dawned clear and bright, so Emmons and I left for station "B," where the others joined us at noon with a picnic lunch. The mountains remained clear and we were able to measure the horizontal and vertical angles to some twenty-five peaks. Two independent measurements were made of each angle, and several additional ones for Minya Konka and the Jara. With a mountain as close as Minya Konka (9.38 miles), and with such an angle of elevation ($10°$ $50.07'$), it is frequently impossible to see the actual summit, as it may be concealed by the rounding or flattening of the crest. We speculated as to the number of feet the summit might be above the point to which we sighted, and said, half in earnest and half jokingly, that we would see when we got up there. As a matter of interest I may state here that the added height proved to be only about five feet.

It was, of course, necessary to tear down the stone beacon in order to set the transit over the center of the spot it had occupied, and then to erect it again so that we could sight upon it from the other stations. I took a complete round of photographs and then made a panoramic sketch, numbering the peaks for future identification. We found the numbers rather difficult to remember, so, for the purposes of our survey only, we named the mountains from north to south after our Eastern States. Emmons was particularly gratified when Massachusetts fell upon one of the finest mountains, (later identified as the Daddomain of Joseph Rock), while I had to be content with a slightly lower one (Nyambo Konka) for New York. While I completed the sketch, Emmons, accompanied by Dr. Lenox, went over to station "D." He arrived in time to take a few observations, made somewhat difficult by a high wind. They were important, as they gave sufficient data to work out results for Minya Konka and the Jara, even had we been unable to again observe them.

This precaution proved unnecessary, however, for the next morning, August 9th, was also clear. Emmons and I climbed to station "D," and made a complete set of measurements, corresponding to those from station "B." The work was more difficult because some of the peaks were hidden by clouds most of the time, and we had to get them one by one, as they appeared for a few moments.[30] Fortunately, by working in this way, we were able to take sights on all of them. Our race against the imminent bad weather had been won! From the day we left Shanghai, eight weeks before, we had been troubled by the thought that it might forestall us. This danger was now over, for the remainder of our survey could be completed even if clouds or rain obscured the mountains. With feelings of relief and satisfaction, we packed up our transit, reërected the beacon, and went down to the camp.

Mrs. Peterson and Dr. and Mrs. Lenox left us the following day. They had been of great assistance in managing the camp and meals, leaving us entirely free for our work. As a permanent contribution, the Lenoxes wrote out for us a list of useful words and expressions in Chinese, and left us a trained cook in the person of

Gaomo. He had been quick to learn and could now cook quite acceptably, and more important still had learned to wash the dishes! Mrs. Peterson left us several recipes, including one for pancakes which we ate with native brown sugar from Tatsienlu. With slight changes, the same formula served for corn cakes, and these became a standard lunch when bad weather kept us in camp.

We considered our meals at Camp Alpine very good. In addition to the tsamba, yak meat, butter, and cheese, which we bought locally, we sent a weekly messenger to Tatsienlu with a list of supplies, which the Cunninghams purchased for us. For breakfast we had little apples, some cereal such as tsamba, cornmeal, oatmeal, or puffed rice (made in Tatsienlu), fried potatoes or eggs; for lunch (when in camp) wheat pancakes or corn cakes; for supper we sometimes had soup, fried meat or a stew, fried eggplant, dried corn, or mien. The last are Chinese noodles which have been cooked and only need the addition of boiling water. For dessert we often had a special dish invented by Emmons—fried bread sprinkled with chocolate malted milk powder. This might not taste so delicious in America, but we can always explain by saying that it should be fried in yak butter. We used about three-quarters of a pound of this butter per day, chiefly for frying, which was the most satisfactory method of cooking. Boiling took a long time, the temperature for that altitude (14,923 feet) being only 186°. A pressure cooker would have been very serviceable. When our weekly messenger arrived we could also have, as a special dessert, some of

Mrs. Cunningham's excellent cookies. We never asked for these on our list, but merely returned the empty tin box and it always came back with a fresh supply! The messenger also carried our mail, and needless to say we looked forward eagerly to his return.

There was a flock of five snow-cocks (*Tetraogallus tibetanus henrici*) which we saw or heard several times upon the ridge. One morning upon awaking I heard them on the hillside above the camp and, hurrying out, managed to secure one by a long shot with our little .22 rifle. It was a hen or young bird, the size of a large chicken, and was barred gray and white all over. When roasted that night we found it good eating, and the bones supplied soup the next day. I also saw a flock of snow-cocks near our southern reconnaissance camp later, at an elevation of about 16,000 feet. On several occasions we saw the pretty little sifan partridge (*Perdix hodgesoniae sifanica*), both in the Yulong Valley and near our camp. It is a brownish bird, a little larger than our quail or bob-white.

China is the home of the pheasant family. The common species in the Minya Konka region, found only in woods, were the Stone's pheasant (*Phasianus colchicus elegans*) with a beautiful green breast, and the white eared-pheasant (*Crossoptilon crossoptilon crossoptilon*), a fine black-and-white bird forty inches long. Later Jack Young succeeded in capturing one of these birds and we took it back alive to the zoo at Nanking. We were interested to note that the change in altitude did not seem to affect it. The Chinese name for this species is "Ma Che," or "horse chicken." We found the meat very tough, but that of the Stone's pheasant was excellent. We saw specimens of the blue eared-pheasant and golden pheasant which Tangier Smith had obtained, but were not fortunate enough to see other species found in this region, probably because we spent so much of our time above the timber line.

Gaomo was supposed to buy his own food. Once we went fifty-fifty with a bag of tsamba which he was able to purchase at a low price. We were interested to see how he would divide it. He put it all temporarily into his empty leather bag and that night poured it all out into our tin wash basin. He made a dividing cut through the flour with a knife, then with a tablespoon he transferred his half back to the leather bag. He was scrupulously exact in the division, and when some of the tsamba fell in a tiny avalanche from our side to his, he showed us that he was leaving an equal amount in our portion. Though the cost of the whole bowlful was less than fifteen cents, we appreciated his exactness, and also the care he took to impress us with it. We allowed Gaomo any scraps of meat and also the potato peelings, which he learned to cut off very thick. We also let him try other items of our food, but he was not at all enthusiastic about them and seemed well satisfied with his diet of tea and tsamba. Later, we found this to be the case with all the Tibetans who sampled our food. Until one is well established with natives it is bad policy to give them strange food, for it may disagree with them and possibly give rise to a suspicion of poisoning.

After supper we used to keep the fire going for a

while, toasting bits of sour yak cheese, writing, and conversing from time to time. Emmons is a good story-teller with a remarkable fund of unusual experiences to draw upon, ranging from the glaciers of Mount Fairweather in Alaska to the turrets of the battleship *Arkansas*. Some evenings we read aloud a story or two by O. Henry, but the light from our lantern was not very good. Our surveying was strenuous work. Whenever we descended into the valley it meant a climb of two thousand feet to return, while station "D" was nearly a thousand feet above our camp, slightly higher than the summit of Mount Blanc. Packing our instruments up these steep slopes and working in the wind all day was conducive to sleep, so we were usually ready to turn in at an early hour.

There were no mosquitoes at camp, but during the daytime huge horseflies were a great pest. At lunch-time they would drive us to distraction, buzzing around our faces and getting into our food. One day we made the important discovery that they would not enter the shade of the tent, even to follow food, and after that we always ate inside.

Gaomo was a native of Yulonghsi and well acquainted with all the Tibetans in the neighborhood. With the "ullah" rate for a riding-animal with caretaker at one rupee for two days, we permitted ourselves the luxury of keeping one horse in camp all the time. We allowed Gaomo the privilege of selecting the recipient of our bounty, who became his visitor and spent the night in his tent. After staying a few days he went down with his horse and some one else came up with another, bringing butter, meat, and cheese to sell to us. This constant company was, I believe, a great help in keeping Gaomo contented and happy.

His position with us doubtless increased his prestige among the inhabitants. Those who paid a visit to our camp admired his ability to prepare the strange food which we required, and he liked to show how easily he could do it. Once he tried to make a flapjack turn over in the air as he had seen me do, but failed, and never mustered courage enough to try it again. We never knew Gaomo's age, but it was probably between thirty and forty. As far as we were concerned, he was a great success, for he was a willing worker and was always good natured, even when we insisted on doing things from which he had tried his best to dissuade us. He was very devout and I clearly recall the expression of horror which came into his face when I indicated a desire to see inside of a locked room at the Konka Gompa.

The horses which we hired were small, sturdy animals with rough coats. They varied considerably in disposition and ambition. I remember one particularly nice black horse. In marked contrast to most of the others, he kept up to a person walking ahead without much urging, in fact even giving him a little push sometimes with his forehead. In spite of much puffing and panting, and stopping every few steps to furiously snatch a mouthful of grass, he was a good climber and, taking turns, we once rode him all the way up from Yulonghsi.

It was fortunate that we had decided to postpone measurement of the base line in order to make all of our transit observations of the mountains as soon as possible. These were completed on August 9th and clouds almost always obscured the mountains after that date. The morning of the 10th looked promising, so I went up to station "D" again to make a panoramic sketch, but could only secure part of it. I was never able to finish it, nor to take a round of photographs from that point, which would have been desirable, though they were not necessary for our survey. From August 18th to September 17th rain or snow fell on every day but three. After that the weather began to improve, and when we were on Minya Konka in October it was fairly good.

The weather, however, did not interfere with our measurement of the base line and of the angles necessary to extend it to B-D, the line between our high stations. A slight complication arose due to the fact that we had chosen the white stone on the tip of a Mani pile to mark one end of the base line. We did not deem it advisable to set up our transit on top of the pile, feeling that, were we the Tibetans, we would object strenuously to foreigners standing on top of our prayer stones. However, by measuring a few feet from the top of the pile, and lining in our instrument exactly on the base line at that point, we were able, after measuring the angles there, to calculate the true angles at the white stone.

We had erected our own stone beacon to mark the other end of the base line. The Tibetans had many little stone cairns set up here and there in the fields, for religious purposes, some of them consisting of but two or three stones set one on top of the other. They apparently disapproved of our addition, for soon after our survey had been completed we found it torn down. They also had cairns on some of the hilltops, resembling our beacons at "B" and "D." These, however, could not have been so objectionable to them, for they were still standing when we passed by early in November on our way back to Tatsienlu.

One day as we were eating lunch beside a little stream in the valley, we were visited by a traveling Tibetan with his wife and little boy. We could not converse by speech, but shared some of our boiled potatoes with them. The little fellow had a good time playing with our tin lunch-box, while the man was interested in my field-glasses, and also in looking through the telescope of the transit. The woman wore a headband of silver coins, rupees. The most popular stones found in the native silver jewelry of this region are coral and turquoise, or imitations of them. It is interesting to note that Marco Polo, who reached the vicinity of Yachow near the end of the thirteenth century, wrote: "Coral is in great demand in this country and fetches a high price, for they delight to hang it around the necks of their women and of their idols." The ethnological boundary between the Chinese and Tibetans was farther east in those days than it is at present.

Both men and women wear several rings set with coral or turquoise.[14] The rings are not continuous circles, but overlap on the inside of the finger, so that their size can be adjusted by bending. The women wear rings in both ears; the men in the left ear only. Decorated charm-boxes are worn around the neck. The men carry, suspended from their belts, leather purses studded with coral and turquoise;[13] also tinder-purses of similar workmanship, which have a blade of steel three-sixteenths of an inch thick, fastened to the bottom. In striking fire with these, a man holds a quartz pebble and a bit of tinder in one hand, and grasping the tinder-purse in the other hand, swings it past, striking the stone with the steel and catching a spark in the tinder.

There were a few bright days which we utilized for time and azimuth observations from the sun to determine the true north and south. In this region the magnetic needle points almost true north, our observations showing the variation to be less than one degree west.

During our twenty-five days at Camp Alpine, we kept the mercurial barometer set up inside the tent and made a series of seventy observations. (See curves, page 260.) Simultaneous air temperatures were taken with a small sling psychrometer. From this data, as described in the appendix, the altitude of the camp has been determined at 14,923 feet. Our triangulation work measured the altitude of Minya Konka above station "B" and a separate little triangulation had been used to measure the altitude of station "B" above our camp. (See triangulation diagrams, page 265.)

On rainy days we spent most of the time getting our records in permanent form and making computations. On August 20th we devoted the whole day to this work. Sitting on our cots, with the rain pattering on the tent, we paid little attention to it, for we were obtaining our first figure for the altitude of the mountain. A rough estimate had shown that it could not much exceed

25,000 feet, but now we were finding out the true figure.

The final result showed the summit to be 9,968 feet above our camp, or 24,891 feet above sea-level. As is the case with all altitudes based on barometric measurements, there is an unavoidable uncertainty in this figure. We believe the probable error to be plus or minus 85 feet, and, as a round figure, call the altitude of Minya Konka 24,900 feet, or 7,590 meters.

This altitude is not equaled on any other continent, the nearest approach being Aconcagua (22,834 feet) in South America. Minya Konka is surpassed, however, by many mountains in the central ranges of Asia. The only one of these whose summit has been reached is Kamet (25,447 feet), which was climbed in June, 1931, by six members of the British Himalayan expedition headed by Frank S. Smythe. Although this is the highest mountain which has been conquered, greater elevations have been attained by three expeditions on Mount Everest (whose altitude is 29,141 feet) and by one on Kanchenjunga (altitude 28,225 feet).

The name Minya Konka means "White Ice Mountain of Minyag." There has been some controversy regarding this name, as "Bo Kunka" has also been used. J. Huston Edgar told us that when he visited the Konka Gompa in 1931, the head lama, without prompting, wrote the name for him as

ཇ་བང་ ཡུལ་ གངས་ དཀར་

a'Bang	Yul	Gangs	dkar
Beloved or revered	region or country	glacier or ice or snow	white

The Bo Kunka used by Count Szechenyi was evidently
derived from this. Joseph Rock, however, wrote :*

In June of 1928, while exploring the Konkaling snow peaks
to the northwest of Muli, I beheld from a ridge, at 16,300
feet elevation, a series of snowy ranges, one of special interest
far to the northeast. My Tibetan guides said this was Minya
Konka. . . .

Herbert Stevens, who was with the Roosevelts, wrote :†

. . . when between Yatsu and Baurong before the descent to the
gorge of the Yalung, I had an impressive view to the east of
snow mountains, which the lama and carriers spoke of as the
Minya Konka. . . .

Minya is derived from Minyag. In his Tibetan-Eng-
lish dictionary, Jaeschke says that, according to the
Tibetan Book of Kings, Minyag and Tangut were the
names of two closely connected provinces in northeast
Tibet which formed in ancient times a separate kingdom. The natives whom we met called the mountain
simply Konka (pronounced somewhere between Gongka
and Gungka). While undoubtedly it is sometimes called
the "Revered Konka," this may also apply to other
mountains in Tibet. It seems, therefore, that the name
Minya Konka, which was used by the guides and lamas
when pointing out the mountain to Rock and Stevens,
is preferable because it is distinctive. There is only
one Minyag, and while there are other konkas in it,
this is the outstanding one.

Heim also uses this name (which he spells Minya

* *National Geographic Magazine,* vol. 58, 1930, p. 385.
† *Geographical Journal,* vol. 75, 1930, p. 355.

Gangkar) and in his book, on page 70, he gives a cut showing it as written for him by the head of this same Konka Gompa:

Men-as   *Kun-gar*

This does not agree with the words as given by the Tibetan dictionaries, and we must conclude that the lama was a little weak in spelling. According to the dictionaries it is written thus:

Mi-nyag	*Kangs*	*dKar*
Minyag	Glacier or ice or snow	White

"The White Ice Mountain of Minyag."

It is interesting to note that Kangs is the same as the first syllable of Kangchenjunga; also that Choma Kankar (Lady white glacier) was once erroneously thought to be a native name for Mount Everest.*

The names of the other peaks given on our map of the Minya Konka region are those used by Rock, with the addition of names given by Heim, the German spelling Anglicized.

The Tibetans believe that Minya Konka is the abode of Dorjelutru and it would be hard to find a more suitable dwelling-place for the Thunder God. Lest we think

* Mount Everest and its Tibetan Names, by Col. Sir Sidney Burrard.

that the Tibetans are unique in entertaining such no-
tions, we must remember that in the Middle Ages the
people of Europe "believed that mountain regions were
haunted by winged dragons, gnomes, goblins, and all
kinds of evil spirits." At Lucerne dwelt the spirit of
Pontius Pilot, which had "roamed over the earth until
a wandering scholar got its consent to remain quietly
in the waters of the lake on the mountain which bears
his name." The Government forbade all strangers to
approach the lake, and in 1307 six clergymen were imprisoned for breaking this rule. (W. A. B. Coolidge in
Swiss Travels and Swiss Guide Books, 1889, p. 45.)

Dorjelutru was usually silent, but one severe thunder-
storm occurred on the evening of August 18th. His
lightning flashed and his thunder came crashing down
over the ranges, echoing and reëchoing from face to
face of the great mountain masses. As we looked out
toward his abode on another evening we beheld a gray
wall of mist; but rifts developed in it, moving rapidly
from left to right, showing that the whole mass of
cloud was in swift motion. And through these rifts, its
base cut off from the earth by solid cloud, appeared
the upper portion of Minya Konka, seeming to float
in space high before us.

That forbidding face, the awful precipices, the snowy
ridges, cold and gray in the evening dusk, appeared for
an instant, to be concealed quickly by the swift curtain.
Again and again the vision was unveiled by those moving rifts, until in the growing darkness we could see it
no more.

Part Two

By

ARTHUR B. EMMONS, 3rd

"And time will close about me, and my soul stir to the rhythm
of the daily round.
Yet, having known, life will not press so close, and always I shall
feel time ravel thin about me;
For once I stood
In the white windy presence of eternity."

—EUNICE TIETJENS

Chapter VI

INTO THE BÜCHU VALLEY

O N THE 22nd of August six inches of snow fell, and with its arrival our enthusiasm for the little Alpine camp by the lake began to wane. The field work of our surveying was complete, and new phases of the expedition's work now claimed our attention. Having triangulated it, the next item on the program was an attempt to climb Minya Konka, a venture which more than anything else had drawn us to this part of Asia.

The expedition was still divided, two of us being already in the field, and the remaining two, Terris Moore and Jack Young, en route from Shanghai, where they had remained to attend to some last-minute affairs. The plan to which we now adhered was that, on completion of the survey work, Burdsall and I should explore the Konka until the arrival of the other two in September. The object of this preliminary reconnaissance was to locate, if possible, the easiest and safest route by which the climbing party could reach the summit. The monsoon had us so thoroughly in its clutches that we rather despaired of accomplishing much until it broke, and the clouds which lay like a pall over peak and plain should dissipate.

To make a complete reconnaissance of a huge, relatively unknown, and remote mountain mass such as that

of Minya Konka is far from being a simple matter,
and where the success of a whole campaign depends
so largely on its intelligent and thorough accomplishment, the importance of such a reconnaissance can hardly
be overestimated.

The problem facing the mountaineer in this respect
has many difficult aspects. In the first place, unless an
obvious way to the top immediately presents itself, the
mountain must be viewed from as many different angles
as possible to insure that nothing be overlooked. The
exploration of such a massif is frequently extremely difficult of accomplishment, when it can be done at all, due
to the confusion of foothills and neighboring peaks
guarding its lower approaches. Such was the character
of the country surrounding Minya Konka. (*See diagram
facing p. 236.*)

Secondly, peaks when viewed from a distance, especially those which rise to great heights above the neighboring country, often present very misleading appearances. Such false impressions are due to the refractive
effect of the atmosphere, the foreshortening of perspective, and the condition of shoulders and ridges super-
imposed against a background lacking in contrast. Under
such conditions it is, therefore, desirable to gain a point
of vantage at some considerable elevation in close ap-
position to the peak in question and to be able to study
its topography from there. The ideal method of making
such a reconnaissance would be from an airplane with
the aid of a mapping camera. In this way photographs
could be obtained from many different directions at

close range. These photographs may then be developed and examined carefully and at leisure, and may also be taken into the field and studied again actually at the scene of operations. This method is sometimes used where facilities are available and expense is no consideration. Airplanes, however, were scarce on the Sino-Tibetan border to the extent of being non-existent, and we resigned ourselves to the fact that our explorations would have to be made entirely on the humble "shank's mare."

No serious attempt had ever been made to climb Minya Konka. Again, due to its isolated position well away from the beaten track, little apparently was known about it and less had been published on the subject. Even from an article by Dr. Joseph Rock appearing in the *National Geographic Magazine* we gleaned but little information that was of much use to us. We studied a set of sketches made by Herbert Stevens of the Kelly-Roosevelt Expedition, but these too lacked enough detail to aid us materially. The mountain had been pronounced unclimbable by several explorers, but as to that point we were inclined to be still skeptical. At least, like the bear, we were going "to see what we could see."

It was from the missionaries in Tatsienlu that we learned more about the Konka than from anyone else. They had often seen it in crossing the passes in eastern Tibet to the north and west, and to them it seemed to provide a source of both pride and inspiration. They greeted our enterprise with much encouragement and enthusiasm, and to them we owe a large debt of gratitude for the interest and coöperation they gave our project. Dr. and Mrs. Cunningham of the China Inland Mission at Tatsienlu were especially generous in both the time and the effort they evinced to give us a helping hand, and our debt to them is especially great.

I am afraid we may have been thought somewhat unappreciative when it became known that our survey figures fell below all previous estimates for their giant peak, though we ourselves felt a distinct disappointment that such was the case.

The southern and eastern approaches to the Konka were relatively difficult of access, and information or photographs from these two directions seemed entirely unavailable. From our camp at Camp Alpine the summit lay slightly south of east, thus precluding any view of the southern slopes. From the west and north the mountain presented no very encouraging aspects.[29] As has been observed, the western face fell away seemingly sheer for thousands of feet, as did that on the north. The only ray of hope was found in the singularly long and uniformly steep ridge extending from a spur on the northwest at about 21,000 feet to the summit. It was a most uninviting sort of ridge, and we gave it but little consideration. It remained then to solve the enigma of the southern and eastern slopes before any route could be picked with finality and the assurance that it was the best one.

Orders were given to the men to obtain ullah and the job of packing up camp began. On the morning of August 25th, seven yaks and two horses were loaded with our worldly goods, and we reluctantly bade farewell to the camp we had first occupied just a month before. It had done well by us and we were sorry to leave, but new fields of adventure beckoned.

The yaks were in a rather boisterous mood that morning, and one in particular was feeling gay. While descending a rather steep bit of trail into the valley, this fellow, carrying two cases, deciding that a short cut is always the best, forsook the trail and plunged straight down a long, very steep declivity. He had reckoned without the added momentum of the load, and we watched him skyrocketing down, all four feet braced, not knowing whether to laugh or cry and compromising by pulling out our cameras to photograph the imminent wreck. It is a commentary on the surefootedness of these great lumbering beasts that he stayed right side up and finally came to a standstill several hundred feet below, calmly looking back, as if to say, "Well, what's all the fuss about?" with the cases still aboard and at least outwardly intact.

The Yulong Valley is typical of the high Tibetan plateau country, being U-shaped in contradistinction to the V-shaped valleys of the more easterly borderland, such as the Büchu. It is enclosed between rounded grassy mountains sometimes surmounted by rocky crags and outcrops. This gently-rolling country was in great contrast with the jagged snow peaks and deep forested valleys that had so recently been occupying our attention. We rode south past several Tibetan settlements[27] until late in the afternoon, when we forded a mountain river and, turning abruptly east, began to climb up into the Tsemei La.

We pushed ahead as fast as possible, for we hoped

to reach a small village in the Büchu Valley at the foot
of the Konka on the morrow. Had we known what lay
between, though, I think our eagerness in this respect
might have diminished somewhat. At dusk we pitched
camp well up in the pass in a cold drizzle of rain, but
despite the dampness and a decided dearth of wood, the
Tibetans soon conjured up enough and got a fire going, a feat which they apparently never fail to accomplish with uncanny ability even under the worst conditions.

The trail from here climbed steeply, winding up
across long talus slopes of loose rock. By ten o'clock
the next morning we had made the remaining seven hundred feet and topped the last rise of the pass. The
Konka greeted us, swimming majestically above a tu-
multuous sea of clouds.[31] Our interest at once turned
to the southern face, which should have been visible
from this new angle. It was shrouded in the clouds,
however, and our curiosity went unsatisfied. I took several photographs while Burdsall set up the mercurial
barometer in the pass and took a reading. This subsequently showed the elevation to be 15,288 feet above
sea-level.

The descent into the Büchu Valley was much steeper
than the ascent had been, the trail zigzagging sharply
down across a steep mountain-side. A few hundred feet
from the top, the sea of mist closed in around us, shutting everything from view. After dropping down about
two thousand feet more, we emerged beneath the clouds
and found ourselves almost at timber line. Shortly the
trail entered a heavy rhododendron forest in which

some of the trees, hardly more than shrubs, as a rule, here reached enormous size. Here in the space of a few minutes the country had changed from one of sub-arctic character to that of a forest of semi-tropical verdure and luxuriance—truly an amazing contrast.[33]

By noon we arrived at the tiny village of Tsemei, consisting of two stone Tibetan houses with possibly twenty inhabitants, the usual size of a Tibetan settlement in this locality. Here it was discovered that the ullah for the next stage could not be obtained until the following day. As Tsemei was within a few miles of the small lamasery on the lower slopes of the Konka, known as the Konka Gompa, we decided to take advantage of the delay and pay it a visit. The men who had brought us thus far wanted to return to the Yulong Valley at once with their horses and yaks. We managed to wheedle a horse from them, however, and having loaded him with the necessary gear for a single night, set out for the lamasery on foot with Gaomo.

The trail dipped abruptly down several hundred feet to the river bottom, where we crossed a wooden cantilever bridge[35] hung with prayer flags, and climbed steeply up the other side through a heavy forest of prickly oak. At length the trail leveled off and ran for several miles along the side of a ridge, when we emerged on a grassy bench above a glacier-filled valley. Here a lamasery had been built. It was composed of one large stone building in the form of a square around a courtyard, and five or six smaller buildings close at hand. The young student lamas, of whom there were possibly half a dozen, lived and studied in this larger edifice. We were shown into the main courtyard and greeted most cordially by several of the older lamas,[27] who led us into a great barnlike room and told us to make ourselves at home. This was to be our private apartment as long as we chose to make it so.

I suggested that we send the flashlight we had brought as a present accompanied by our cards to the head lama, the "Living Buddha of Minya," and ask him for an interview—the usual procedure in such cases. We gave them to a lama, and in our meager Chinese asked him to convey them to His Holiness with our compliments. He expressed his regrets and said the Living Buddha would be away, we understood, for another three weeks, so we took back our flashlight, saying we would give it to him when we returned later on. The incident was closed, but I mention it as it has relation to a later episode.

Early the next morning Gaomo came running to our private apartment shouting, "Lookee! Lookee!" This was his interpretation of our exclamations of "Oh, look" when something attracted our attention, and was the sum total of Gaomo's grasp of the English language. We rushed out half dressed into the chilly courtyard to see what had occasioned this outburst of English from our faithful Tibetan. There stood the resplendent Konka in the clear morning air, the very embodiment of majesty and awe, with a golden plume of sunlit snow streaming from its summit in the early dawn. It seemed so remote that it was almost ethereal in its aloof austerity—a thing quite apart from the petty world below. No wonder the Tibetans of this whole region worshiped it as a holy mountain! It was not difficult to imagine what had given rise to the legend that on its summit there reposed a golden crown whose radiance was now so much in evidence in the light of the rising sun.

We stood silently and gazed in wonder. Climb it? There appeared not the remotest chance! It seemed almost a desecration even to attempt such a thing. Then the bite of the frosty air penetrated our preoccupation and reminded us that we were still decidedly in a state of *deshabille* and that this condition had best be remedied immediately.

Cameras were unlimbered and little attention paid to breakfast, for not only the Minya Konka, but many of the lesser peaks, put on an appearance, conspicuous among which was the Nyambo, in whose very shadow lay the monastery. Our first enthusiasm for photographs having been satisfied, we sat down to study the riddle of the northwest ridge, now visible at a very favorable angle. A pair of eight-power field-glasses brought the ridge into sharp relief. It appeared rather fearsome and presented several difficult-looking stretches. One of these was a decided gap at the point where the northern shoulder joined the peak; a difficult thing to cross. Then there were two ice-and-rock buttresses breaking the contour of the ridge itself, one just below the summit and a second at about 23,000 feet. Could these be circumvented or must they yield to a frontal attack only? These were questions which could only be answered when the attempt was made.

Despite these problems, however, I felt decidedly

more optimistic about this ridge than heretofore, an opinion not shared by Burdsall. In any event, the scaling of the northwest ridge should not be thought of, save as a very last resort in case no other way could be discovered. And even then the chances of success in this direction seemed scarcely worthy of consideration.

Before many hours of the morning had passed, long gray fingers of cloud came creeping up the valley, and soon the ranges were again blotted from sight. We bade farewell to our hosts, the lamas, and headed back towards Tsemei village with the feeling of having accomplished a little at least in the work of reconnaissance.

At Tsemei it was discovered that only five pack animals could be produced by the ullah, and with the addition of our present pack horse, we would be still one short even if we ourselves walked. We hated to waste more time, as the season was advancing, and we must indeed get busy if much climbing were going to be accomplished before the winter set in. There followed much talk, and then, as always, the faithful Gaomo came to the rescue by arranging with the villagers to have the surplus gear "baied" or back-packed along the line of march towards Pawa, our ultimate destination.

Our road crossed the river on a second bridge lower downstream from the first and followed the river for five or six miles to a single Tibetan house perched on a bluff and dignified by the name of Boka. Although the afternoon was well advanced, we felt it desirable to press on to Pawa with our present aggregation. The Tibetans, however, were of a different mind and claimed

that no road existed beyond Boka. We had been otherwise informed and were much inclined to doubt the
verity of this statement, but the Tibetans were adamant,
and so the caravan was unloaded and we became guests
of the mayor of Boka for a night. I continued a short
way on along the river and found that the trail did
indeed dwindle to a mere track and in places all but
disappeared. At all events, no self-respecting yak could
be expected to traverse it with a load, and I came back
thoroughly disgusted. This was truly a blow to our eastward progress.

Chapter VII

SIGHT UNSEEN

A COMFORTABLE base camp was pitched in the river bottom close beside the rushing Büchu not far from Boka. We received no little help in clearing the stones away from under the tent given by a four-year-old Tibetan boy whom we christened "Tony," an individual of insatiable curiosity as to these queer white men.[36] Several cloudy days were spent in camp going over equipment and getting things into some semblance of order; then the weather cleared and an opportunity presented itself to do a bit of exploring and to orient ourselves somewhat.

Dick Burdsall was nursing a pair of blistered feet, so I donned nailed climbing-boots and set off alone with my camera to have a "lookee" at what was to be seen. The Konka was now shut off from us by the range of the Nyambo and its 20,000-foot neighbors which formed a complete barrier running east and west. It would be necessary, then, to find a break in this barrier wall farther to the east through which we could effect a nearer approach to the mountain from that direction.

I crossed the Büchu on a shaky log footbridge and climbed for several thousand feet in a narrow gully which eventually gave access to a shoulder above. At this point the clouds again began to gather, reducing all visi-

bility to a few feet of dank rocks. I kept on, hoping
to climb above this fog, and finally managed to do so,
only to find another layer higher up which soon began
to pelt me with rain and hail. By this time I was some
5,000 feet above camp at an altitude of nearly 16,000
feet.

Seeing no use in going farther, I sat down to eat my
lunch and to curse the weather. The bad language may
have had some effect, for a break in the clouds suddenly revealed the chain of mountains across the valley which we were interested in penetrating. They
seemed to form an unbroken line, hopelessly inaccessible. Then far down the valley I espied something that
brought my binoculars up into focus in an instant. A
deep valley ran north, extending far back towards the
Konka and breaking through the barrier chain. It lay
some eight or ten miles to the east. Only part of it was
visible, but there was a suggestion of greater things now
unseen. The clouds soon rolled across and it was no
longer visible, but I had seen enough and felt that a
great find had been made.

For a few fleeting seconds the Konka showed its tip.
A hasty compass-reading showed it to be nearly northeast, much to my disappointment, as we had hoped by
now to be at least due south of the mountain. Perhaps
my newly discovered valley wasn't such a find, after all.
It would be well worth investigating, at any rate. After
taking a few more compass-readings to augment our
survey map, I made a quick descent to camp.

The sun again failed to appear on the succeeding day
and I took this opportunity to explore the trail, if it

deserved the name, to the eastward along the Büchu Valley to see to what extent it would help our efforts to reach the new valley. There were the marks of horse's hoofs plainly discernible in several places, and I became more hopeful, for, although the path was atrociously bad, at least a man could go where a horse had gone. After some six miles I was satisfied that the mouth of our valley could be reached, and feeling much encouraged returned to Boka.

The day following we had a snowstorm and remained in camp, preparing for an extended reconnaissance of a week or more, which was expected to include a fair amount of snow and ice climbing. The 1st of September dawned clear and bright, but we were not deceived. The monsoon still had us in its grip, which was not due to be loosened for some weeks yet. Burdsall's feet seemed well enough to stand more punishment, however, and so, leaving Gaomo in charge of the camp, we started down the valley in high spirits, for now the game began to get interesting and adventure was at hand.

Accompanying us was an ancient Tibetan woman leading a horse carrying our two packs. After several miles the trail became really bad, and our female attendant became highly agitated when she perceived our intention to continue. Our mutual language consisted of very poor Chinese. With the aid of much pantomime she conveyed to us that she was afraid the horse would step off the path and slide into the river below. This thought was not farthest from our own minds, but we took pains not to express it. She was all for returning to Boka at once with friend horse in tow, but we had other and conflicting ideas, inasmuch as our cry was now, as ever, "On to Pawa." Furthermore, we had paid in part for our transportation to that point and could not see ourselves shouldering heavy packs at this early juncture. The majority prevailed and I relieved her of the halter rope as we scrambled on along an almost precipitous bank above the Büchu River.

At one point disaster was imminent. Here the track was cut in a steep hillside above a particularly swift place in the river. For a short distance the trail had been undermined by the water and had partly dropped into the torrent, the rest being in a fair way to follow. It was decidedly not a place to linger, so I hurried across. The horse scrambled over, but miscalculated his distance and the protruding pack glanced off a projecting rock, throwing him from the trail. For a few seconds there was a *mêlée* of plunging horse and loosened packs, punctuated by a series of wails from the woman, who strode back along the path tearing her hair. Fortunately, here there was a grassy shelf just below the trail and this alone saved the day for us. I quieted the horse as best I could and held his head while Burdsall went to the rescue of the Tibetan. He soon returned with her somewhat calmed, and then came to my aid.

The pack-saddle was *en renverse* beneath his belly, and after some trouble we got it free and led the horse to a safe place farther down the trail, whence we carried the packs and reloaded them. During this latter process our friend emitted a tirade of Tibetan that met only deaf ears. We assured her that we would pay her

well for the horse if anything untoward should befall
him, and resumed the march. She became resigned to
these crazy foreigners after consigning them in her
native tongue probably to the Lower Regions and all
went smoothly forward.

At length we rounded a bend and, joy! there we were
greeted by a wide gently sloping valley that extended
some six or eight miles northward, penetrating into the
very stronghold of the Konka itself. Its headwall, to
be sure, consisted of a ring of formidable-looking
21,000-foot peaks, but on closer inspection these might
disclose a vantage-point from which the whole situation
would be exposed to view. Something of value was
bound to come of an exploration of this valley in any
event, we both felt, so laid our course accordingly.

Here lay the much-vaunted Pawa, a filthy hut of
even less pretensions than any we had yet seen. The inhabitants told of a pathway leading back towards the
mountainous headwall. The woman who had brought
us thus far refused to go farther, and neither bribes,
threats, nor pleading could move her one iota, so we
were forced to shoulder our own loads, and headed for
timber line.

Towards evening we forded a turbulent glacier stream
and pitched camp on its opposite bank. Good progress
had been made and Pawa lay well behind us. Tomorrow would undoubtedly reveal what this line of approach was going to accomplish.

The weather turned cloudy the next morning as we
climbed up along an old glacial moraine flanking one
side of the valley, and we moved in ignorance of what

lay ahead or above. The going became more difficult and the footing less secure, with our sixty-five-pound packs. Darkness found us still far below the glacier which had been our goal for the day. Camp was pitched among the rocks in a cold drizzle of rain. We had made only three or four miles, and a thousand feet in elevation, a disappointing record.

The rain still continued the day following, but the fog lifted a few hundred feet and our immediate surroundings now became visible. We were at a point where the valley turned abruptly eastward not far below the tongue of a glacier that descended from a basin higher up, and were completely encircled by peaks whose summits were still hidden. To gain the higher level of the glacier a steep rocky slope must be climbed for a thousand feet or so. Above that nothing could be seen but swirling wraiths of mist.

We carried our packs to the foot of the glacier and I climbed to the upper basin in search of a camp site to serve as a base for further reconnaissance. Meanwhile Burdsall returned to our last camp for part of a load which still remained there. I found an excellent site on a grassy bench overlooking the entire valley. On returning to where Burdsall was waiting, camp was set up after much yeoman-like work with an ice-ax in clearing and leveling a place for the tent, as there was not time enough left to climb higher that day.

The next thirty-six hours were spent in our snug alpine tent. The walls from time to time had to be cleared of the snow, which fell continually, by pounding the canvas from inside with our fists. At night the frequent rumble and roar of avalanches falling from the heights above, thundering like a fast express train on an iron trestle, would startle us into wakefulness. Sometimes they continued for several minutes at a stretch before they died away in a distant grumble, portending death for the unwary climber.

We pushed on again in six inches of wet snow, after crawling from warm sleeping-bags to put on wet clothes and frozen boots, an operation requiring one's utmost will-power. Half the loads were left for a second trip, as the climb ahead of us was too strenuous for full packs. By noon we reached the new tent site and dropped our first installment to return for the second. By five in the afternoon we had the new camp consolidated at about 16,000 feet.[37] As we were clearing away the two feet of snow for a tent space, the clouds broke and the sun came through.

What a sight greeted our eyes! We were in a tremendous amphitheater hemmed in on all sides by jagged snow peaks which towered many thousands of feet above us. Huge walls of blue-green ice menaced the lower slopes with the potential danger of mighty avalanches from their crumbling sides; razor-like ridges were fantastically capped by coxcombs and cornices of snow so huge and weird that only in the Himalayan system do such formations exist. We forgot our tent, supper, and everything else to stand enthralled by the magnificence of the scene. The Alps, the Canadian Rockies, even the great mountains of far Alaska would fade into the background before such glory and splendor displayed, as it was, in the rays of the setting sun.

To our relief, several breaks in the northern ramparts disclosed themselves. The lowest of these looked quite inaccessible, but one other, from which a broken glacier descended, seemed to yield greater possibilities. Through the field-glasses a route was picked to a shoulder at one side of this higher gap, a point which, once gained, we felt should offer a splendid view of the Konka from the southeast.

A day intervened before we could attempt any more climbing, a day which I spent in the tent with my eyes bandaged, ruefully penitent of a few minutes spent in presence of the sun without my snow glasses, even when it was about to set. Fortunately, the day was not a wasted one, as the bad weather again closed down on us, and nothing could be seen of the higher peaks.

On the seventh, after a day's rest, I was again fit, and by eight in the morning we were off across the valley glacier under clear skies. By this time we had christened our present abode "Cloud Camp," and this was by no means a misnomer.

A heavy terminal moraine of loose snow-covered rocks confronted us; a worse footing would be hard to devise, and we lost considerable time before we reached the sloping tongue of ice which descended from the gap. As we neared a rocky outcrop, a herd of bharal, or Himalayan blue sheep, was spotted crossing a cliff face just above. We counted forty-two sheep, and among them were some beautiful heads. How I longed for my rifle!

We put on that invention of the devil, crampons, and a rope, and began to climb in earnest. Three feet of wet soft snow on top of steep glacier ice made the going doubly arduous, when working, unacclimatized as we were, at 17,000 feet. A few hidden crevasses lay across our path, but these were of minor character and were easily discovered by sounding through the snow with an ice-ax, and, as the rope between us was always kept taut, risk of a fall was minimized.

The grandeur on all sides increased as the horizon receded before our advance, and cameras received much attention. A brief halt was made for lunch and a rest, but soon we pressed on, realizing that there was yet a long way to climb before we topped the shoulder at 20,000 feet. The snow became softer and deeper, reducing progress to a snail's pace. Soon it became evident that we could not possibly reach our goal that day, but we decided to break the trail as far as time would allow for a second try later.

The depth of the snow increased so much that it became impossible to touch bottom with our axes, thus materially increasing the danger of a nasty fall into a crevasse. In fact, in several suspicious-looking places I crawled across on my stomach to distribute my weight while Burdsall anchored me with the rope. By 4 P.M. we arrived at the base of a large area of badly broken ice and a number of huge cracks that cut the glacier transversely at about 18,000 feet.

As clouds had now begun to gather, we decided to call it a day and, feeling much disappointed that we had fallen so short of the mark, began the descent. Now it is a curious fact that in cloudy weather on unbroken snow certain conditions of diffused light sometimes prevail which render all sense of perspective false. Hummocks of snow only a few feet away appear as full-fledged mountains, and one stumbles into depressions or over ice blocks without seeing them at all. This effect has been remarked upon by several Arctic explorers and is especially prevalent in the polar regions. We encountered just such a phenomenon that afternoon in making our descent, but, fortunately, we had our tracks to follow and so experienced but little trouble, arriving at camp in two hours, whence it had taken us eight to climb. On the whole, it had been a rather disappointing day, but we both were better for the added acclimatization.

Our food and fuel supplies were by now running low, with hardly enough of the latter for another day, but to save, if possible, another trip to Cloud Camp from Boka, we determined to eke out our stores and, weather permitting, would try again to reach the gap in the barrier wall before going back to our base.

The day following the climb we were held in camp by another snowstorm. This meant that if the weather permitted no advance on the morrow, we would be forced to return to Boka to renew supplies, and incidentally change our chronically wet clothes. For the next day I refer to my diary:

Sept. 9th. Rain, snow, and sleet, so decided to head for tall timber. Broke camp, leaving everything except sleeping-bags. Collapsed the tent and secured it, leaving the pole stuck in the ground as a marker. Only three Meta tablets (patent fuel) and two bars of chocolate left. Off at 9:30 A.M. Reached Pawa at 2 P.M. in a cold drenching rain somewhat ahead of Dick.

We both arrived at Boka after dark, to find Gaoma and several other Tibs in charge of camp. No sign of the boys (Moore and Young), as we half expected. The Tibs gave us a good welcome and seemed worried, as we were two days overdue. Fifteen miles today in the snow and rain; surely good to be "home" again. At least we've a good climbing base now, even if it took ten days to establish.

Dry clothes for the first time in over a week, and piping-hot food, soon made life worth living again, but it was not long *that* night before we crawled into the eiderdown!

Chapter VIII

DEFEAT ON THE EAST

DURING the days that followed occupations became somewhat varied. We planned not to return to Cloud Camp until the personnel of the expedition should be completed by the arrival of Moore and Young, who were due at any time. Young, chiefly in whose hands lay the collecting work, made a prophecy before we left Shanghai, that, since we were human beings and in such a capacity inclined to indolence, we would not exceed the limit of twenty-five birds toward the collection by the time he rejoined us in Tibet. Until now our score had been zero, but as the honor of the Vanguard must be upheld, a sudden strong interest in local bird life developed, and one or the other of us could often be seen slinking through the forest with our .410-gauge shotgun to bang away at anything that flew or looked as if it might be capable of it. It was indeed a brave and hardy bird that ventured near our camp those days!

As I knew relatively nothing of the art of taxidermy, it devolved solely upon Burdsall to prepare the specimens, and I found myself with much free time on my hands. On several occasions I took my Mauser 30-06 rifle and went after sheep or muntjac deer, but game was either very high in the mountains or else scarce in the valleys, due to the extensive depredations made upon it by the Tibetan hunters, and I had poor hunting.

The monsoon, like the poor, we had with us always, and few and far between were the days on which it did not rain. My diary had fallen much in arrears, and this was a welcome opportunity to bring it up to date and also to do some more work on the unfinished calculations of the survey. The Jara, a spectacular snow peak lying northwest of Tatsienlu which the Tibetans believe to be higher than Minya Konka, very disappointingly came to only 19,383 feet in elevation; but then the Tibetans are not blessed (or cursed) with such conventional instruments as theodolite or mercurial barometer, and their ignorance is more apt to be bliss than otherwise.

Each day we expected the other two men to put in an appearance, but our eagerness to see them probably rendered our expectations a little premature. By now the required twenty-five birds had been victimized and ten to spare. Our honor was saved and we could now face Jack Young with perfect equanimity.

On the 19th of September I conceived a compelling hunch that the day had arrived when the Büchu Valley would witness the coming of the Moore-Young contingent. Burdsall made light of my prediction, saying in an irreverent tone, "Oh they'll be here when we see them, and not before," but I took this omen more to heart and resolved to be a brass band and a welcoming committee-of-one should this premonition prove correct, and, as the day was sunny, started off towards the Tsemei La alone.

The warmth of the air made it feel like spring, and so the brass band hurried not. Having reached Tsemei village, I began the ascent of the pass. As I reached timber line, the Konka became divested of clouds save for a long streamer whipping from its glistening summit. A photograph was decidedly indicated, and climbing a bank above the trail, I jockeyed for the best position from which to shoot. I was in the very act of sighting the camera when a series of whoops and yells from above drove all thoughts of photography from my mind, and thereby was lost what might have been one of the world's best photographs.

The Tibetans are no mean hands at rending the air with vocal disturbances, but such caterwauls as then smote my ears could never have come from any but American lungs. I dashed up the trail and greeted two of the handsomest bandits that ever ran wild. There, complete with beards, slouch hats, rifles, and flea-bitten horse, were Moore and Young.

Leaving Shanghai early in August, they had followed our footsteps closely, proceeding up the Yangtze by river steamer to Kiating, and thence to Chengtu by bus while their baggage went overland by coolies to Yachow. Arriving at Yachow, they hired another coolie caravan and, after a seven days' trip over the mountains, reached Tatsienlu and the generous hospitality of Dr. and Mrs. Cunningham. A note from the Vanguard awaited them here, urging them to lose no time in joining us at Boka and telling of the work so far accomplished.

They camped one night below the Djezi La, and on saddling up the next morning discovered one of the horses missing. The Tibetans reported that a small band of soldiers had passed and had probably "adopted" the animal, a practice of commandeering transport frequently indulged in by the military factions along the border. Moore and Young, however, did not display the usual *laissez-faire* attitude generally accorded this procedure. An armed posse was organized which included Tsong-gombo, a Tibetan servant, and the soldiers were trailed up over the Yachiagan pass on their way into the Lolo country.

They overtook a group of soldiers making off into the hills some hours later, high up in the pass. A command to halt was shouted at them, but it went unheeded. When two shots whistled close over their heads, however, the fugitives quickly changed their minds and stopped. Young rode up, questioned them in Chinese, while Moore covered them with a pistol. They had with them a horse soon identified as the one stolen that morning, although the mane had been clipped in an effort to disguise him. As there seemed to be no officer in charge, the man leading the horse was disarmed of a large Tibetan knife and a bayonet and marched back to the magistrate of the nearest town, protesting that it was a mistake and he did not know the horse belonged to any one! The horse was thus recovered and the thief brought to justice, but a whole day had been wasted in the process. I think Burdsall and I both felt we had missed something.

After four days consumed in overhauling equipment and organizing a caravan, they crossed the Djezi and Tsemei passes and—well here they were!

At Tsemei we waited for their caravan to catch up, and then continued on to Boka. Burdsall was greatly surprised and pleased when I proudly displayed my two highwaymen, and I had the always joyful opportunity of saying, "I told you so." The Sikong Expedition was now all present and accounted for.

Ensued a council of war which lasted well into the night, and plans were laid for the continuance of the reconnaissance. We would continue the work of exploration where it had been dropped, and, once a route had been decided upon, would throw our whole weight and resources into a concerted assault on the Konka. When the season became too far advanced to allow of any more climbing, or when, through good fortune, the peak had been conquered, there was the zoölogical collection to be made for the museum of the Academia Sinica at Nanking, which up to now had been sadly neglected.

Moore and I made preparations to leave at the first opportunity for Cloud Camp, while Young and Burdsall planned a hunting-trip for blue sheep during our absence. We hoped to reach our climbing-base in two days, spending one tentless night out on the way and praying for clear weather.

This time we engaged several Tibetans to carry our loads to avoid a possible recurrence of our experience with the horse on the previous occasion. A cold drizzle was falling and leaden clouds clung to the mountain-sides and filled the valley with their gloomy presence, but we could ill afford to wait for good weather now, for it was "touch and go" as to whether the winter storms should beat us to the summit as things were.

In due time we passed through Pawa, where we stopped only for a short rest, and continued on up the valley. This time the porters went with us to a point four miles above, where we paid them the customary ullah rate of half a rupee apiece. This amounted to only about three cents in United States currency at the then prevailing rate of exchange for a whole day's work, but they went off down the trail quite content with this amount plus a small tip, bidding us good luck and probably wondering what these crazy foreigners were up to now.

A huge overhanging boulder that in some ancient cataclysm had crashed from the cliff above proved an excellent shelter from the rain and soon our sleeping-bags were spread beneath it. By dint of much fussing and blowing we got a fire started. As we sat before it, drying our clothes and smoking, my thoughts went back to the youthful tales of Rob Roy and his Scottish mountain fastnesses. The setting was one well suited to such tales, but we had even that gentleman beaten in one respect; he could boast no such surroundings for his wild glens as the towering snow-clad giants which, though now invisible, made their presence ominously felt through the distant rumble of avalanches that broke the stillness.

Awaking sometime after midnight, I saw a full moon riding high in the heavens—our storm had cleared! The pale moonlight made the peaks seem utterly beautiful and fantastic as it shimmered on distant snows. I nudged Moore, but he only emitted a grunt and burrowed deeper in his eiderdown bag. I repeated the process and drew from him a "whatdyowant" as he opened one eye. In a second both were open and he sat up wide awake.

As the first rays of the sun glistened on the highest nevé we again shouldered our packs and set a brisk pace, for much ground had to be covered ere we found ourselves in Cloud Camp. One of my pet theories had been that most of our bad weather was perpetrated at comparatively low altitudes below 16,000 feet, and that by climbing to higher levels one might for the most part come out above the zone of clouds. This we found to be more or less well borne out on reaching our destination that afternoon, as all the snow in the vicinity of 16,000 feet had melted away where there had been two feet of it before. In many places higher up the rocks were now bare, indicating that, while we were enjoying (?) almost continual rain at Boka, the sun had here been frequently shining. We were much elated at finding conditions to be thus, for it meant that most of the snow, which previously had so hampered Burdsall and me, would now have either disappeared or formed a strong crust, and our chances of reaching the top of the wall without protracted effort were considerably enhanced. The weather was so warm and clear that we set the primus stove up outside the tent and spread our sleeping-bags on the grass for a night under the stars.

On awaking the next morning we were covered from head to foot with white frost, and the thermometer showed a minimum of 23° Fahrenheit. Another beautiful day; perhaps the monsoon had indeed broken. For this momentous day I again refer to my diary:

September 23:
Up at 6 A.M. Gorgeous weather. Breakfast and off for the North Col by 8. Took to the moraine at the right of the ice instead of on the left as before, and found much easier going (this route on the previous trip had been avoided, as it seemed badly exposed to avalanches, but on closer examination a rock arrête was found to shield it from any such danger). Put on crampons at 17,000 feet and turned out onto the ice, joining the old route. Much less snow and a good surface. Arrived at the base of the ice fall by 10 A.M. where Dick and I stopped on the last trip. Worked up through the fall for several hundred feet, but were forced back by a huge crevasse. Lost an hour, but finally got around the difficulty on an avalanche fan (a huge pile of debris deposited by an avalanche, where it had spread out on the glacier below in the shape of a fan. As a rule they are good things to keep away from because, unlike lightning, avalanches are very apt to strike many times in the same place. Under certain conditions, however, crossing them is considered a legitimate risk). Climbed diagonally upward towards the shoulder for some distance, crossing several more extensive fans. Encountered a rather stiff bit of ice work in a steep couloir, badly exposed to a hanging glacier above—rather ticklish (at this point steps had to be cut in the ice for a hundred feet or so, only one man moving while the other belayed him with the rope). From here plain sailing to the shoulder in the col, kicking steps the whole way. Arrived at a point at about 20,000 feet by 2 P.M., taking six hours to do the 4,000 feet from camp—not so bad for what little acclimatization we've had.

A few clouds hung around, but nothing to worry about. We were about three miles from the Konka, and the summit, to my surprise, was only 15° to the west of us. The south face was in plain view and was separated from the east face by a singularly jagged ridge, through a low gap in which, we could see the upper 3,000 feet of the latter and a flank of a ridge to the northeast behind. Both the eastern and southern faces had much the same appearance, dropping away in the stupendous rock cliffs too steep to hold much snow.[38] Everything visible from here entirely out of the question—not a prayer! An extensive nevé lies on the lower southern flank, but it leads nowhere. Looks like the northwest ridge for us. Away off to the south a jumbled mass of snow peaks, some of them well up around 20,000 feet.[39] Some photographs and a bit of lunch. Started down at 3 P.M., making camp by 7. Successful day, although the results are disappointing.

I had cut my leg superficially with a crampon spike while on the descent, and, although able to walk, felt that I should get back to Boka as soon as possible, before any complications should set in, now that our work in this direction was finished. Accordingly, the day following the climb we broke camp again, leaving the tent and a primus stove behind to be recovered later, as I could not carry a full load, and started for the valley. We saw the herd of blue sheep again running across a hillside below us, and resolved to lure Young and Burdsall here to get a fine family group of them and incidentally rescue the gear that had been left in Cloud Camp. Our work had borne fruit—lemons!

On returning to the Boka base camp we found that both of the men had shot fine rams[40] during our absence and would not be so anxious to go after our herd of bharal as we had hoped.

We described our findings, and a new course of action was laid. It was evident that, if Minya Konka were to be climbed, our point of attack would have to be shifted to the uncertain and hazardous northwest ridge

—our last resort. The season was so far advanced that if our climb succeeded at this late date, it would be almost unprecedented in the annals of Himalayan mountaineering, and severe winter storms could be expected at any time from now on. The route appeared difficult in the extreme. Our total climbing personnel consisted of only four men, two of whom had had little previous mountain experience; a woefully small number to tackle an unknown 25,000 foot giant, with the necessary extended string of high-altitude camps and the communication and support required for a conservative attempt on such a peak. Our food and fuel supplies, while perhaps adequate, left little or no margin in case of emergency. We had little or no faith in the local men as porters. In the face of such tremendous odds was it worth the chance of failure, which might be attended by serious personal risks, for the mere satisfaction of standing for a few icy minutes atop even so glorious a peak as Minya Konka? Most unanimously and emphatically it was!

Burdsall and Young volunteered the undesirable task of retrieving what was left of Cloud Camp and the off chance of getting a record head, thus allowing Moore and me to make a further reconnaissance from the west and north in the vicinity of the Konka Gompa.

A day of rest in camp did wonders for my injured leg, and leaving Gaomo in sole charge, we took Tsong as a servant and started for the Gompa with only a light kit, while Burdsall piloted Young back to Cloud Camp once more.

At the Gompa we were again cordially received by the

lamas and were once more conducted to the hall room that we had occupied previously. I related to Moore our attempt to see the head lama, who by this time should have returned. On requesting a lama to take our cards and the flashlight to him, the man gravely took the things, but said that, unfortunately, the head of the lamasery was away on a trip of three months' duration and we should not be able to see him. Having accepted the hospitality of these people and wishing to uphold the traditional courtesy due such an august personage, we gave instructions that our gift be presented to him when the Living Buddha of Minya should return, as we ourselves did not expect to be in this vicinity at that time. The lama bowed, thanked us, and withdrew with the gift.

Later I laughingly remarked to Moore what a joke on Burdsall and me the "three weeks" theory of ours had been. To our further great chagrin, we learned a few days later from Jack Young that the grand lama was on an extended trip far into Tibet and would not return for three years! At least when the poor man receives a useless flashlight with the batteries long since dead in the years to come, its sheepish donors will be many thousands of miles away, and at least no one can say we did not try, in spite of this horrible commentary on the accuracy of our sketchy Chinese.

Snow kept us indoors for a day at such domestic duties as writing letters or sewing up pants. That evening we sat long around the fire in the black hole that passed for the lamasery kitchen, watching the Tibetans, adding the smoke from our pipes to the already murky atmosphere, and amusing ourselves by trying to teach Tsong the English alphabet. He was rather astute and we soon had him writing his A B C's on everything that came handy.

In due course the snowstorm cleared away. The fresh snow flashed so brilliantly the next morning we had to put on snow-glasses as we climbed the shoulder behind the monastery with the hope of making a closer acquaintance with the northwest ridge from a new and better position. Four thousand feet fell away beneath us in four hours as we followed up along the crest of the shoulder, at last finding ourselves on an eminence which we estimated at about 17,000 feet in elevation. From here the long northern spur lay directly opposite at a distance of only two miles, whose crest, once gained, would be a direct road to the higher reaches of the Konka.[41]

We studied the situation long and carefully through the field-glasses. One fact became apparent at once. From this new angle the northwest ridge, which from below had appeared so razor-like, was now discovered to be considerably wider and seemed to merge with the northern face for the last several thousand feet. Perceiving this new state of affairs, things looked much brighter, for now we would have greater latitude of movement in the vicinity of the most difficult parts of the ascent. On the other hand, the ridge for the most part assumed a steeper appearance, but remembering that such appearances are usually false anyway, that did not worry us so much. The gap at the foot of the summit ridge looked problematic and decidedly treacherous. It, however, could be attended to when the time came, and our immediate problem was to find a way to the top of the spur.

We finally agreed on a route as well as could be determined from such a distance, although many variations were likely, once we were actually traversing it. A triangular rocky formation extended from the valley floor well up through the snow line, and henceforward was spoken of as the "Pyramid." From its apex a passage was picked around huge hummocks of ice and up a long snow slope broken at intervals by crevasses. By this devious path the top of the spur, we felt, could be gained at about 20,000 feet.[43] The only "if" in this line of assault was, could the Pyramid itself be scaled with heavy packs? Then, too, a trail must be found giving access to the base of our spur. The next step would be to find such a trail.

On returning to the lamasery, Moore left immediately for Boka, where, with the aid of Burdsall and Young, who should by now have returned from Cloud Camp, he would strike the base camp, bringing everything to the Gompa, where our headquarters were to be. Meanwhile my job was to scout out a trail in to the base of the ridge and locate a site for the main climbing base.

The glacial valley leading in from the west looked the most promising, and I started early the following morning for the glacier, but not before the mists had begun to form. Despite their presence, however, there was hope of getting something accomplished, and even the chance of catching a glimpse or two of our spur, so I kept on.

Things went badly from the start. Following a trail down to the river, it soon dwindled to nothing, but rather than retreat I indulged in a bit of bushwhacking, that bane and bugbear of all mountaineers in wild country. Forcing my way through, under, over, or around a nearly impenetrable jungle of live oak, rhododendron, and bamboo grass interspersed with a generous number of windfalls, I finally emerged in the river bottom just below the snout of the glacier, rather the worse for wear.

I had a difficult time in crossing the river, resorting to a bit of rock-climbing and several breath-taking leaps, but at last I landed safely on the farther bank. Yes, without a doubt conditions of travel that morning could so far have been greatly improved upon.

The course of least resistance now seemed to lie along the lateral moraine which formed both the bank of the stream and the northern limits of the valley glacier. About noon I reached the upper limits of the cloud bank and came out into the brilliant sunshine. On rounding a bluff I was suddenly confronted by a beautiful little alpine meadow lying at the very foot of the Konka and its northern spur. The peak seemed so dominant that anything dropped from its summit nearly eleven thousand feet above must inevitably land at my very feet. I noticed several piles of Mani stones and altars for burning juniper boughs decorated with prayer flags. The valley was evidently considered sacred by the lamas and it was here that they came to make sacri-

fices to the God of the mighty Minya Konka. I was probably the first white man ever to venture into its sacred
precincts and felt as though I were gazing upon a
scene which I had no right to see. Soon, however, there
were to be more alien spirits here to desecrate its sanc-
tity, as this was a perfect place for our base camp.

My attention now turned to the Pyramid and its problems. It consisted of a rocky arrête surmounted by several huge towers or pinnacles and merging at about
18,000 feet with the extensive snow slopes above. It
was a forbidding-looking mass and could be approached
only over a glacier descending on its flank, though this
necessitated coming under the baleful presence of a
menacing cliff of ice that at any time might shower
ice and rocks on whatever lay below.[45] Yes, with luck
it would go all right, although perhaps with some difficult pitches to overcome. Thus the last stage in the line
of march against the gleaming heights above was disclosed, and I turned homeward.

I returned to the Gompa by a new and easier trail
and found Moore there ahead of me. He reported that
everything had been brought down from Cloud Camp,
and that Young and Burdsall were moving to the lamasery the following day.

The expedition was duly united, and an afternoon
of strenuous preparation spent in sorting equipment and
making up loads in the proper sequence to be carried
to our new base camp. Jack Young conjured up six
Tibetan porters, five men and one woman, to help in
the consolidation of the base. Both of our servants,
Gaomo and Tsong, were asked to go with us and re-

main at the base to help with the work there. Gaomo begged off and gave a dissertation on the vengeance of the Thunder God of the Konka, whom it was well not to displease, and mentioned several varieties of evil spirits that would "get you if you don't watch out." In fact he was so genuinely opposed to the idea that we told him to stay at the lamasery, where it would be convenient in any case to have a man to act as agent and maintain liaison with Tatsienlu.

Tsong, however, was made of different stuff. Neither thunder nor evil spirits held any terrors for him, and he was our man—until, at the psychological moment, he fell down and struck his spine in such a way as to entirely destroy his ardor for the venture, and he, too, had to be left behind.

That evening a bombshell landed in our midst. Young came into our "apartment" wearing a rather long face, and remarked, "Well, maybe we'll go tomorrow and maybe we won't." He explained that the lamas seemed to object to our summary invasion of their holy little valley, and, furthermore, did not care to have us tamper with the holy mountain. It was evident that a crisis had arrived and that some quick thinking must be done. The lamas felt that we would bring famine and pestilence on the land should we anger the gods of the Konka, chief among whom was the dread Dorjelutru. Unless they could be persuaded that their fears were unfounded, we had run into a situation which might spell defeat before even setting foot on the mountain. With our little knowledge of the Chinese language, the entire responsibility for the fate of our enterprise fell upon Young. Should he fail to win the lamas over, there was little chance of our being able to carry on.

Young told the lamas that it was to pay homage to their sacred mountain that we had come from the other side of the world. To prove our sincerity they were asked to burn juniper and repeat many prayers for us, each liberally paid for in silver coin. Through Young's skillfully diplomatic handling of this delicate situation the lamas changed their attitude of suspicion and hostility towards the expedition to one of benediction and encouragement. Thus a "high purpose" for our project now existed in more ways than one!

Chapter IX

THE ATTACK BEGINS

THE morning of October second saw the usual confusion attendant upon the assembling of a Tibetan caravan. By 9:30, however, some semblance of order was in evidence, and soon the loaded porters began to move out of the courtyard, bound for "Surprise Valley." The fight was now on, and I think that realization brought somewhat of a thrill to us all (see Analysis of Ascent Chart, page 273).

It was the rushing turbulent glacier stream that nearly proved our downfall both literally and figuratively. Its bed, composed of large smoothly rounded stones invisible beneath the waist deep tide of milky ice water, which all but bowled one over, made very insecure footing at best. It was small wonder that the laden porters hesitated on the brink. They said there had once been a bridge, and stood looking hopelessly at the torrent, as if trying to conjure up another one.

Moore was the first across and I followed close at his heels to show the men that there was no danger. Despite our efforts and those of Young and Burdsall in exhorting them from the rear, the porters seemed unconvinced. Two schools of thought arose among them. One group roved up and down the bank, looking for a place to cross, while the other just sat down to await developments. Finally, after it seemed that we had become properly stalled, several of the men consented to be led across by the hand, and the rest soon followed, all save the woman, who had different ideas as to how the thing should be done. Even in far Tibet the women always get the last word in.

Moore recrossed the stream. Then, dripping wet, barefoot, with only a pair of short underpants to maintain modesty, he gave chase up along the bank, shouting and wildly waving an ice ax to head her off. She had too good a lead, however, and the hotter his pursuit became the faster she went, until Moore stubbed his toe and with one last fierce shout sat down on a boulder and gave up.

Finally one of the porters, Chelay by name, went to the rescue of the fair maiden. He was a stocky individual with a wild-looking visage and a large silver ear-ring in his left ear. He would have made a wonderful pirate for any roving Spanish Corsair. The pair balanced for what seemed to us an eternity on the brink of a cascade, while we held our breaths and visioned beds and clothes swirling down the stream. At last they came on and got safely ashore.

We rewarded the man with a rupee for his good work, and thereby won a most valuable friend, for from then on he led the van and showed fine spirit. He later became one of the mountain porters, rendering excellent service. Subsequently his faithfulness came home to me personally in a most forceful and surprising way. But that is another part of the story.

Young worked like a Trojan and produced wonderful results by his skillful handling of the men in getting their best efforts from them. Whenever a porter came to one of us with some excuse as to why he could not continue, we would send him back to Young and the trouble would at once be smoothed out.

That day ten loads were landed at the base-camp site (we each carried a pack in addition to those of the six porters).[45] This meant fourteen more loads to come, and these could be brought up in two trips, exceeding our fondest hopes.

An alpine tent was pitched, as Moore and I were to reconnoiter the first stage of the route at the earliest opportunity, while the other men returned to supervise the transportation of what remained at the Gompa.

A more ideal spot for a camp could hardly be wished for. Both wood and water were readily available, and the valley was well sheltered from the high winds so prevalent throughout Tibet. The meadow lay at an elevation of about 14,400 feet, dotted with blue gentians, and hemmed in by snow peaks, beetling cliffs, and huge grinding rivers of ice. A more sublime setting could hardly be conceived for the drama that was soon to be enacted there.[46]

Moore and I climbed for hours up over interminable slopes of loose moraine rocks, a very tedious and treacherous kind of ground to cover, as the boulders were often so nicely balanced that, when in the least disturbed, they would suddenly tilt or roll in a very disconcerting way. When struggling uphill with a load over such terrain, one must truly step lively to avoid serious injury. It was wearing work at best, and rests were frequent.

Just below the 17,000-foot line, we reached the lower end of the glacier flanking the Pyramid. We had hoped to establish our first camp on the snow at the apex of this Pyramid, but as this was still nearly a thousand feet higher, we felt no desire to strain ourselves in reaching that point on the first day's climb, so left our loads close under a protecting cliff which formed part of the upper tower. This spot later became known as the "Dump," because here we continued to leave loads until they could be relayed higher, and also eventually established a small cache of gasoline, extra crampons, etc.

A climb of several hundred feet more brought us beneath the ice wall, whose menace we should have much liked to avoid, but the only feasible route to the snow line seemed to lie in a steep rocky couloir which lay close under the ice. To be sure, there were no signs of any recent avalanches, and the ice seemed fairly firm. Such edifices, however, give way with little or no warning, and anything in the path of the tons of falling ice and rock would be most swiftly and effectively annihilated. It might even be necessary to ascend this bit only at night or in the early morning when the ice, being more solidly frozen, would be less apt to fall.

From where we now stood, we were satisfied that the apex was at least accessible without an undue number of difficulties to be overcome, and a motion having been made and carried that enough had been done for one day, we made short work of the descent.

All but six of the loads had by now arrived and the large tent set up, bearing witness to the efficiency of

Young and Burdsall. The Sikong Expedition was all present at the base camp.

To save the expenditure of useless time and effort it was necessary to make a trip to the top of the north spur without delay, for once this point at 20,000 feet were attained, we were fairly certain of our ground to at least about 23,000 feet, on the main summit ridge. With this idea in mind, we determined to establish a camp at 18,000 feet on the snow just above the Pyramid, and stock it with supplies for two men without delay.[43] This was to be occupied by Moore and me, from where we would strike immediately for the ridge, establishing a route to the crest (Analysis of Ascent Chart, page 273).

Young remained at the base camp on October 4th to await the final relay from the lamasery and to engage porters for the higher mountain work. The rest of us shouldered packs containing items for the establishment of a complete camp for two men and, by a varied and somewhat easier route, proceeded to the Dump at 17,000 feet. We kept on, however, and reached the bottom of the couloir beside the ice cliff. Here we encountered a short pitch of steep rock, but it provided nothing worse than an easy rock climb, though our large packs rendered it rather a clumsy bit of work.

Above this point the couloir extended for four or five hundred feet, but, to our disappointment, did not give access directly to the nevé, being cut off from it by a rock wall. It was now late in the afternoon, and Burdsall left for the base camp. As there was no room for a tent where we stood in the col at the head of the couloir, we worked our way up the wall to the snow above.

Great was our dismay, when we had climbed the rocks, to find ourselves on a snow-covered knife-ridge badly corniced on one side, with not the slightest sign of a place to camp. As it was nearly dark, I climbed back down to where Burdsall's load had been left, and brought it up. Moore meanwhile knocked off part of the cornice and the crest of snow that capped the ridge and made a space just large enough for our small 5½′ x 7′ alpine tent with absolutely *nothing* to spare on either side, where the ridge dropped away nearly sheer from the very canvas.[47] We anchored the tent as best we could and prepared to make the best of the emergency. Lucky it was for us that there was no wind, else this precarious perch would not have been at all tenable. I must confess that I did not sleep very well that night, and it wasn't entirely due to the altitude!

A day was spent in relaying loads from the Dump to Camp I. We established connections with Burdsall and Young, who with two porters[48] had brought loads to 17,000. The porters were sent back, as we wished to accustom them to the new conditions of ice and snow by degrees and avoid dampening their ardor prematurely for the work later on. We four then climbed to the new camp, finding a much-improved passage around the upper cliffs. All hands felt the altitude considerably as yet, especially as we were carrying between forty and fifty pounds apiece, and halts had to be made constantly to catch up on our panting and puffing. We would truly need much of that elusive and all-important factor, acclimatization (see Acclimatization Chart, page 283) before we could hope to be efficient at twenty and twenty-two thousand feet, much more climb to twenty-five. There would have to be much physical and mental metamorphosis before any such feat were possible. Burdsall and Young departed, and we again crawled into our precarious tent for the night.[50]

The 6th of October saw our attempt to reach the northern spur. Our first obstacle lay in an ice buttress which was ultimately rounded by cutting steps and hand holds, a short but somewhat delicate traverse until one got the hang of it. Another fifty-foot wall of ice barred the way completely, but we gained the slopes above by means of a vertical crack half filled with snow.

The snow above was fairly steep, and we plowed our weary way upward through nearly three feet of it, taking turns at breaking trail. This lasted for five hundred feet, and three hours after leaving camp we gained a small depression behind a hummock of snow and paused to reflect and take cognizance of our situation.

From here a narrow passage ran steeply up between two immense insecure-looking seracs and finally gave on the last long slope below the top. Several hidden crevasses of no mean proportions were uncovered gingerly, and we had to be continually on the *qui vive* for such pitfalls. Finally, after negotiating a small bergschrund (a type of crevasse in which one lip is much lower than the other), we traversed a short exposed stretch of wind-blown snow whose lower limits verged on empty space below and found ourselves on the coveted spur.

The spur was broad, with an easy gradient, and consisted of a series of rounded humps rising one above the other, very reminiscent of the lower Valot ridge of Mount Blanc in the Alps, terminating in the Gap at the foot of the summit ridge. The whole length of the spur on the east revealed a huge snow cornice that it would be well to keep away from, and one which would call for added caution in stormy weather when visibility was poor.

The main summit ridge now drew our attention. From here the slopes between the Gap and 23,000 feet looked fairly easy, but above that the angle became decidedly greater and the issue became more involved by several evil-looking pitches of ice-covered rocks; those which we had discerned from the valley. There appeared no obvious solution of these difficulties from where we stood, but then one could never be sure of appearances until actually on the spot; at least, so far we knew there was a fairly safe and comparatively easy climb to our present position at 19,800 feet. We could now go ahead with the establishment of higher camps, and provided the Gap would go, we felt assured that we could push far up onto the flanks of the Konka itself. Our determination to continue the campaign was thus all the more strengthened by a strong desire to cross the Gap and see the summit ridge at close quarters.

An icy wind was whipping across the shoulder and had such a numbing bite to it that there was little inclination to linger, and before long the descent began. In crossing an open slope not far below the top Moore, who was ahead, suddenly, without the slightest warning, dropped from sight, with a consequent heavy pull on the rope. I managed to brace in time to take most of the shock with my body, and then drove my ice ax into the snow, belaying the rope around it. This all took place with an unexpectedness and rapidity which left little time for thought, a characteristic of most such accidents in the mountains. I waited a full minute, yelling to him several times, but my voice was drowned by the wind and there was no reply. I was getting rather apprehensive, when I heard a faint subterranean shout, "Pull up on the rope." This I did with alacrity, taking in the slack until a head and shoulders appeared above ground as if from nowhere, and then a body followed, presenting such a ludicrous appearance that I nearly burst out laughing as Moore crawled forth.

"Rather close, that!" was all he said; and with my reply of, "Yes, rather," the matter was closed. He had fallen through the roof of one of those insidious snow-covered crevasses which have ended the career of more than one skilled mountaineer, and whose presence it is often nearly impossible to detect. This particular chasm was forty to fifty feet deep, and the rope had checked Moore's fall in mid-air about ten feet below the surface, where he hung until he collected his wits and took stock of his predicament. By reaching out with his feet he was able to touch the walls, and by means of his crampons managed to climb back to the outside world. After shaking the snow out of the back of his neck and sleeves, we made a quick descent to 18,000 feet, always on the alert, however, for any more of such dangerous traps as the one just encountered, arriving just as a glorious sunset flamed across the hills and plains of the Tibetan hinterland.

On October 8th the last of the loads was brought to Camp I, thanks to the excellent work of Young and Burdsall. A new site was selected in a less precarious situation.[51] With the addition of the last-named men all hands were now present and accounted for and everyone was feeling fit and eager to come to grips with the Konka. The porters had been dispensed with, as we felt they would prove more a liability than an asset in the higher camps, and as they themselves had no stomach for snow-climbing.

Our feet were now gathered beneath us for the final spring—the supreme effort in the struggle against altitude, cold, and snow, enemies worthy of any man's mettle. Let the odds be what they might, four men were determined to fight it out.

Chapter X

THE SPUR

AS I crawled stiffly forth from the tent, a delicate roseate hue was just diffusing itself over some of the highest slopes and ridges, transforming their dull whiteness into a beautiful dazzling fresco of light. Far across Tibet the land still lay in dim shadows. On the sea of clouds lying at my feet the huge bulk of the Konka was silhouetted in every detail, its immense profile stretching away for miles, a visible yardstick to its tremendous height. Such a morning as this made one almost visibly expand in its utter glory.

Camp I was still held in a shadow cast by the ridge behind, from whose presence it would not be freed until 9:30 A.M., so steep were the slopes above. The cold was penetrating, and I looked longingly at the sun-gilt snows of the peaks across the valley. The thermometer hanging from one of the tent ropes read 14° Fahrenheit.

The inmates of the larger tent, Young and Burdsall, only groaned when I shook it and showered them with the frost clinging to the canvas inside, the frozen condensation from their breathing. But this was the cook tent, and when reminded of that I could hear their vague stirrings within. It was not long before the primus stove was roaring merrily away beneath a pot of snow.

That morning we made up packs averaging close to forty-five pounds, including only those articles not essential to the maintenance of the present camp. This practice of advancing first loads of general supplies was necessary because of our limited number of tents, sleeping-bags, and stoves which always remained in use until the last moment.

We roped together in a single party, Moore taking the lead. The sun topped the ridge just as we left camp. Almost immediately its warmth was greeted by a crashing volley of avalanches from one of the tottering ice-walls to the north. These continued throughout the day with spectacular volume, sending thousands of tons of blue-green ice far across the valley four or five thousand feet below.

Fortunately, our route was not exposed to such bombardment. We did, however, have another and more subtle menace with which to contend, that of the loose snow avalanche, or "surface peel." This phenomenon occurs when a layer of light snow lying on a steep open slope is set in motion by the sun's heat or the feet of an unwary mountaineer. These avalanches are most to be feared because they start unannounced and sweep down upon a climber and overwhelm him with a suddenness that leaves no time for thought. Their lair may be any innocent-looking slope of sufficient steepness, whereas a fall of ice always has its origin in a hanging glacier or tottering serac, whose area of destruction below can usually be detected and avoided.

The track was well broken and we made good progress up across the first long slopes, climbing at a steady pace, with rests at hundred foot intervals. At 19,000 feet occurred the only distinct break in the flank of the spur. Here on a level spot sheltered from the wind it became our custom to pause for half an hour's rest and a bite of lunch. It was generally conceded to be the halfway point in altitude from Camp I to the spur, though the steeper and more involved part of the climb lay above.

On reaching the scene of Moore's former subterranean exploit, extra caution was observed in preventing its recurrence, each man in turn being carefully belayed as he jumped the crevasse. Here, too, a nasty biting wind from the south was usually encountered that whipped the snow into our faces in an unpleasant fashion. In an hour's time, as we neared the top of the spur, it had increased to a steady lashing blast that bullied us at every step.

As we approached the place where Moore and I had traversed out across a particularly precipitous bit above an ice wall, a variation of the route was decided upon. This amendment made use of a safer though more arduous course and involved crossing a small bergschrund and negotiating a forty-five-degree slope above it for several hundred feet. Fortunately, the latter could be accomplished by kicking steps. This variant had the advantage that, in the event of a slip or under conditions of poor visibility, the slope eased off below enough to provide at least a fighting chance of preventing a forced landing in the valley beneath.

We four topped the spur at 19,800 feet in only three hours' climbing from Camp I. Both Young and Burd-

sall felt the altitude rather badly, not having had the
benefit of our previous acclimatization, but we were
rather pleased with our rate of ascent of five hundred
feet an hour with over forty-pound loads.

The ferocity of the wind soon drove us from where
we were sitting, and after several minutes we crossed
to the eastern side of the spur to avoid it. On its eastern
flank a hundred feet below the crest we found a shelf
backed by a fifty-foot wall of ice which completely sheltered it from the gale, apparently an ideal site for Camp
II. Depositing our loads here, without further cere-
mony we began the descent.

The wind, as we faced it with bent heads, fairly
staggered us. A few wisps of gray cloud came boiling
up from below and went streaking close over our heads.
No one was sorry to quit this exposed position and
reach the comparative shelter of the slopes below.

It was a cold, tired group of men who returned to
Camp I that night. This was really our first severe
taste of high-altitude work, and it had been an un-
savory one. None of us felt particularly cheery at the
thought of facing such a gale of wind as we had met,
aided and abetted on the higher reaches of the Konka
by increased altitude and cold. Still, "sufficient unto the
day was the evil!"

That evening, as supper was being prepared, Burdsall
went outside to adjust a tent-rope without putting on
a parka. In a moment he returned and immediately experienced a severe chill accompanied by the "jitters."
We wrapped him in all available coats and sweaters
and offered him some of that universal remedy put up

by a Mr. Hennessey. This last he refused, so we plied him with as much hot soup as he would hold, and after a considerable period the chill passed off. It was an alarming performance, and although he recovered with no ill effects, it taught us that we could not be too careful in the future about keeping warm, especially at the end of an exhausting day when a man's resistance was at a low ebb.

It snowed heavily during the night and the cold became intense. Morning dawned dully and the weather gave promise of more snow. Because of the strenuous work of the day before and the fact that the track must be entirely rebroken, a day off was proclaimed by mutual consent.

Four of us crowded into the 7' x 7' tent, there to spend our waking hours. We held a chess tournament with a small pocket set of mine. Its owner was speedily put out, however, and the contest continued between Burdsall and Moore. Burdsall was finally hailed the winner after marching and counter-marching against Moore for an entire afternoon.

I consumed my spare time in sewing up a crampon tear in my trouser leg and in reading Kipling. Young curled up behind my back and was soon dead to the world. Thus does one take a "holiday" at 18,000 feet!

Moore and I planned to move up to Camp II on the following day, as only four more loads were needed there to establish residence. From here we would push on up along the spur, establish Camp III, and from that point reconnoiter as high on the summit ridge as our food and fuel supply would allow. Such a move was necessary to ascertain at close quarters whether the situation there justified our continuing the campaign, or whether its inaccessibility rendered reaching the summit a forlorn hope. In the latter event we had decided to attempt one of the lesser 21,000-foot peaks to the north of the Konka.

While we were thus engaged, Young and Burdsall planned to work on the lower stages, carrying supplies through from the base camp as fast as possible and further consolidating Camps I and II.

By the next morning, October 10th, eighteen inches of snow had fallen, completely obliterating our tracks. This meant a slow, laborious climb, and again the possibility of a "surface peel" lurked in the back of our minds.

Moore and I led on the first rope, taking turns at breaking trail. The second party left camp somewhat behind us and dogged our steps. The loads consisted of tents and supplies for two camps, II and III, to provision the reconnaissance party to work for a week above 19,800 feet without returning to the lower regions.

The going was exhausting in the extreme, for plowing one's way up over steep slopes at 19,000 feet with a thirty-five-pound load, knee deep in snow, is no child's play, however regarded!

We had got away to our usual late 9 A.M. start, and it was almost 4 P.M. before we reached the site of Camp II on the eastern edge at 19,800.

The inevitable wind was present, blowing from the southwest. The clouds began to close in, and so, after assisting in digging in the tent, our support party left for Camp I without further delay.

Moore and I scrambled into our new abode and proceeded to make the place livable—*i.e.,* inflate our air mattresses! An hour later the primus was beginning to reduce some blocks of ice to water for supper, when we heard an indistinct shout borne on the wind; "Hey, Terry! Hey, Terry!" repeated several times. We looked at each other with dismay clutching at our hearts. What could this mean? What disaster had befallen our comrades? The possibility of a catastrophe involving another snow-covered crevasse flashed into my mind.

Moore, who still had his boots on, struggled hastily into his parka and mittens. I began frantically to pull on my boots, but he disappeared through the door head first and was gone before I was ready.

In another two minutes, the sound of approaching voices was heard and, thus reassured, I abandoned my hasty efforts at dressing and relit the stove.

When their crampons had been removed Moore crawled inside, followed, to my great relief, by both Young and Burdsall. Both were badly played out and suffering from exposure.

Their story was brief. Beyond the shelter of the ridge they had encountered driving snow which obliterated everything beyond a radius of a few feet. They had followed the track with difficulty to the open slopes below the first bergschrund where they found it completely covered.

They therefore took the wisest course and retraced their steps before it was too late, climbing back five

hundred feet to the spur. Once there, they again lost the
trail in the welter of flying snow, and knowing that a
large cornice ran along most of the eastern side of the
spur, and not being sure just where the camp lay, they
raised a shout for help. The wind drowned our answering yells, but once outside, Moore soon made out
the two figures in the gloom and piloted them in.

Young was in especially poor shape, and we got him
into the smaller of our two sleeping-bags, where he immediately fell asleep. The only other bag was a larger
one (90" x 45"), and, as we jokingly remarked, it was
meant for a man and a half; that is, two of these eiderdown bags opened out and laced together would hold
three men.

After a round of hot food, watches were told off,
for one man must sit up. Moore drew the first watch, so
Burdsall and I compressed ourselves into the remaining bag.

Two hours passed, then Burdsall took his turn, sitting bundled up in all our spare clothes. Feeling that
Moore and I had a very hard and trying time ahead of
us in the next few days, he generously refrained from
waking me when my turn came, and sat alone all through
the long frigid hours until dawn. Gasoline was too
precious a commodity to expend in keeping the stove
alight except to cook our meals, and he was in utter
darkness.

The weather, fortunately, cleared and we bade goodby to our two companions for better or for worse until
another week should pass. They departed for the base
at an early hour without breakfast, wishing to con-

serve the utmost amount of our food supply at Camp II.

Moore and I got off at a reasonable hour to see how the land lay along the spur as far as the Hump at 21,000 feet. We both felt a bit done in through an uncomfortable night in the crowded tent, and the fact that our present state of acclimatization was far from perfect. We decided therefore not to take loads but make it an easy day of exploration.

The spur continued to rise gradually, broken only at intervals by short abrupt pitches of snow between the rounded hillocks. The nevé was wind-packed, providing an excellent footing for crampons, and we were able to proceed unroped, so conspicuous were crevasses by their absence. The cornice on the eastern edge gave us but little worry as it could be easily avoided.

In the two miles from Camp II to the Hump, the spur rose only 1200 feet, making this stage a reasonably easy one. The crest of this shoulder was the only part of the entire climb where skis could have been of the slightest use to us.

We made good time, so good, in fact, that we loitered in every sheltered spot to study the summit ridge above the Gap. Through the binoculars, the going to about 23,000 feet seemed fairly straightforward, the terrain consisting mainly of a series of folds of wind-swept snow one above the other, similar to those which we were now encountering, only set at a far steeper angle.[58] In several places an element of uncertainty was presented by a bergschrund or an icy pitch. However, once across the Gap, which was still hidden, we were per-

suaded there existed no insurmountable difficulties until the first band of rocks was reached at 23,500 feet.

Above this latter point, however, the angle of the
ridge increased markedly and the issue became involved
by a number of out-cropping rocks covered with snow
feathers—a rather disconcerting spectacle. There
seemed no way around them from our present view-
point.

Again, just below the summit, it appeared that we
might have to leave the ridge entirely and traverse out
on to the precipitous north face, for here the ridge
seemed to be broken by a decided rock wall which from
our present vantage-point looked practically out of the
question. It must be remembered that, while such climbing might be well within the realm of possibility in the
Alps or other ranges of lesser altitude, here on the wind-
blown ridge of Minya Konka at over 24,000 feet such
feats are scarcely to be thought of. We were still far
enough off, however, to make us hope that some route
through these barriers might have been overlooked.

As we approached the Hump, the clouds, which
every afternoon blew up from the southwest and enveloped the peak, shut the ridge from view. It was useless to go higher, for nothing was discernible above
save an occasional bit of rock or snow. We returned to
camp at 3 P.M. feeling at least somewhat gratified to
find the route feasible to within fifteen hundred feet
of the top, excepting, of course, the Gap, about which
we knew relatively little. Concerning the last fifteen
hundred we felt far from optimistic, but determined to

get as high as possible on it before admitting absolute defeat.

In our yet unacclimatized condition sleep was an elusive luxury (Acclimatization Chart, page 283). One would doze off, only to awake with a sudden start, half choked for lack of oxygen. A spell of deep breathing would follow and the feeling of semi-suffocation subside after a few moments. Sleep would again claim one, only to be rudely dissipated by a repetition of this breathing cycle. Such a phenomenon has frequently been noted by men at high altitudes, and is known as "Cheyne-Stokes Respiration." It is truly exasperating to one who is trying to rest from a hard day's work in the blinding glare of wind-swept snowfields. It required several nights spent at 20,000 feet before sound sleep again allowed us complete relaxation.

On October 12th, Moore and I again set off along the spur, this time with packs in order to establish Camp III across the Gap at the foot of the main northwest ridge, if possible. We determined that above 20,000 feet we should limit our loads to a maximum of thirty pounds to avoid undue strain.

The carrying of loads by the climbing party itself has, to a certain extent, a definite advantage. It breaks the men in at relatively lower altitudes, so that in the final supreme effort to gain the summit without packs they will be in better condition physically when the test comes. At least such was markedly our experience. Aside from that, there is a certain satisfaction in feeling that you are doing the entire job by your own self, to say nothing of obviating the worry and care at-

tendant upon maintaining a porterage staff high on a
snow peak. It must not be supposed, however, that there
are no limits to which a climbing party can go and still
be self-supporting. We felt that the Konka was very
near our "ceiling" in this respect, and on such peaks
as Kanchenjunga or Everest one far exceeds the point
of diminishing returns should one fail to make use of
high-altitude native porters.

Today, however, our loads, though under the limit,
seemed double their weight, and sat so heavily upon
us that we would have given much for a corps of stout
Darjeeling Sherpas. Despite the slow pace set by Moore,
we both felt ineffably weary after only a short distance
had been covered. It was as if a great leaden hand were
squeezing the breath from our lungs and our feet
seemed to freeze to the snow at every step. Lassitude,
that great enemy of the mountaineer, claimed us, and
everything connected with climbing the Konka seemed
purposeless and utterly futile. Why struggle and work
our very hearts out only to add to the burden of stress
and discomfort which was already ours, just for the
empty glory of claiming victory over an unknown mountain, to satisfy some transitory feeling of conquest?
How much easier and more sensible to sit down in
some sheltered spot in the sun and doze comfortably
to sleep.

Then a fresh breeze eddied around the shoulder behind which we were climbing, and as it struck our faces
the lassitude dropped from us like a cloak. The old
zest returned and the loads seemed pounds lighter. Our
step regained its old spring and we settled joyfully into

the rhythmic, measured stride which is the secret of successful high-altitude climbing. Rhythm was a god! Rhythm was life! And what occasioned this sudden change from the depths of indifferent indolence to the heights of renewed energy and enthusiasm? Until that time we had been climbing in a pocket of still, dead air behind the shoulder. Then the breeze found us, bringing with it a supply of vitalizing oxygen. We found that when climbing in a stiff breeze our lungs labored far less than when the air was quiet. There were other aspects to the wind, however, far less enjoyable!

Although following the track of the previous day, we found that nearly double the time was consumed in covering the same distance with loads.

Upon reaching the foot of the Hump we dropped our packs to do a little investigating. Moore climbed the remaining hundred feet to its summit. On gaining the top, he hastily drew back, calling for me to get a careful belay on the rope.

The upper side of the Hump dropped abruptly 250 feet into the Gap, even overhanging it.[53] The cliff was topped by a large cornice of snow, of which Moore had suddenly become aware from above by seeing daylight through a hole made by his ice-ax in exploring the crest!

Before long he clambered back to where I stood, shaking his head dubiously. The western side of the ridge we knew, from previous observation, to be too steep to cross at this point. It became a question either of roping ourselves down into the gap, an awkward and hazardous procedure at best, or of attempting to traverse around on the eastern slope.

The latter course was adopted, and retreating to a point slightly lower down, Moore led out onto the open flank on the east. It was steep and covered with two feet of fresh snow. Neither one of us cared much for it, feeling that it had a decidedly treacherous appearance. However, there was no other way of circumventing the Hump.

We advanced cautiously and I gave Moore almost the full hundred-foot length of the rope, so that we would be more widely separated in the event of a snow slide. We were both pretty well out on the flank and a few feet below an ice buttress when, without the slightest warning, there came a low hissing sound. We stood gazing in fascinated horror as the entire snow-field to the depth of two feet slid away from immediately *below* our tracks. We had cut the slope as neatly as with a knife.

Several seconds passed and then on the glacier a mile below a great fan of tumbled snow spread out, making a large blotch on its white surface. Over it there hung a vaporous wisp of powdered snow which might well have marked an unknown grave for us both.

Nor were we yet out of danger. At any moment the snow above us might give way, sweeping us down with it. A realization of our insecure position broke upon us and we made careful haste to reach the safety of a small level spot behind an icy protrusion. We had been more fortunate than cautious, and our experience left us with an unpleasant hollow sensation at the pit of the stomach.

The platform on which we now stood at 20,700 feet was barely large enough to accommodate a 7' x 7' tent and depended for its existence on a small serac. It was, however, the only place discernible on the face of the ridge level enough for a camp. The loads were therefore deposited and a space cleared for the tent. The return trip across the slope was executed with much caution. By keeping well at the upper end of the remaining unstable area close beneath the ice buttress, we obviated the danger of being carried down should another "peel" occur. Thankfully gaining the spur once more, we made short work of the trek back to Camp II.

Neither man slept well that night and we both awoke feeling decidedly jaded. Consequently, when Moore poked his head forth and reported the camp buried in clouds and that it was snowing, we unhesitatingly declared a day off. Our physical efficiency would be bettered by merely remaining at 19,800 feet, though no advance was made in our position on the mountain, so the time was not entirely wasted.

Days off were consumed largely in cooking and eating, for by the time one meal had been leisurely prepared and done away with it was nearly time to begin on the next. Thus it was that on the morning of October 13th, breakfast lasted until eleven and supper began at three in the afternoon, lunch being omitted entirely. Still ensconced in our eiderdown bags for warmth, the interim between meals was passed in contented ease, reading and smoking.

One circumstance, however, served somewhat to destroy our placidity. The level of the tent floor had been sunk several feet below the surrounding nevé to render the walls less exposed to the buffeting of the wind. Now the snow blowing from the shoulder above began to fill in around the tent. The walls bulged inward with the weight of it, and so reduced the floor space within that, instead of four, there was barely room for the two of us.

Bracing our feet against one side and our heads and hands against that opposite, we heaved and pushed with all our might until the tent assumed some semblance of its former shape despite a few irregularities. When this process had been several times repeated, however, the snow outside became so compacted that it refused to yield even to the strongest blows from within. Its added weight exerted such a strain on the canvas that we feared it might tear or the pole break.

We tried to console ourselves with the thought that it might stop snowing, that we *could* possibly find room to sleep somehow as it was, or that it would keep on snowing and only make ours a wasted effort—anything to excuse ourselves from work we knew to be inevitable.

We procrastinated thus as long as we could, but the situation became inexorable in its call to duty. Reluctantly we were forced to admit defeat! Summoning up that supreme effort of will essential to pulling on our clothes, we crawled forth dejectedly into the cold.

After several false starts, the chilly air commanded action. Grabbing ice-axes, we fell to with a will and attacked the offending drift about the tent. It was frozen, and required utmost care in breaking it up lest we puncture the tent. An hour's work proved sufficient to remove the snow, and the tent again assumed its original shape and extent.

The weather cleared late that afternoon, though the temperature sank and the wind still raged out of the southwest in devastating blasts. The peaks to the north, especially those of the number 57 massif of our survey (Mount Edgar),[55] stood out sharply defined in the declining rays of the sun. The Konka was hidden by an intervening ice ridge, but to the east the long shadows of our range reached out upon the tossed array of cloud banks that inevitably cloaked the Chinese plains. I dove into the tent and dragged forth our cameras to try to record a little of so sublime a spectacle.[54]

That night the temperature fell nearly to the zero mark, and we could hear the distant undertone of the wind, like the far-off bellowing of a locomotive whistle, as it tore at the ridge above camp. We well knew that to be caught out away from camp up here on such a night could have but one ending, not pleasant to contemplate, and thanked fortune for the comparative warmth and shelter of our tent.

The following morning the last loads necessary to complete Camp III were made up. It was decided to take only the larger of the two sleeping-bags and try to sleep double in it again, thus saving the weight of an additional one. Such a course in our experience proved a decided mistake, for where conditions are severe at best and sleep so imperative, the mountaineer should consider his comfort and well-being above all else. The practice of self-denial on the part of the mountaineer in unnecessarily stinting himself under such adverse conditions as ours only leads to the reduction of his physical fitness and hence his chances of success. We therefore rued the day on which the second bag was left behind.

Both of us felt a little worn as we bade farewell to Camp II, but as the day progressed we once more fell into our stride. The trip to our platform at 20,700 feet on the side of the Hump, was made in good time, and it was not many hours before we were staking out Camp III on that site.

That evening, while cooking supper, our primus stove, one of the type with a small base, began to exhibit alarming symptoms. It sputtered and flared and then went out completely, hissing viperishly and filling the tent with choking unburnt gasoline fumes. Apparently it had reached its "ceiling" and there was not enough oxygen to properly support combustion.

This was indeed a serious predicament, for the life of a climber at extreme altitudes centers about his stove. Heat is essential to his existence, for while a man might live on food which required little or no cooking, he would have to depend entirely on melted snow for water to drink. In addition, the valuable psychological effect of the cheering roar and heat given off by a primus stove is not to be ignored. High mountains are climbed on "morale." This precarious mental condition must be maintained at all costs.

So perturbed were we over the failure of our stove that we contemplated a trip to the base camp for one of the larger and, we hoped, better ones. Fortunately, I had included in my pack a limited number of "Meta" solid fuel tablets. When one of these was lighted and placed in the priming ring of the burner it kept the vaporized gas alight. One of us fed our meager supply of "Meta" into the stove, tablet by tablet, while the other melted snow and cooked the supper. In this way a crisis was for the time averted until our supply of "Meta" should give out.

That night we ceremoniously christened Camp III, as we had all the others, with an ounce bottle of Cognac, toasting with due solemnity The First Ascent of the Konka, each with a spoonful of the precious liquid. If we triumphed, the success of the enterprise could be laid at the door of our assiduity in carrying out these sacred rites. The gods of the Konka could not help but smile upon such faithfulness; for if the lamas were to be believed, repetition is the essence of piety.

We wedged ourselves into our one sleeping-bag, drawing for who should sleep on the outside next to the zipper fastening. It had been found by experience at Camp II that, whenever one of the inmates stirred in his sleep, he so expanded the bag that the zipper would unzip, projecting the unfortunate outside man onto the frozen canvas floor. Hence the inside position was always at a premium. Whenever one of us wished to turn he must of necessity gain the coöperation of his bedfellow, a process which was frequently apt to invoke the latter's ire, as he would have undoubtedly dozed off by that time. There was little turning done!

We both lay in a state of semi-consciousness through-

out the night watches, listening to the demoniacal fury
of the wind as it lashed and battered the tent, sending
showers of fine snow sifting through the crannies of
the door and ventilator. Somehow we preserved our
sense of humor at the ridiculousness of the situation and
remained on the best of terms despite it all.

This new altitude of 20,700 feet made itself felt.
The slightest exertion in moving about the tent brought
on a prolonged bout of panting. It took fifteen minutes
to put on and lace a pair of boots, five minutes to don
a parka and mittens; all accompanied by much heavy
breathing and pauses for rest. The cold as well as the
rarefied atmosphere slowed us down, until every action
was done at one-third speed.

We slept with our clothes on for warmth and usually added a few extra ones. The entire process of
dressing seldom occupied less than three-quarters of
an hour.* Several layers of sweaters had to be removed
and then a gaberdine parka put on, in turn covered by
an outside parka of light wind-proof material. This evolution could be executed with the lower half of the
body still in the sleeping-bag. Then slowly and painfully each leg was withdrawn and the outside pair of
heavy wool socks—those "for sleeping only"—were
removed and shoved back into the bag to keep dry.
Groping hands searched blindly its inner recesses for
two pairs of felt inner soles, which had been taken
from our boots and slept with to dry out any moisture they might contain. When these had been inserted, came that superhuman effort of will necessary

* See Appendix C, page 274.

to force one's warm feet into half-frozen boots. Thus fully dressed, we would lie back on our air mattresses, thoroughly tired, and rest for five or ten minutes, before pulling on a flying helmet and goggles for the plunge into the stark frozen world outside.

There was not room in the tent for more than one man to dress at a time, and while one of us was thus engaged the other would set about getting breakfast. Provided there was still a supply of snow blocks within reach outside the door, the preparations for the morning repast could go ahead uninterrupted. If, however, the supply which had been placed there the night before had been exhausted, then the poor unfortunate whose fate it had been to dress first must put on mittens and goggles, and, holding his breath for the final plunge into the cold, would disappear headfirst through the tunnel door like an Esquimo emerging from his igloo.

The stroke of his ice-ax prizing up blocks from the crusted snow would resound through the morning air for several minutes. Then with much stamping of feet would come a shout, "For the luva-Pete, open that door!" Once the strings were loosened from the inside, the requisite number of snow blocks was passed in, followed precipitately by a breathless human form on hands and knees. The chores for the morning done, breakfast would go merrily ahead.

Breakfast over and water-bottles filled,* the loads must be sorted and lashed to pack boards outside the tent. To manipulate ice-coated lash ropes, frozen crampon straps, climbing-ropes and the draw-string of

* See Appendix C, page 276.

the tent door, all with three layers of mittens on one's hands, was a function which required no little proficiency, a proficiency gained only through much practice. To remove one's mittens even for a few seconds was to court disastrous frostbite, for where in comparable temperatures in low altitudes one might do so with impunity, here at 21,000 feet the circulation was so sluggish as to make danger of frostbite at all times imminent. The frost god was our lord and master and he was indeed a jealous god!

One can easily see, therefore, why, although try as we would to get an early start, it was well nigh impossible to do so. From the time of awakening it was usually between two and three hours before we were ready to set out.

Chapter XI

THE NORTHWEST RIDGE

O UR original plan of placing Camp III across the Gap having gone awry, it now remained to find a route by which we ourselves could cross it. We were up at daybreak on the morning of October 15th. It was exceedingly cold and brilliantly clear. The air even in the tent had that bite and dryness to it in the nostrils which bespeak sub-zero temperatures. One of the maximum-minimum thermometers had been inadvertently sat upon, much to its detriment. The other remained at the base camp. Though without a definite check, we estimated the temperature at between —10° and —15° F., which on mature reflection I do not think was an exaggeration.

The jagged array of peaks north of us loomed so clearly in the morning air one felt almost able to reach out and touch them. So extravagantly beautiful was the scene that it resembled some fantastically painted backdrop.

There was little time or inclination, however, for such rhapsodizing. It was too cold and we must be off. Somehow we managed to get away by 8 A.M., breaking all precedents, and set off without packs in order to work our way unencumbered as far as possible up the summit ridge.

An intervening shoulder of the Hump cut off a view into the Gap, so there was nothing for it but to follow blindly the course of least resistance, without, however, losing more altitude than necessary.

The entire northeastern face of the Hump was excessively steep, but by good fortune the preponderance of loose snow on it had avalanched away, leaving exposed a solid footing for our crampons.

Immediately on leaving camp we were forced to descend fifty or sixty feet, cutting steps in the ice to round a vertical bulge in the slope, below which the angle eased a little.

Moore led off and I envied him his exertion in cutting the steps, for the Konka still held us in its icy shadow. The cold was numbing, and the altitude reduced one's resistance to it in an alarming manner. I felt as though I were slowly turning to ice, but our position was too precarious to indulge in any of the usual evolutions calculated to speed up circulation. Fortunately, we were out of the wind.

At length we circumvented the bulge, only to find a new barrier in our path. The slope we now confronted was set at a fifty degree angle and was badly broken by an ice-fall. A hundred feet below us the slope dipped so steeply that it was lost from view. Above, our sphere of action was limited by a perpendicular wall of ice. There was nothing for it but to take the ice-fall by frontal attack at our present level and battle our way through it.

Moore continued in the lead, doing a fine job in picking out a passage through the tangled maze of precarious-looking ice blocks. I constantly belayed him with my ax—not that either of us felt much security in such a belay here. The slope was too abrupt to hold a man in case of a slip. One just *did not* slip, that was all!

Our first problem lay in crossing a deep vertical fissure in the slope, a type of crevasse not before encountered on the mountain. At one point it was divided in two by an ice island halfway across. On the nearer side the island was connected by an insecure-looking snow bridge. The second part, about three feet, must be jumped.

I took up a position close to Moore and a few feet above him. Scraping away the loose surface snow, I drove the shaft of my ax almost to the head into the firm crust beneath, taking several turns of the rope about its head. After getting a good stance, I then signaled Moore to go ahead.

With admirable coolness he tested the bridge. In two strides he reached the island, there cutting a small platform for both feet. Then he proceeded on the next stage of the crossing. At arm's-length he managed to reach over the next chasm and chip away enough of the farther lip of the crevasse to make a landing-place for one foot.

After recovering his breath sufficiently, he turned to me reassuringly and asked, "All set?" I nodded and gripped the rope tighter, paying out just enough for his next move.

Again reaching out, he drove the point of his ax deep into the opposite side and with a great effort swung his foot across and up to where the step was. There

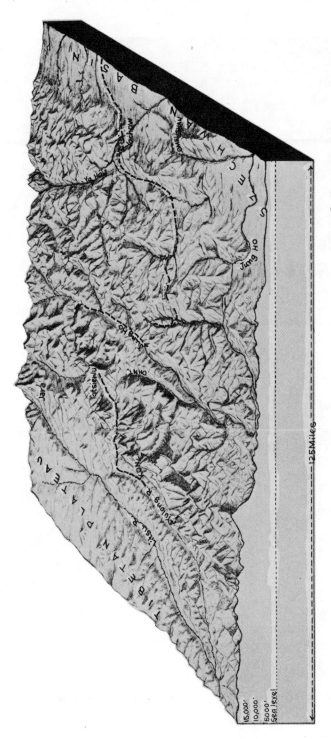

Block diagram of Minya Konka (24,900 feet) and vicinity

by A.B. Emmons III.

1. *Minya Konka Range from Tahsiangling Pass, 45½ miles distant (p.3 and map p. 236)*

2. *Junk on Upper Yangtze (p. 12)*

3. Windbox Gorge (p. 13)

4. Chungking (p. 17)

5. *Buddha at Kiating (p. 23)*

6. *In the Tung Valley (p. 30)*

7. *Tatsienlu Road above the Tung (p. 33)*

8. *360 pounds per man — tea bound for Tatsienlu (p. 34)*

9. *Tea at Lengchi — Yang at lower right (p. 35)*

10. *Tung Valley at Waszekow (p. 42)*

11. East Gate of Tatsienlu (p. 43)

12. Westbound freight – tea caravan leaving Tatsienlu (p. 51)

13. *Gaomo (p. 53)*
14. *A Tibetan smile*
15. *Tibetan boy*

16. *Southward toward the Djezi La (p. 55)*

17. *Chiburongi Konka from north (p. 56)*

18. A barometer reading on the Djezi La: Emmons and Burdsall (p. 56)

19. A Tibetan Herdsman (p. 56)

20. *Tibetan camp*

21. *Tibetan house and Mani pile, Yulong Valley (p. 59)*

22. Mani pile at Yulonghsi (p. 60)

23. "Om Mani Padme Hum"—a Mani stone (p. 60)

24. On road to Konka Gompa: Emmons (p. 61)

25. Konka Gompa (p. 61)

26. *Lamasery courtyard (p. 62)*   27. *Lama (p. 62)*

28. *Camp Alpine (p. 67)*

29. *Minya Konka from Camp Alpine (p. 69)*

30. Transit work on Station D (p. 74)

31. Tsemei La—Minya Konka (p. 94)

32. *Yulong Valley from Station B*
(p. 70)

33. *Büchu Valley, north from Tsemei*
(p. 95)

34. *Chorten, Yulong Valley*

35. Crossing cantilever bridge over Büchu River (p. 95)

36. "Tony" (p. 100)

37. *Cloud Camp—note avalanche track on right (p. 106)*

38. *South face of Minya Konka from 19,000 feet on reconnaissance: Emmons (p. 119)*

39. *View south from 19,000 feet on reconnaissance; top of Mt. Tsemei in clouds (p. 119)*

40. *Young and Burdsall with blue sheep at Camp Boka (p. 119)*

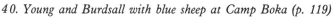

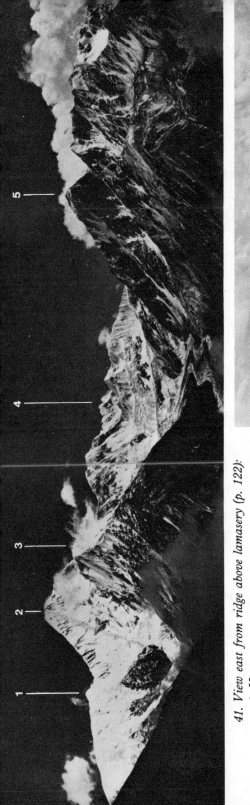

41. *View east from ridge above lamasery (p. 122):*

1. *Hump,*
2. *Minya Konka,*
3. *Peak 111,*
4. *Mt. Chu,*
5. *Nyambo Konka*

42. *Moore on reconnaissance looking south-southeast from 17,000 feet above Gompa Lamasery; sea of clouds (not glacier) below (p. 122)*

Summit

IV

III

II

Base Camp
(behind shoulder)

43. Route and camps (p. 123)

44. Prayers at Base Camp

45. *Porters at Base Camp (p. 130)*

46. *Base Camp, early morning (p. 130)*

47. *Camp I, Nochma Peak (p. 133)*

48. *High porters: Chingwa and Chelay (p. 133)*

49. *The Pyramid*

50. *Cold (p. 134)*

51. Camp I, *new location (p. 137)*

52. Camp II *and view north: Emmons and Burdsall (p. 180)*

53. *The Hump, looking back across gap: Emmons (pp. 150 and 166)*

54. Sunlight and snow—Camp II (p. 154)

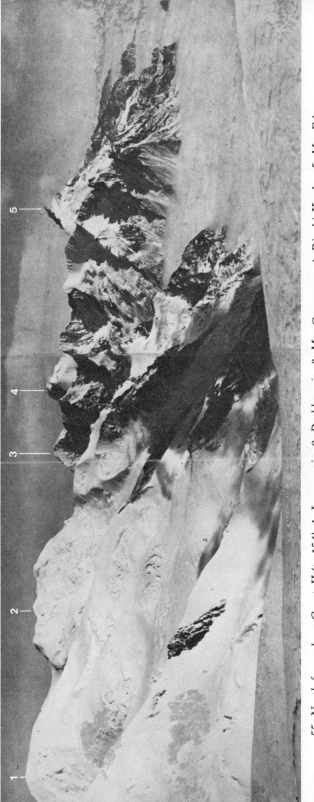

55. *North from above Camp II (p. 154): 1. Longemain, 2. Daddomain, 3. Mt. Grosvenor, 4. Riuchi Konka, 5. Mt. Edgar*

56. A "back and knee": Emmons (p. 165)

57. *Glaciers southwest from Camp I; Base Camp near bend of stream (p. 176)*

58. *Solitude*

59. Work: Burdsall and Moore (p. 180)

60. Camp IV: Emmons and Nochma (p. 190)

61. The northwest ridge: Burdsall and Moore

SOUTH

Peak 148   Peak 153   Peak 156

WEST

Nyambo Konka

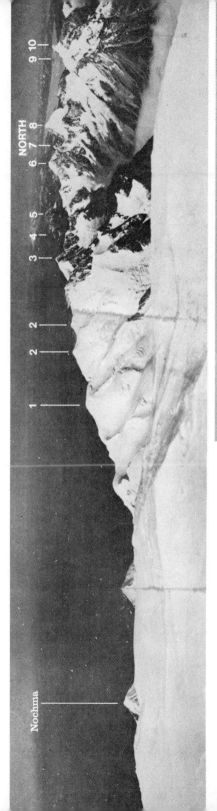

NORTH

9 10

6 7 8

3 4 5

2 2

2

1

Nochma

EAST

Mt. Sunyatsen

10

62. Panorama taken on summit of Minya Konka, October 28, 1932 (p. 199): 1. Longemain, 2. Daddomain, 3. Reddomain,
4. Jara, 5. Mt. Sherap, 6. Mt. Grosvenor, 7. Chiburongi Konka, 8. Riuchi Konka, 9. Tatsienlu (below the clouds), 10. Mt. Edgar

63. *Moore on summit* (p. 200)

was room for only one foot, and he seemed to balance for an eternity on two or three points of his crampon before finally gaining a good footing.

When several more steps had been cut he took up a good position, and then came my turn. As I crossed the bridge I caught a fleeting glimpse of several pieces of snow I had dislodged cascading down into the abyss below, a decidedly disturbing spectacle.

The second part was more trying than the first, for one must swing one's weight up and outward to reach the foothold, relying solely upon the purchase of the ax to keep from overbalancing and hurtling down the slope. When I started to cross this bit I realized with admiration the apparent ease with which Moore had done it, for it was assuredly a delicate maneuver.

Once across, we found our troubles had but begun. We were now forced to traverse a narrow strip of snow at the base of an ice buttress. The shelf lay at a fearsome angle and below it yawned a bergschrund, the lower lip of which was not visible. It was too dangerous a place to exchange the lead, so Moore continued to cut the steps, though feeling badly winded.

Where this snow shelf would ultimately take us we could only conjecture. It was our only possible line of advance, however, and we therefore followed it.

After progressing at the same general elevation for a few yards, the shelf ended abruptly in a second ice buttress. Moore reported that he had passed the mouth of a narrow snow-filled couloir running up between the two buttresses, though it was so steep, he was not sure that we could negotiate it.

I joined him, and together we studied the couloir. It rose so steeply that standing upright in our tracks we could reach out and touch the snow in front of our faces. It provided the only avenue of escape, and as we did not relish the thought of recrossing our double crevasse, we decided to have a go at it. Moore again took the lead, while I cut two substantial footholds just to one side of the couloir where I could anchor him and be out of the line of fire of the débris dislodged from his step-cutting.

I shifted my weight with impatience from one foot to the other and gazed down between them to the glacier nearly a mile below. The Konka no longer threw its frigid shadow upon us and in the sun the temperature rose to more comfortable heights.

Nearly an hour passed before the entire hundred-foot length of the rope had been payed out. At last a cheering "All right, Art: Come along up," and I started the ascent. Resting every five or ten feet, it was twenty minutes before I came out on top of the declivity where Moore had taken up his stand.

From here I took the lead and plowed my way along in deep snow, skirting another crevasse at the foot of another ice wall. We were now well into the Gap, but found ourselves considerably below its lowest point. To further complicate matters there was a huge cornice running its entire length, completely cutting off all access to it from where we stood. Our only hope appeared to be a détour out on to the extremely precipitous north face of the Konka and an attempt to gain the ridge from there. Here on the leeward side the wind had drifted powdery snow to great depth, and for an hour we floundered waist deep in it, making very little headway at an enormous expenditure of energy. One place in particular, a small level platform, gave us trouble. The snow here appeared bottomless, and to add to our embarrassment there were signs of crevasses underneath. We finally got over by lying flat and literally swimming our way across, a pastime in the thin air of 21,000 feet scarcely recommended to those subject to severe cardiac disturbances!

Gaining firm névé once more, we sat down for a council of war and a spot of lunch. It was now 1 P.M., and five hours had been consumed in making good scarcely a third of a mile with no gain in altitude. Very definitely our route thus far would have to be radically amended, or else we must resort to roping directly into the Gap from the Hump.

On closer examination of the cornice above us, I discovered a small vertical crack, about two feet wide, leading up to the floor of the Gap twenty feet higher. It had been formed by the outward drag of the cornice, where its weight was beginning to split it off from the consolidated snow behind. It looked stable and ponderous enough not to be easily dislodged.

By cutting several steps I gained a position from which it was possible to squeeze into the crack. Using the technique employed in ascending a rock chimney, I managed a "back and knee" with the aid of my crampons and ax and easily gained the top.[60] Moore followed, and together we stood in the Gap at the very foot of the northwest ridge.

Though it was late in the day, we ascended the first five hundred feet of the ridge over easy snow terrain. Standing at 21,200 feet, we were just slightly higher than the crest of the Hump. To our great relief, an obvious route across its near face presented itself from our new point of vantage.[53] This new route was steep and again presented danger of avalanching, but it was so infinitely preferable to our morning's method of reaching the Gap, we unhesitatingly adopted it.

A lively gale sprang up from the west and howled through the Gap as we again descended into it. This time we crossed easily and ascended a snow ridge to a point where a traverse could be made of the side of the Hump, a few hundred feet above the place along which we had so laboriously climbed that morning.

The snow lay deep along this new route and at such an angle as to cause us no small anxiety as to its stability. It seemed well attached to the ice beneath, however, and stayed put.

After several hundred yards of cautious progress, we turned a corner and were confronted by an unpleasantly steep bit, bare of loose snow. Moore had done the lion's share of the work that day, and I volunteered to do cutting across this new barrier. Half an hour's strenuous ax work brought us to a position on top of a bergschrund immediately above Camp III. Jumping down over it, we half slid, half stumbled into camp, thoroughly spent by the day's exertions.

At dawn on October 16th Moore and I sallied forth from Camp III and started again for the northwest ridge without loads. It was our intention to climb as far up along the ridge as possible and examine the first rocky band at 23,400 feet, could we reach that point.

In two hours we had crossed the Gap and reached the high point of the day before. Climbing steadily, we advanced over uniform wind-swept slopes of firm snow into which our crampons sank with a satisfying crunch. It was excellent footing.

We now felt well acclimatized and climbed at a steady rate of over 350 feet an hour with only infrequent pauses. I personally felt in better condition than I had for many a day, and Moore also seemed very fit.

The sky was clear except for a few fluffy cumuli off in Tibet and the ever-present pall over China. Above, the ridge remained clear to the summit and was sharply etched in the mid-morning sunlight. As we stopped at intervals to study it we got the impression that this ridge was impossibly steep. Several of the rock projections near the top seemed fairly to overhang us. Whether such a route were feasible only actual experience with it would tell.

The lower part of the ridge, as we had foreseen, was devoid of technical difficulties, save for a rather exposed snow bridge across a small bergschrund and one or two short bits of hard ice. Belays were necessary in only a few places. We congratulated ourselves on the simplicity of the climb thus far, though, to be sure, the ridge was seldom less than thirty-five degrees in angle of elevation and in places exceeded forty degrees.

At 1 P.M. we stood at an estimated elevation of 23,000 feet. Here we sat in the snow for half an hour's rest and a snack of lunch. We were now higher than any of the other peaks in the entire range; all had sunk into relative insignificance below us. The hills of Tibet assumed the aspect of one vast dun-colored plain, with scattered snowy ranges breaking the remote horizon. One of these distant ranges, in particular, attracted our attention. Until now it had remained hidden below the horizon, but as we had neared 22,000 feet it began to make its appearance. Now at 23,000 feet this group of peaks stood out impressively. One of the group was in the shape of a huge cockscomb, another a gigantic pyramid somewhat resembling Minya Konka, and a third a jagged wedge. From their distinctive shape and general southwesterly bearing we believe them to be the Konkaling peaks explored in 1930 by Dr. Joseph Rock. In fact, he mentions having seen Minya Konka from that vicinity, and gives their location as approximately two hundred miles southwest of the Konka group (undoubtedly much less), and their altitude in excess of 20,000 feet.* Rising as they did from the brown Tibetan plateau, they presented a spectacular sight, and will, no doubt, some day provide new fields of adventure for the mountaineer, perhaps at no distant date.

* "Proceeding over a rocky trail, we halted on more gentle slopes, and then, at 15,300 feet, decided to pitch camp. I ascended the spur back of our camp to 16,320 feet, hoping to obtain a view of the other Konkaling peaks, but in vain. Looking east, however, the sky was clear, and more than 200 miles away rose two distinct snow ranges. There was one mighty peak that fairly pierced the sky. Not finding any in that direction on the maps, I then and there decided to spend the following year exploring those mighty peaks and clear up the mystery which hedged them in. The vast snow range I then beheld proved to be the unexplored Minya Konka."—"Konka Risumgongba, Holy Mountain of the Outlaws." Joseph Rock—National Geographic Magazine, July, 1931.

Farther to the north, the lone spire of the Jara had
sunk well down beneath the skyline and lay an incon-
spicuous white patch on the landscape. At our backs rose
the Konka, solitary and forbidding, reigning in lone
majesty in a stark, empty domain of its own.

Far below, the world of man seemed so remote and
detached that one was seized with a poignant loneliness. The firmament existed only in austere black and
white; the blinding glare of the sun on the snow, the
black sky, and the forbidding dark facets of rock slic-
ing through their mantle of gleaming ice—all conspired
to give one a burden of mental depression, which was
overpowering. The eye sought vainly for a haven of
refuge, for some fair nook in this dazzling waste of
desolation in which to rest, but none was vouchsafed
in the cold thin air of 23,000 feet.

And yet there was relief. Lifting and falling with
motionless outspread wings on a rising column of air
below us were two or three choughs, black birds the
size and shape of crows. Occasionally in a lull in the
wind we could hear their hoarse croaks. They were
repulsive-looking creatures, but we welcomed them, for
they provided a link with the familiar world we had
left so far below. The spirit drew comfort from their
presence, for here, after all, was life where death ruled
supreme. We wondered what these birds could find to
interest them on such barren heights. They no doubt
wondered the same of us. At any rate, we felt a friendly
kinship towards our winged companions and envied
them their ability to rise so effortlessly to a point we
had spent such weeks of desperate exertion to win, and

then, in one sublime minute of speed, sweep down to that green meadow so many thousands of feet below.

To be sure this latter feat might almost be accomplished by merely stepping over the western face a few feet away, though at this time such a thought had but little appeal! No, we were chained to the earth; they were free.

After exposing a set of consecutive photographs, we again started upward. By 2.30 P.M. we reached a point just below the first band of rocks, estimated at 23,400 feet. On closer examination these rocks looked somewhat less formidable, though we still felt far from optimistic about them. There would have to be some nice discernment in the matter of routes before the barrier would give way to attack. In addition, from here on the steepness of the ridge increased considerably, making it doubtful whether we could proceed safely without step-cutting.

The afternoon clouds began to gather with startling rapidity and made higher reconnaissance not only futile, but inadvisable. Neither Moore nor I felt unduly fatigued, and so it was with some regret we took a parting look at the last fifteen hundred feet of the ridge through the binoculars and did an about-face. This point, 23,400 feet in elevation, was the highest I reached, though, fortunately, at the time I did not know the fate that was to befall me.

The wind began to get up as we descended, and before long became unpleasantly strong, frequently throwing us almost to our knees. It drove before it a hail of ice particles with such force that one could not face the blast. With heads averted and hands held before our faces for protection, we retraced our steps down the ridge, at times immersed in the flying obscurity of a vagrant cloud, only to emerge abruptly into the blinding glare of sunlit snow beneath. The wind fairly beat the breath from one's lungs and turning one's back to it, some seconds were required to regain normal respiration.

The prints left by our crampons in the hard pack became nearly indistinguishable in the uncertain light. The holes quickly filled with drift, so that at times there was danger of losing the track. We determined that over certain parts of the route trail markers would have to be employed for safety under such conditions.

Not until 5 P.M. did we regain Camp III. There we discussed the situation. By now we had been living for two weeks above 18,000 feet, and each of us felt inordinately tired of both our diet and our surroundings. The work of preliminary reconnaissance was over (Analysis of Ascent Chart, page 273), and the prospect of several sunny days lying about in the grass at the base camp had an overwhelming appeal. In addition, the low state of our food and fuel supplies necessitated a retreat at least as far as Camp I for their renewal. It was therefore not a difficult decision to make to descend to 14,400 feet on the morrow, where Burdsall and Young awaited news of us.

The prospect of a third night jammed in one sleeping-bag was so unattractive that we put it to chance to see who should descend to Camp II the same afternoon, for we knew that by now the drift had rendered the tent there too small to accommodate more than one man.

The lot fell to Moore to go on to 19,800 feet, where there was a sleeping-bag, food, but no primus stove. He must therefore spend a waterless night.

I remained outside the tent at Camp III to watch his progress until I saw him emerge well down the spur. A large black thundercloud came rolling in out of the west and caused me some apprehension until I saw that Moore would outdistance it.

That night the worst storm in our experience lashed along the spur, beating the snow into a perfect fury of flying spindrift. The lightning struck frequently, once or twice along the shoulder just above Camp III. Its concussion shook the ground so much that I could hear small pieces of ice coursing down the slope outside near the tent. My peace of mind was disturbed by the possibility of the slope above avalanching and sweeping the camp away, or of the serac upon which it was perched giving way and dropping me into the abyss.

The lightning was terrifying in its brilliance even inside the tent. The thunder reverberated deafeningly from cliff to cliff, dying away in a low grumble only after several minutes.

At length the storm died away slowly in the distance, but the wind increased in violence until I thought the tent would be torn to pieces by its ferocity.

Despite the noise of slatting canvas I finally dropped off to sleep. Suddenly there came a crash, and I awoke to find myself smothered beneath a wildly flapping tent. The stakes on the windward side had let go and the

pole came down amongst a *mêlée* of stove, candle-
lantern, cans, and clothes. I had purposely slept on the
windward side of the tent to steady it, a fortunate move
as, even with the tent collapsed, the wind was strong
enough to roll me half over. Had I picked the other
side, I should have received the pole full in the face,
accompanied by a large proportion of my belongings!

Although somewhat uneasy lest Camp III be blown
bodily over the edge, I was in no mood to disentangle
myself in the darkness and go out into the cold to do
battle with the gale for the possession of the tent.
Leaving the pole flat, I weighted down as much loose
canvas as I could from inside. Then placing a dunnage
bag where it would keep the cloth from my face, I spent
the long weary hours from midnight until dawn half
awake and thinking if I survived the night how wonderful the base camp was going to look on the morrow.

I verily believe the wind that night reached velocities
well in excess of one hundred miles an hour, to have
exerted such force in air of less than one-half the density
of that at sea-level.

Crawling out of the wrecked tent the next morning,
I found everything enveloped in a confusing swirl of
gray mists. I noted with satisfaction that the tent remained untorn despite the beating it had received.

The wind had dropped, but the air was bitter cold.
After replacing the missing stakes, I breakfasted on
chocolate and raisins. Then tying the tent flat, I set
out for Camp II through the fog, leaving everything
behind except the recalcitrant primus stove.

The tracks as far as the spur were easy enough to

follow. Once on its broad crest, however, they became indiscernible.

I again experienced that queer defying diffusion of light on the snow which rendered all sense of perspective false. A few feet on my right lay a cornice, which, if ventured upon, would precipitate me several thousands of feet to the glacier. To the left lay the great western face of the spur. Neither had much appeal to a lone climber immersed in the fog.

Proceeding cautiously a few paces at a time and checking my course by a pocket compass, I made my way from landmark to landmark along the top of the spur. Occasionally I was reassured by the sight of Moore's footprints where the wind had not destroyed them. Keeping well to the left where the more obvious of the two dangers lay, I several times caught myself within a few feet of the edge, headed for destruction, and promptly changed course. On one occasion, upon reading my compass, I found that I was headed back up the mountain. On another, I thought I discerned through a rift in the clouds one of the rock peaks north of Camp II. Thinking at last I was emerging below the cloud level, I increased my stride, and after several paces walked directly upon the peak! It turned out to be a black film paper frozen into the snow and had only been a few feet away when I mistook it for a mountain!

Had it not been for the fact that I had a rendezvous to keep with Moore at Camp II, and that Camp III was now almost untenable, due to the low supply of stores there, I should have let discretion play the better part of valor and retraced my steps. However, luck was with me, and after two hours of mental strain I came out below the clouds at Camp II.

I was astonished to find how badly snowed in was the tent. Had I not seen where Moore had burrowed a hole down to the doorway, I should not have thought there was room enough inside for him. I gave him a shout and shook the tent. Despite the fact that it was nearly noon, there was only a muffled subterranean groan. When Moore at last crawled forth, I saw that he had been sleeping cornerwise, there not being room enough inside to stretch out any other way!

On arriving at Camp I, two hours later, we found both Young and Burdsall in residence. With them was a large depot of stores, including a five-gallon tin of kerosene which had come out by courier from Tatsienlu.

What delighted our hearts more than anything else, however, was home mail for both of us. This was rural free delivery *par excellence*, at 18,000 feet on a Tibetan peak! The letters were dated two months earlier.

We sat in the snow in the warm sun outside the tent and, while a delicious feeling of contentment penetrated our souls, read the home tidings of how Hoover's campaign was progressing and how devastating was the Depression. To add to the utter delight of the situation we each consumed our entire respective shares of the carefully rationed cookies Mrs. Cunningham had sent out with the runner. Ah, but life had its sweet moments!

During the ensuing conversation Moore and I reported our findings and what we felt were the chances of success. All hands agreed that it was definitely worth while to carry on, even though our hope of defeating the mountain was decidedly slim.

Young and Burdsall were eager to renew the attack at once. Though there was no time to waste, Moore and I felt the need of several days at the base camp to recuperate, and so a plan was evolved whereby we should descend immediately to 14,400,[57] while the other men remained at Camp I to acclimatize. When Moore and I had rested sufficiently, we would join them at 18,000 feet and continue the campaign as a foursome.

Chapter XII

AT CLOSE QUARTERS

MOORE and I had the base camp to ourselves, the porters having returned to the valley. For two delightfully warm days we lay in the grass about the fire and exulted in the caress of the warm sunshine, a scene such as to gladden the heart of any bucolic muse.

Occasionally the distant murmuring rumble of an avalanche drew our attention to the silvery bulk of the Konka rising over ten thousand feet above us, straight into the blue smiling sky.

We could hear the far-off roar of the wind along the ridge, two miles away—a low monotone—and enjoyed the more our seclusion. Otherwise we forgot the stern, grim fight of the past three weeks, and exulted in the present relaxation and a well-earned rest. Life seemed like one long pleasant dream from which we would fain not be awakened—the more so because of the hard work which lay ahead.

Our diet here consisted solely of fried potatoes—all that had been left by the support party in their zeal to stock Camp I. Even the lowly potato took on the likeness of food for an epicure to our jaded appetites. We had wanted a change of diet, and here it was with a vengeance!

On the second day of our sojourn at the base we were

joined by Young from Camp I. During our absence higher up he and Burdsall, with the two high porters, Chingwa and Chelay, had moved some two hundred and fifty pounds of stores to 18,000 feet, each night returning to the base. When everything had gone up, including new stocks of provisions from Tatsienlu, the porters were sent down, while Burdsall and Young moved to Camp I to acclimatize and await our return from the upper regions.

Young now joined us to confer about the porters. The men were too untrained and without discipline to be of much use without supervision. It seemed essential that one of us should remain at the base camp or at the monastery to hold the men in readiness should an emergency demand their immediate services. Also, when the campaign was over we should need them to help in the speedy evacuation of the mountain.

Young realized that he was the best qualified to assume this all-important post as head of the support party, both through his knowledge of the language and his previous experience with the natives. He also felt that his physical reaction to the altitude thus far had been less encouraging than might have been expected, and that his lack of mountain experience would tend to lessen the chances of success for the rest of the party.

To be sure, his record both on the reconnaissance and thus far on the ascent did not altogether bear out such a premise, for in both cases he had done much excellent work. He had, however, suffered more from the effects of altitude than the rest, and I think, on the whole, his choice was a wise one. He generously resigned his place in the summit party and volunteered to take charge of the porters, returning to the lamasery the following day.

The last phase of the assault began. We now knew the strength and deadliness of the weapons with which the Konka could defend itself. It was to be the last dire thrust we could make at the heart of our gigantic adversary. Were we beaten back, there could be no rallying. Defeat and possible disaster would be the result. It was now a case of risking everything in one last supreme effort, an effort requiring every atom of skill and strength we could muster. We were going the limit.

October 20th saw a renewal of the activity. Moore left the base camp at an early hour to join Burdsall at Camp I and push on through to Camp II on the spur the same day. I remained until late in the afternoon to cut some willow sticks to be used as trail markers.

It was after three before I started for Camp I. On reaching the Crampon Place in the gully, darkness descended, but I climbed steadily to where the original Camp I had been. From here it was only a matter of seventy yards to the present location of the tent, but a damp mist enveloped everything, making the intervening distance hazardous going in the dark. I nearly stumbled over the tent without seeing it.

As I half expected, both Moore and Burdsall were in residence. The threatening weather had made their continuing on to 19,800 feet inadvisable. The present situation was awkward because three of us must somehow cook our meals and sleep in a tent scarcely large enough for two. To further complicate matters, it began to snow, rendering some one's suggestion to sleep outside impossible. Somehow we all managed to get inside, though the walls bulged alarmingly. The tent was wide enough to allow one foot eight inches to a man, and we slept with shoulders overlapping. Apparently we all slept soundly!

Nearly a foot of snow fell during the night, and higher up considerably more. Getting away at 8.30 A.M., we shouldered forty-five-pound loads. The going was heavy indeed, and it was slow work breaking the track.[59] Ten steps and rest. Ten steps and rest. One hundred and change the lead. All three of us took turns at plowing up through a heartbreaking mass of clinging snow. Crampons clogged. Footsteps gave way. On we fought. Three hours to reach the halfway point. Yet Camp II still seemed infinitely far away.

To our relief, we found that in the zone above the wind had done its work. The area above the crevasses had been blown clear and the footing became firm once more. Our pace remained the same, however, for by now we were so badly worn that each step required a tremendous amount of our failing energy.

It was late afternoon before we attained Camp II. Only the top two feet of the tent showed above the snow! It was hopelessly buried,[52] so we merely dumped the loads alongside and started back for 18,000 feet and a second night wedged into the two-man tent there.

We took pains to climb carefully and deliberately at all times, especially while descending, for then it is that by far the greater proportion of mountaineering accidents occur. It is desperately hard, if not impossible, when one's knees are fairly caving in with weariness, not to relax for an instant, and such relaxation sometimes proves fatal.

The two-man tent was left at Camp I and stocked with provisions and a double sleeping-bag in case a hurried retreat became necessary. The three of us the next day again started up for the spur. The tent at II having been so badly snowed under, we decided to finesse it entirely and go on through to Camp III in a single day. Our present loads would complete the stock of necessities for all camps, including the establishment of a fourth one on the main northwest ridge itself. Thus until the Konka campaign was over, Camp I would see no more of us.

The day was perfect, and although we had a great distance to cover, we did not hurry. The light conditions were excellent and our cameras got plenty of use. Until now we had been so absorbed in merely consolidating our various camps that little attempt had been made to make a photographic record of our surroundings.

We had no moving-picture equipment, for which we were doubly thankful, both because of the considerable additional weight involved and because of the expenditure of time and energy required in the exposure of film where conditions made such an undertaking extremely difficult. To film such a climb properly there must be one man whose sole responsibility is to do nothing but "shoot" the film. Our personnel was far too limited for any such extravagance. Moreover, we were there to climb the Konka, not to take pictures of it.

Hence a few characteristic "stills" for purposes of record had to suffice.

A couple of hours were spent at Camp II in digging down to the tent door and in readjusting loads. Once the door had been cleared, I crawled inside to retrieve the remainder of the food and unexposed film. There was barely room to squeeze in, and I noticed that, although the canvas remained untorn by the weight of snow, the pole had snapped, leaving the surrounding drift still supporting the walls to which it had frozen.

We continued on up the spur that afternoon.[58] Now our shortage of equipment and man-power made itself markedly evident. By the time Camp III was reached, we were all utterly worn, especially Burdsall, who, through poor acclimatization, felt badly exhausted. This was his first experience above 20,000 feet. All day the thin air had sapped his strength, and though we repeatedly demanded that he share part of his load with us, he grimly and steadfastly refused.

Had he had the acclimatization and orientation which Moore and I had gained on our high reconnaissance, he would have been as fit as either of us in all probability. If we had had sufficient tents, equipment, and personnel to accommodate a corps of high-altitude porters above Camp I, he could have become inured to the present severe conditions less rapidly and more completely by being able to work at a slower pace. In this way a self-sufficient party is usually handicapped at high altitudes by lack of porters.

We all felt the unspoken realization that we were rapidly nearing the end of our tether, though not one of us would ever have admitted it, even to himself. It was touch and go as to whether we should be able to carry a camp up the steep summit ridge to 22,000 or 23,000 feet, and from there force our way through unknown obstacles to the summit. Trivial happenings at such extreme altitudes take on a new significance and can have the most decisive and overwhelming influence where a man is reaching the outer fringes of his endurance. The breaks must be with us, and by far the most important of these was the weather—an uncertain quantity at best in these ranges. If the weather held, then, it might be possible—just possible—to win through to the summit.

We found Camp III in order, and, after setting up the tent, crawled wearily inside, but not before the stakes had been reinforced with all available ice-axes. My experience of the last night spent here during the storm would not gain in pleasure by repetition.

It was estimated that six more loads remained at 19,800 feet. These could be brought to Camp III in two relays in a single day. By tomorrow night we should be fully consolidated here at 20,700, and ready to carry on with Camp IV on the northwest arrête.

Next morning, Moore started ahead for II to dig out the tent there if that were again necessary. It was our custom to go unroped over this section, and Burdsall and I followed him at a more leisurely pace.

The day was cloudless and almost without wind. As we strode down along the spur, a sense of well-being pervaded me. The rarefied air no longer laid a heavy hand on body and mind. I felt exhilarated by a strong

sense of superiority lent by the tremendous height of
the spur, as I glanced contemptuously down across the
vast tableland of Tibet, spreading off to that distant
gray line where earth and sky met.

Exalted lords of the earth we were until, turning to
see how Burdsall was progressing, I gazed up across
the savage cliffs that dropped away with magnificent
symmetry from a bastioned ice-bound summit, a long
silvery pennant of snow whipping from it to the northeast. For there, nearly a mile above me, was the goal
we had set out to win. I felt subdued and oppressed
by its huge and awful presence—this Holy Mountain of
Minya. How utterly futile it seemed to match one's
pitiful strength against so relentless a foeman.

And yet one felt irresistibly drawn towards a thing
of such utter beauty and majesty whose moods and
changes were never the same. One sympathized with
those untutored, simple-minded Tibetans that here was
a Being to be at once feared and loved. How incom-
parably glorious it looked in the morning light!

We met Moore just leaving Camp II with his first
load. He reported that there were only four loads left,
which on later consideration we narrowed to three and
a half. Burdsall and I decided we might stretch a point
and clean up the lot, obviating a second trip. When the
loads had been made up I found that mine was in excess of fifty pounds, and Burdsall's somewhat less. Camp
II was officially "closed for the season."

I began strongly to regret my exuberance as I swung
up the pack, but to save my face I could say nothing.
As we started upward our pace was funereal, and we

made up our minds to taking the whole afternoon to cover the distance to Camp III. Again, however, once a rhythm was well established in our respiration as well as our stride, the loads seemed miraculously pounds lighter, though still a crushing weight to lift uphill at over 20,000 feet.

Having climbed seven hundred feet, we met Moore returning for his second installment. When he was informed that there was nothing left, he was at first incredulous, then righteously indignant that we had been such fools as to overload ourselves in this fashion, when we had all agreed to make two trips and take equal amounts. To soothe his injured feelings we shared part of our packs with him. And so The Camp by the Hump was reestablished.

On October 24th a much-begrudged day off was taken on our meager food supply, a windy day along the spur with clouds enveloping everything so thickly that visibility was literally zero. A prolonged game of chess consumed whatever of the day was not occupied in cooking and eating our two meals. To cheer lagging appetites we made up a hypothetical list of "The Most Luxurious Foods One Could Possibly Take on a Canoe Trip!" a pastime in our present situation we felt to be slightly irrelevant, but entertaining withal. Much interest and amusement was also found in reading all the labels and directions on our various tins of food.

It was a great relief to listen to the steady, comforting purr of the primus stove, one of the larger type, as its blue flame licked about an aluminum pot packed with snow.

We were now using kerosene in preference to the gasoline of the former occasion, and, contrary to the general belief that gasoline was superior at extreme heights, the kerosene seemed a decided improvement. Whether this difference was due solely to the better stove now in use I do not know, and I suspect the grade of gasoline we obtained in western China, when it could be got at all, left much to be desired. At any rate, our stove troubles seemed to be over.

Our appetites above 20,000 feet were never strong. Eating became rather an onerous duty than a pleasure. The diet consisted largely of concentrated foods,* and was high in sugar. The sugar had an undeniable taste of gasoline, but was just as welcome. Among the things obtainable in Tatsienlu were eggs. These eggs, though three weeks old, were nonetheless considered as a great delicacy. They had been solidly frozen for days, and one could shell them raw as though they had been hard boiled.

We used to make an egg soufflé which would make any Waldorf chef wilt with envy. Two of the aforementioned three-weeks-old eggs were peeled and fried in yak butter in an aluminum bowl. The whites would have been long since cooked before the yolks had even melted, a condition which, though inconvenient, did not seem to spoil the taste. The whole was then beaten up with granulated yak cheese into a delicious concoction —my mouth waters yet at the thought! But we survived and lived to tell the tale.

The *pièce de resistance* of our diet consisted of three-

* See Appendix C, page 276.

minute oatmeal which invariably took at least twenty minutes to cook. So low was the temperature of boiling water at 21,000 feet that one could plunge one's hand into it without suffering undue discomfort. We tried to disguise the oatmeal in various ways with malted milk, sugar, and butter, but its flavor was not to be thus easily defied. Oatmeal was oatmeal, and before long we became so inordinately tired of this food that a solemn oath was sworn whereby, once away from the mountain, we could never be coerced or cajoled into touching it again. Once back in Tatsienlu, however, this resolution died a premature death, for when a bowl of Mrs. Cunningham's steaming Scotch porridge was set before us, there was no resisting it. We ate it prayerfully, joyfully, and with great gusto!

Each man was allowed but one spoon and one aluminum bowl. With these implements, a pocket knife, and any accessories nature provided, he had to eat and drink everything that came his way, and be as merry as he might. There was no water to spare in which to wash dishes—water meant fuel—and fuel here was more precious than fine gold. He simply used the Tibetan system of licking his bowl clean with his tongue before the next course, or cleaned it with snow.

On the morning of the 25th we recorded 5° F. at 9 A.M., as we started for the Gap with substantial loads of food and extra clothes. The steps around the Hump were filled and took some time to clear. On reaching the floor of the Gap we saw that our crack, instead of being a mere two feet wide as on the former occasion, had widened to ten, and still the cornice did not fall.

We never ceased to wonder at the elasticity and toughness of this ice.

The southwest gale was on the job as always, and so battered and bullied us that we felt almost bruised by its impact. The skirts of our parkas flapped viciously about our knees. Flying snow particles clung to our clothes in a white rime. Icicles formed on our eyebrows and beards. Again and again we were beaten from our tracks despite thirty-pound loads. Balance regained, again the slow rhythm of our feet timed to our breathing, the trip-hammer pounding of heart against ribs, as we labored on.

Short rests to lean, gasping, over one's ice-ax, back to the wind. Stamping of feet to keep them alive. Pauses that seemed like heaven itself as long as one were only not moving upward. Then the response of tortured lungs as we struggled on again.

Five hours of steady plugging and we breasted a sharp rise at 21,700 feet to throw off our packs and lie panting in the snow. My feet began to ache with the cold and grew steadily colder despite my efforts to revive them.

Another hour we fought our way upward, and finally sank to rest behind a low ice bastion at 22,000 feet. By this time my feet were becoming numb, and I told the men that I was worried about them. It was well along in the afternoon and we had reached the point of exhaustion where to continue much higher would not have been possible. Furthermore, here occurred about the only place on the ridge so far which offered even a vestige of shelter or of a level spot for a tent. Within three thousand feet of the top we considered that we had a fighting chance of making the climb from here, though we had hoped to put the camp five hundred feet higher.

All things taken into account, it was decided that our present elevation would have to suffice. We might possibly have to advance our position higher, but only after a determined try at the summit from here.

Leaving our loads securely placed, we made a quick descent to Camp III. My feet recovered on the way down, accompanied by the painful return of circulation. Once in the tent, I removed boots and socks. One or two toes seemed a little white, but a massage soon brought back good color and sensation. I spent a very comfortable night.

October 26th saw the dismantling of Camp III, for we had need of the tent above. Leaving a small cache of extra fuel, clothes, and exposed film, the climbing party again turned its collective face toward the ridge.

The thermometer hovered around zero, and as we entered the Gap the wind again struck us with numbing force. This day was a repetition of the previous one, save that there was no return to Camp III.

When we reached the 22,000-foot level and the site of Camp IV, my feet were again giving trouble. After a prolonged rest in the lee of the ridge, we attacked the lower lip of a small snow-filled bergschrund with our ice-axes, hewing a platform from the living ice.

The top half of the 'schrund protected the tent in some measure from the battering of the wind, and the snow-filled crack, when augmented by part of its lower lip, made a space just large enough for the tent. It was an hour and a half of hard work before the platform was ready. Its architectural points, to be sure, would not have evoked much praise from a landscape gardener, and it had a very decided outward tilt not conducive to a feeling of security. Nevertheless, we had to make the best of it, so eyes were cut from the solid ice at great labor, large enough to admit tent ropes, and the tent was literally tied to the mountain. Still, it was "home," and after putting the finishing touches on Camp IV, we crawled thankfully inside.[60]

That evening the discussion revolved about the next phase of the campaign. Burdsall was in poor condition through lack of sleep and acclimatization, but both Moore and I were feeling perfectly fit. In view of these circumstances, Moore and I decided on the morrow to scout a route up through the first band of rocks, cutting steps where necessary and marking the route. We hoped with luck to force our way through to about 24,000 feet. While we were thus engaged, Burdsall was going to take a day of rest in Camp IV to recover some of his strength. On the first good day thereafter the three of us together would make a determined attempt at the summit.

Scarcely had this plan of action been evolved when I attempted to slice a frozen biscuit with my pocket knife. The biscuit was tough and its frozen interior yielded but little to my efforts. Suddenly it gave way and the knife broke through, cutting a deep gash in the palm of my left hand nearly two inches long. The wound was so deep that a number of the sensory nerves in the two little fingers were severed.

I sat and dazedly watched the thick drops of blood ooze out and drip slowly onto my sleeping-bag. Suddenly the significance of what had happened penetrated my altitude-benumbed consciousness. Moore assisted me in sterilizing the cut and adjusting a tight compress.

Now at the eleventh hour fate had struck us a dire blow. Our plans had to be changed. We knew from what we had already seen of the final fifteen hundred feet of the ridge that its ascent, if possible at all, would exact the last atom of skill and strength from every man. The climbers would be taxed to the very limit of their endurance. If indeed it were possible to win a way through the various obstacles, we fully expected to encounter some very ticklish pieces of ice-work and even a bit of rock-climbing might be expected. My left hand would be of little use to me in holding a rope or ax, with two fingers partly paralized. Furthermore, both the wound and its tight compress would so tend to cut off the circulation from the two injured fingers there was almost a certainty of freezing them on such exposure as the ascent entailed.

At the high camp there was hardly enough food for another five days. It was scarcely conceivable to us that the summit could be reached on the first try. Burdsall, though suffering badly from altitude, stubbornly insisted that he was fit to carry on. There was no time to be lost in making the first assault. Therefore, with the keenest pang of disappointment I made the decision to remain in Camp IV in reserve while the other two made the attempt. If they failed, then perhaps I could join them in a second attempt when the hand had been given more time to recover.

The reconnaissance was abandoned, and on the following day the entire party rested out of deference to Burdsall's condition. We felt our quest but the forlornest of hopes, and watched with despair our hard-won victory slipping through our fingers. That day we spent literally holding down the tent to keep it from being blown away. Again my little chessboard saw good service in possibly the highest chess game ever played, and certainly one of the weirdest. Despite the wind, it was not excessively cold, nor did the usual afternoon clouds cloak the ridge. The weather, at least, boded well for the morrow.

That evening breakfast was cooked for the following morning, to save time in getting off. Moore and Burdsall talked over the plans for the climb in every detail. The items to be taken to the summit were placed in two rucksacks. These included emergency rations, a flashlight, cameras and film, a compass, and American and Chinese flags. Preparations complete, we all set our mental alarm clocks for 3.30 A.M.

The wind continued with unabated force throughout the night, hammering the tent unmercifully despite the shelter afforded by the ice wall behind it. I, for one, got little sleep, dozing fitfully with nightmarish dreams in which I climbed desperately for the top, within a few feet of it, only to be dragged back by some huge magnetic force each time.

Suddenly I heard Moore's voice off in the distance. I awoke to see him strike a match to look at his watch. It read only 11.45 "Glacier Standard Time," as we called it. Our watches had now been set for months by guess alone.

I lay awake for some time, wondering what the morrow would bring forth, scarcely daring to hope that it would be crowned by success, and then dozed back to sleep.

At 3.40 on the morning of October 28th, Camp IV was astir. Moore looked out through the door and proclaimed the stars were shining brightly and that there were no clouds visible. The wind still blew out of the west, sending showers of fine powdered snow sifting into the tent. Our day had come!

I reheated the frozen blocks of oatmeal and brewed a pot of hot malted milk, while the two climbers busied themselves in dressing. Four o'clock in the morning was a deadly hour at which to do anything save sleep at 22,000 feet on a cold morning. The work of dressing was almost more than human patience would stand.

It was an hour before the men were ready and fed. Then they crawled out into the black night, and I could hear them grumbling as they tried to adjust frozen crampon bindings in the dark with numb but mittened hands.

It was just five o'clock when I wished them good luck and a safe return. Moore took the lead and, with a perfunctory wave of his flashlight, was swallowed up in the frozen darkness, his only link to his companion a strand of flaxen rope paying out slowly through Burdsall's fingers. When fifty feet of it had slipped away, Burdsall drew his parka hood closer about his face and with a brief salute he too disappeared into the gloom.

I was alone!

It was a bitter pill being thus relegated to a passive rôle when my two companions were fighting their way up along that ridge, somewhere "out there." I had grave and not unfounded misgivings about ever seeing them again. One slip on the part of either man on those upper slopes and only a miracle could save them—places where one must walk with the nicety of a ballet dancer while fighting for breath and keeping one's balance against a lashing gale. It was not hard to conjure up pictures of disaster under such circumstances, though I had great faith in their ability and judgment.

Crawling back into my blankets, I extinguished the fluttering candle-lantern and lay half awake until seven o'clock. The weather was beautifully clear, and the thermometer somewhat above zero. At dawn the wind had lulled and the tent no longer shook with its impact.

In order to speed their getaway I had delayed my breakfast. The meal, though frugal, consumed a large part of the morning and the cheering roar of the primus did much to alleviate my feeling of loneliness. I turned my attention to a pocket edition of Kipling's ballads in an effort to forget the vague fears to which my mind was prey.

About noon I donned boots and parka for a short excursion outside to see if the men were visible up along the ridge. An intervening ice buttress shut off all view of the higher slopes, and my effort was wasted.

After working half-heartedly to clear away the drift about the tent walls, I went inside to await the party's return. I felt ill-at-ease, and a vague foreboding seized me.

Chapter XIII

THE CITADEL FALLS

A S TO what actually befell Moore and Burdsall on that fateful 28th of October, I will quote the following from an account by Terris Moore:

As we left the tent and Emmons, there was yet no suggestion of dawn. The stars burned from a black sky down to the eastern horizon. The lightness of the snow, however, faintly revealed our frosty crampons biting into the hard-packed nevé. I led the way with a tiny flashlight, occasionally coming upon one of our old tracks in its pencil of light. The snow rose steeply, and Dick crawled along slowly at the end of the fifty-foot line, at times feeling for the steps with his heavily mittened hands. At intervals I drew from a fold in my parka one of a small bundle of willow sticks and drove it upright in the snow to mark the trail.

Traveling in this fashion, we had risen some two hundred feet when, topping a sharp rise we found the first light of dawn illuminating the upper slopes. Here we rested in glad anticipation of the sun's warmth.

Not a cloud could be seen in the entire sky of our upper world. A deep purple line marked the rim of the horizon one hundred and fifty miles away in Tibet. Jupiter still glowed brightly above and to the east of the summit. The wind swept us powerfully in isolated gusts. It was getting lighter and the flashlight was no longer necessary. As I adjusted my goggles, my leather face mask, temporarily pushed up over my forehead, was seized by the wind and whisked away across the smooth slopes below and disappeared. Its loss was a serious matter, but there was no returning for another. We pushed on.

The sun began to rise, though we still climbed in the shadow of the peak, its great purple outline lying at our feet across the brown hills of Tibet. It receded with visible rapidity as the sun lifted higher above the horizon. Gazing down at the vast territory still blanketed by the mountain's shadow made me at this moment peculiarly aware of our great height.

We continued on slowly, rising at an average rate of three hundred feet an hour. The brilliant edge of the sun pushed above the shoulder as we approached the highest point reached by Emmons and me ten days before.

Here the smooth rounded contours of the ridge were broken by a series of frost-smothered rocks. Burdsall and I climbed upward through them cautiously, moving with one man continually belayed, the ax driven well into snow-filled cracks and the rope paid out from a turn about its head. The angle of the ridge increased very considerably, and every care was used to prevent a slip. Our crampons held beautifully in the firm crust, and we rejoiced that it was not necessary to waste precious time and energy in cutting steps.

Having surmounted this first band of rocks by a small

snow couloir, we found ourselves at the foot of another open slope. Above this, however, we were disconcerted to see that the ridge narrowed sharply and was topped by a number of unpleasant-looking surface features. What lay beyond was hidden behind this maze of snow blocks and cornices.

A slight mistake now in our choice of route might easily spell defeat, for while it would soon become evident upon advancing higher, it might cause a delay in retracing our steps—a delay so disastrous that there would not be time to reach the summit and yet leave a safe margin for the descent.

I therefore had to rely solely upon my memory as to the tentative route traced through these intricacies with the field-glasses from below on our reconnaissance, when we had obtained a composite though distorted view of the terrain.

We advanced upward at a slow, steady pace calculated to produce a minimum of fatigue. Our altitude was by now nearly 24,000 feet, and all the other peaks in the range had sunk into insignificance below the line of the horizon. I was surprised to find myself not much more affected by breathlessness and lassitude than on the two days of carrying loads to 22,000 feet. Probably the greater altitude was compensated for by the day of acclimatization at Camp IV and by the absence of packs. Burdsall, too, seemed better than before and climbed splendidly.

The sun was just leaving the meridian as we encountered the first of the broken ice. We wound our way up through the tangle of towering pinnacles and top-heavy blocks of ice. Although able to see ahead but a short distance, we felt the top was not far off. We spurred ourselves on to greater effort, though our pace was scarcely more than a slow crawl. A few steps and we would pause to lean panting with bent heads over our ice-axes. Looking back and down between my feet along the length of the rope, it appeared impossible that I had taken such a very long time to climb those few steps from where Burdsall stood.

We found, to our dismay, that what we had taken for the summit was in reality just another bump on the ridge. On reaching it I traversed to the right out on to the huge western face, while Burdsall held me carefully belayed. The view thus afforded showed me what was unmistakably the summit some three hundred feet above; obviously there was nothing to be gained by continuing in this direction. I retraced my steps and we changed our course more to the left.

At last, cutting steps up over a low wall, I saw that our present position was connected with the summit by a very narrow though unbroken crest. Though it appeared but a short distance above, it was fully an hour before we stood at 2.40 P.M. on the highest point after nine and a half hours of steady climbing.

There were three small summit platforms grouped close together. These we ascended in turn and sank down thankfully in the snow on the third. Here we had some protection from the wind, which apparently came from below, most of its force shooting well above our heads.

This was the first time we had really had an opportunity to view our surroundings at leisure, so engrossed had we been in the struggle to reach this point.

The horizon surrounded us in one unbroken ring.[62] No mountain massifs nor even clouds relieved the vast expanse of blue-black sky. At such great height the visible horizon is seen at some considerable distance below the true horizon. Its depression was very evident and I fancied I could actually see the curvature of the earth. The panorama of tremendous snow peaks, which had so dominated the sky at our 19,800-foot camp, had now dwindled to a series of mere white patches against the brown plain.

Rested, we rose and warily approached the eastern edge of the summit, fearing cornices. At our feet, nearly three miles below, the great sea of clouds lapped at the bases of the peaks. As the eye traveled eastward it moved away across the endless plains of China to the distant line where earth and sky met. Here and there rugged black islands of rock protruded through the mists in bold relief.

North and south the entire range lay at our feet. To the west stretched the vast undulating plateau of Tibet, broken here and there by isolated snow ranges, mysterious and remote.

We spoke of Emmons lying in his blankets below, and heartily wished him with us to share in this moment of victory.

Despite the intense cold, the sun exerted a real force in this thin air, which could scarcely, however, be described as heat. We tried to converse above the rushing of the wind, but the thin atmosphere only weakly conveyed our shouts to muffled ears. Cameras were got into action to perpetuate these fleeting moments. I removed two of the three layers of my mittens to operate mine, but I saw, to my consternation, that Dick had bared his hands completely to adjust some small mechanism. We exposed some twenty negatives, including a complete panorama of the distant horizon and the serrated topography beneath it.

Flag-waving was certainly not one of the purposes of our expedition, yet, since this was the highest point of land (24,900 feet) which Americans had ever reached, we flew the American flag for a few brief seconds from my inverted ice-ax while Dick photographed it.[63] The same courtesy was shown the Chinese emblem because of the many kindnesses extended to us by that country whose guests we were.

The sun was sinking well into the west before we abandoned the summit. We found, to our dismay, that these simple operations had consumed over an hour, and we began the descent immediately.

As we crept down along the narrow crest just below the top, the wind mounted to truly alarming proportions, certainly the worst in any of my experience. The loss of my face mask earlier in the day had painful results, for I now found it almost impossible to face unprotected the devastating blast that swept up along the ridge.

It was necessary to negotiate these ticklish bits with face averted, clinging desperately to maintain my balance. The parka hood beat about my ears with a noise not unlike gunfire, and the air was charged with a sand-blast of driven snow.

As we gradually attained a lower altitude, however, the wind abated somewhat and we could proceed with some semblance of comfort and assurance. Once clear of the upper difficulties of the ridge, our descent, though still requiring extreme care, was more rapid.

———

The sun was well down on the western horizon and my watch read six o'clock. Still no sign of the returning climbers, and my apprehension for their safety increased with each fleeting minute of the time for their safe return.

Then above the clamor of the wind I heard a faint shout. Hastily I undid the door, just in time to see Burdsall come stumbling down the slope, closely followed by Moore.

Both men presented a weird appearance, their beards and eyebrows a mass of ice and their clothes sheathed in a white rime of frost. They sank exhausted in the snow, unable for the moment to rise or remove the rope. Moore looked the more done in of the pair, but his recovery was more rapid than Burdsall's.

Unable to restrain myself longer, I posed the momentous question, "Well, what luck?" Moore smiled wearily and said simply, "We made it." Made it! The thrill was electric! What an eloquent story those three words told. We had traveled over halfway around the globe, spent nearly a year in attaining our present position, and now at last the Konka had fallen!

My own feelings were somewhat confused. Great

elation that we had at last triumphed over the Konka, a tremendous feeling of relief that the men were safely back, the job finished, and that we could now go down and leave these inhospitable surroundings, and a gnawing disappointment that I had been *hors de combat* for so glorious an exploit.

Burdsall complained of a numbness in some of his fingers and on inspection found that seven of the tips were suspiciously white. After massaging his hands, the color returned a little, but on the following morning the tips began to turn black and swell. It was frostbite acquired when his mittens had been removed to take photographs on the summit, where only a few seconds of exposure to the air had been sufficient to do the harm.

One might say that logically the story should end here, our goal having been won. Did this story deal with fiction, not fact, such a happy ending might be all in good order. Unhappily, that was not the case.

For one of our number, at least, the sequel to this tale of high adventure was fraught with events which to him, anyway, presented no anticlimax whatsoever. The Konka had gone down in defeat, but it still had power to strike back—and did.

Chapter XIV

WHAT PRICE VICTORY

THE strain, physical and mental, to which we had all been subjected began to manifest itself in an all-consuming desire to get down and away from the mountain as fast as ever we could, now that the campaign was over. This desire was augmented by the depleted condition of the stores in our high camps. At Camp IV there remained but two or three days' food. Should a severe winter storm beset us, our predicament might be serious in the extreme. We therefore determined to quit Camp IV and strike out for the base the very day following the climb.

A late start was made in demolishing Camp IV. All items were jettisoned which could not be carried down in one trip. Those removed included only things of some intrinsic value or items which would be necessary on the trek back across the Tibetan uplands to Tatsienlu.

I was packing a rucksack with some extra clothes and personal effects in the door of the tent. I looked away for a moment, and when my attention again returned to my packing I was just in time to see the bag go rolling down the slope and bound joyfully over the edge of the great western face, where it must have dropped nearly four thousand feet to the glacier. I did notice that in its gyrations, however, the chess-board, which was in an outside pocket, dropped out and was saved for another day. Camp IV's front steps were assuredly steep ones![60]

We started down about noon, and, descending slowly, took two hours to reach the Gap, and from there another to the cache at 20,700 feet.

Here the party unroped in order that each man might choose his own pace to Camp II.

Moore went ahead, accompanied by Burdsall, to dig out Camp II and salvage some film and a camera that had been left there. I stopped to pack up several things at the cache.

It was here that I first began to feel sharp jabbing pains in my right foot, though at the time I thought little about them. On carrying my load a few yards farther, the pain increased to such an extent that I sat down before long to have a look. It was so swollen that I had difficulty in removing my boot, and further inspection revealed that the entire foot was nearly double its size and had turned a purplish black nearly to the instep—a rather unpleasant sight with which to be suddenly confronted. Then it was that I realized with a shock that both my feet must have been numb for several days at least without my having realized the fact.*

The left foot was still without sensation, and I did not have to look at it to know its condition. In desperation I replaced my socks and boot. The others were far ahead along the spur and could not hear my shouts. I was alone at 21,000 feet with a pair of frozen feet.

* See Appendix C, page 278.

My pack, fortunately, contained a sleeping-bag which might possibly save my life should I be forced to bivouac, so I dared not leave the load behind. With each passing minute the pain in my foot increased until to place my weight on it became almost unbearable torture.

Luckily for me the left foot remained numb and I knew that my salvation lay in keeping it so until I could get off the mountain or at least join the other men. Using my ax as a cane, I managed to hobble along, and after two hours reached Camp II just behind Burdsall.

I began to experience that feeling of resignation which has led more than one man to a death in the snow. But Camp II was completely buried and I *had* to go on. Moore had been forced to cut the peak from the tent and fish out the contents from its dark interior with an ice-ax!

Realizing that in my unstable condition I could never negotiate the steep slopes below the spur with a pack, I threw it down on the shelf, where it undoubtedly remains to this day. We roped and climbed over the brink of the slope. Moore anchored, being the only fit member of the party, for Burdsall's fingers were giving him trouble. He was also decidedly unwell and our progress was reduced to a snail's pace.

I soon saw that if my other foot thawed out up here, I would place not only myself, but the rest of the party, in a very grave position. Knowing that, unencumbered as I was, I could make better time alone than if I stayed on the rope, I removed it and struck out by myself in a last desperate effort to reach the base camp, though both Moore and Burdsall were reluctant to let me do so. In any event, they would be following in case I got into difficulty.

Much fresh snow had fallen and it was a delicate job maneuvering through the hidden crevasses I recalled from our previous trips. Once free of these, I glissaded slopes which anyone in his right mind might have shunned for their steepness.

Luck favored me and I made famous time to Camp I, experiencing difficulty in only one or two places. I arrived here just as a golden sunset flamed across Tibet, and scrawled a large "O.K.—Art" in the snow beside the tent, which they later found.

Then began the descent into the gully, and there my troubles began in earnest. While I was on the snow its softness acted as a cushion for the feet. The hard rock, however, gave me the full benefit of my painful condition. My left foot, moreover, had also begun to thaw out, and I found it well-nigh impossible to stand up. Reaching the Crampon Place at the snow line, I discarded my crampons for the last time with thankful sigh, and then began to hitch myself slowly down the gully in a sitting position.

During our absence high up, the sun had got in its work here at 18,000 feet. Many rocks had melted free of the snow and were hanging precariously balanced. Several came crashing down the gully, narrowly missing me in the dusk.

I had got fairly beneath the menacing wall of ice which had always made this route so hazardous, when the tottering mass cracked like a pistol-shot. Six times I could hear the ice being split asunder from within. By the time the last report had died away I was scrambling well up the opposite wall of the gully, the pain of my frozen feet forgotten in the presence of this new peril.

I sat for perhaps fifteen minutes perched on a ledge, waiting to see the huge bulk of ice crash down across the track below.

Nothing happened. The silence was unbroken save by the trickle of running water somewhere beneath the ice and the tinkle of an icicle as it fell and broke in some rift in the glacier wall.

Darkness was upon me and I had no time to lose, so screwing up my courage, I scrambled on down, feeling the glacier's icy breath upon me and glancing up fearfully at the one-hundred-foot front of ice as it glinted evilly in the evening light.

The short pitch of steep rock at the lower end of the gully gave me considerable trouble, but I managed it somehow, feeling for hand and footholds in the darkness.

At last, after what seemed an eternity, but in reality could not have been more than fifteen minutes, I rounded the corner where the Dump lay protected by the abrupt cliffs of the Pyramid.

I contemplated spending the night here, and I would have been wise had I done so. To be sure there was nothing here save a leaking tin of gasoline and several pairs of crampons, but it was a sheltered nook and I would have been assured of seeing Moore and Burdsall, for they must of necessity pass this point.

The idea of trying to reach the base camp still predominated, though by now all I could do was to stumble from boulder to boulder, using my hands for support as much as I could. I blundered on in the semi-darkness over the loose rocks of the moraine which punished my feet cruelly. It took me an hour to descend another four hundred feet to the lower portion of the glacier. By now only the light of the stars faintly illumined the confused desolation of rocks over which the path led. The pain in my feet was fast becoming unendurable and the base camp was still far away.

Seeing the folly of trying to proceed farther, when I reached the glacier floor at 17,000 feet I made for a point several hundred yards away, out towards the center of the ice where I could hear running water. It was desirable to have water should I be marooned here for some time.

Half walking, half crawling, I at last reached a small trickle on the surface of the ice, though it was fast freezing up with the evening chill.

Not having eaten since morning, I consumed several of my few remaining malted-milk tablets—the only sustenance I would have until I should be rescued, which might be a day or two. I had therefore religiously to conserve my supply.

A sudden realization came upon me that in leaving the trail I had placed myself in an even more serious position. After taking a prolonged drink of water, my last for a good many hours, I tried to retrace my steps to a point where the trail skirted close beneath a shoulder of the Pyramid.

To my dismay, my feet and legs refused to function. It was rather a dismal feeling to know that I was helpless here alone at 17,000 feet on a remote Tibetan peak, a week's travel across the mountains to the first outpost of civilization, over two weeks from the nearest doctor, and probably two thousand miles through war-torn China to the nearest railhead.

But I think I can say, without boasting that I rather enjoyed the novelty and sheer drama of the situation. At any rate, I was stimulated by it to the point of yodeling at the black empty cliffs above. Perhaps the triumph of yesterday had something to do with this exuberance now that the stress of the recent struggle was over. Certainly the relief brought by being no longer on those deadly white snowfields, but on terra firma again, had a decided influence. It may have been that I was beginning to crack under the strain of the last few weeks and hours, but if so, at least I felt in a joyful mood about it.

On one good hand and my knees I crawled back over the moraine, hitching myself up one side of mound after mound of broken boulders and slithering down the other. After what seemed an interminable period I again reached the trail, where I stretched out on a rock, worn out. My knees were so cut and bruised that this form of locomotion was no longer possible. I had come to the end of my tether. As to whether I were rescued I was too exhausted for the moment to care. The Konka had been climbed, so what else mattered!

Chapter XV

BASE CAMP REGAINED

IT WAS too cold to sleep and far too uncomfortable. The feet mercifully regained some of their former numbness, and I had not the strength of will to try to revive them. I sat through the long weary hours, occasionally shifting my position on the boulder, which soon became uncommonly hard, and stared up at the stars. The Pleiades were setting behind the dark bulk of a mountain ridge, and moved with painful slowness. The night dragged on its interminable length.

A low dank cloud came sweeping up from the valley below, and whatever its clammy fringes touched became coated with frost. Nor was I spared. Before long my clothes were sheathed with frost crystals. Fortunate it was that my stanch high-altitude clothes were warm enough to keep me from freezing.

I wondered how Moore and Burdsall had fared and whether they had reached Camp I. If not, would they descend and find me on the morrow? I was not at all sure I wanted to face another two days and a night of exposure without food, water, or shelter.

I was awakened from such reveries by the reverberating roar of an avalanche. I turned just in time to see a large section of the glacier front under which I had passed but a few hours before, topple and cascade down over the track below like a mammoth waterfall. Huge blocks of ice were hurled into the air as they bounded down the slopes to land far out on the glacier below. Our route beneath was white with shattered ice in the dim starlight.

Though I was half a mile away and out of danger, the ground shook with the concussion and several stones came tumbling down from the shoulder not far from me. It was certainly one of the largest falls of ice I had ever seen, and its sinister possibilities made me shiver. At least Burdsall and Moore would have little to fear from it within the next day or so. Its bolt was spent.

The night wore on. Though it was not excessively cold, I was thoroughly chilled. Centuries passed in marshaled array. There was no sleep. Oh, if the dawn would only come!

When hope had been given up of ever seeing the sun again, an almost imperceptible lightening of the highest snowfields heralded the dawn. No Mayan sun-worshiper ever greeted the sun with more ecstasy!

By nine o'clock the sunlight found and bathed the slopes below me and soon its warmth crept to where I lay. Tying a white handkerchief to the shaft of my ice-ax as a flag, I propped it up and then fell asleep.

When I awoke several hours later I was so warm that I peeled off two layers of sweaters. I tried a halloo, but it brought only answering echoes. I was reasonably sure, however, that the men had not passed me on their way down.

I ate three more of my malted-milk tablets to ease

a ravenous hunger. There were six left. A strong thirst assailed me, engendered by the hot sun. About every fifteen minutes I gave a shout, hoping that Moore and Burdsall were on their way down. Three short blasts on a police whistle was our signal for help, but even these brought no response.

Two hours passed. The sun began to sink towards the mountain across the valley. My apprehension about the two climbers grew as the day wore on. The base of the gully was visible from where I lay, but it revealed no signs of the men. Perhaps they had passed me when I slept. At any rate, on not finding me at the base camp, I knew they would instigate a search.

Then in response to one of my shouts came an answer—but from *below*. In a few moments a shaggy Tibetan head appeared above a mound of moraine, closely followed by a second. Here were Chingwa and Chelay.[48] They ran forward on seeing me, and their faces broke into delighted smiles as they greeted "Ngan Hsien Sheng," as they called me.

I inquired as to the whereabouts of Young, and they pointed towards the lamasery. Then I remembered that this was the tenth day after our parting, the day on which we had hoped to return. The two porters had been sent ahead to look for signs of us. Young himself had remained at the Gompa to engage an aggregation of men to dismantle the base camp. Neither Burdsall nor Moore had yet made an appearance.

These two stalwart porters took turns carrying me on their backs down over the precipitous slopes of loose rocks and underlying ice with never a false step.

On some of the steeper bits I sat down and, grasping my legs, they towed me along, to the decided detriment of my trousers.

At 5 P.M. we reached the base camp. Never was there a more welcome sight than the cheery fire of juniper in front of the tent.

Moore came in with a load twenty minutes later, having spent the night at Camp I, and reported that Burdsall was following at a slower pace. They had been rather anxious as to my fate, especially when they came upon the débris-littered slopes below the ice wall, and he expressed relief at finding me safely in the valley.

I soaked my feet in ice water.* They appeared in such poor condition that both Moore and I felt it imperative that they should have medical attention without delay before any serious complications should set in. Accordingly, Moore at once set out for the lamasery to seek Young and engage horses and a retinue for the trip to Tatsienlu. He was benighted halfway down and spent a supperless night beneath a boulder, arriving at the lamasery at an early hour on the following morning.

Burdsall came in at dusk with his load, very tired. His fingers, though not seriously frozen, had developed painful blisters. But the last of the expedition was safely off the mountain, so no one complained.

It snowed six inches that night. The wood became wet and our fire was decidedly sickly the next morning. We attempted to construct a stretcher from a folding camp cot, but its folding propensities were too pro-

* See Appendix C, page 280.

nounced and the idea had to be abandoned. By lashing two cross-bars on to a pack-board, a system was evolved that proved more successful. I sat on the lower bar, straddling the pack-board, and hung my arms over the upper one, thus maintaining balance.

Chingwa and Chelay once more shared the work of carrying my 170 pounds, only this time under less difficult circumstances.

I bade farewell to Burdsall, who stayed behind to assist in demolishing the base camp. For ten hours the two Tibetans took turn and turn about at carrying me down over as rough a five miles of country as one could find; so rugged was the trail that no horse or yak could ever have made the trip.

When it came time to ford the stream, my two hardy men hesitated. And well they might, for in the late afternoon the icy water was waist deep and of terrifying swiftness as it boiled along the boulder-strewn bed. I climbed as high on my improvised sedan chair as I could without overbalancing, in an attempt to keep my feet dry.

The stocky Chelay was carrying me at the time and he looked like a small terrier beneath my relatively huge bulk. Chingwa took his hand to steady him and together they stepped into the milky water. At times we balanced on the edge of one submerged boulder for an interminable period before stepping to the next. Disaster seemed impending. At last the men climbed safely out on the farther bank, dripping and shivering, but smiling as ever.

It was not until dark that they staggered up the steep

trail to the door of the lamasery, where I was enthusiastically welcomed by Young and Moore.

Horses had been engaged for the morrow, and it was planned that Moore and I should make the trip out to Tatsienlu with all possible speed, accompanied by Gaomo, leaving Young and Burdsall with the porters to bring the remaining gear down to the lamasery.

Young had shot a large grizzly of a little known species while we were making the ascent. In addition to the bear, he had bagged several pheasants, and that evening we dined royally on roast pheasant and bear's paws. The latter are reputed to have brought two hundred dollars a plate in New York restaurants! To cap the climax, home mail had just come in by courier. Frozen feet, aches and pains, hardship and high altitudes, were nearly, if not quite, forgotten as we sat around the fire in the smoke-filled lamasery kitchen and swapped tales with Young of the events of the past ten days.

The lamas seemed incredulous when we told them we had scaled their Holy Mountain to its summit. Still more incredulous were they when, asking if we had brought back the lump of gold, we replied that it had been left there, being too heavy. The story of our porters, however, that they had seen us descending one of the high ridges lent our tale considerable prestige. At any rate, our hosts looked upon me and my misfortunes as a horrid example of what befalls a man who is indiscreet enough to tamper with the awful power of Dorjelutru. Perhaps they were right, but despite my offense, they felt I had been punished severely enough and did everything they could to make me comfortable.

Both Chingwa and Chelay were rewarded with ten rupees apiece for their fine work, a sum which to them constituted a small fortune. Such good friends had we become that they asked me to take them with me to America, which they supposed to be a mere two weeks' travel down the river!

Chapter XVI

TO TATSIENLU

WE PARTED, Young to assist Burdsall and then make a three weeks' trek south into Lolo country to continue the work of collecting, while Moore and I, with Gaomo and another Tibetan, rode for the Tsemei La and Tatsienlu. There was no time for us to await the removal of the gear from the base camp. We had with us only the clothes we wore and two light sleeping-bags. We hoped by fast riding to spend only three nights on the road, depending on Tibetan hospitality for food and shelter.

A morning's ride brought us to Tsemei village, where we enjoyed the hospitality of the head man for lunch. I crawled on hands and knees up his front steps and across the room to his fireplace, much to the evident amusement of the younger generation.

From Tsemei we must climb steeply 3,600 feet to the top of the pass and descend 2,500 more into the Yulong Valley by nightfall. It was now nearly two o'clock, and the pass usually required a full day to cross. The Tibetans were reluctant to attempt it until we managed to convey to them the urgency of the situation. Then with their ever-present smile and deprecating shrug they acquiesced.

All afternoon we rode up into the pass. The other

men walked, and my poor pony made heavy weather of carrying my weight up over the steep rough trail. I clung to the saddle with my good hand and tried unsuccessfully to keep my feet clear of his short legs and the bank. He fell continually behind, and one of the Tibetans was forced to take the halter rope and literally tow him along.

An hour before sunset we breasted the pass. I turned in my saddle and gazed for the last time at Minya Konka, rising in supreme majesty above the clouds—again a Being of indescribable beauty and mystery, aflame in the golden light of a dying day. I felt a swelling in my throat and a tug at my heart as I waved her farewell and dipped over the divide.

Darkness caught us about halfway down into the valley, but we rode on for an hour and a half through low scrub bushes which tore at my sensitive feet. Gaomo thought he knew where there was a yak-herder's encampment in which we could spend the night. The open veldt where the camp supposedly lay revealed only empty trodden grass in the wan light of the moon.

We camped close beside a stream. The Tibetans for some reason were too apathetic to build a fire or even eat. Moore did both, after lifting me from my pony, cooking an excellent supper, at which our spirits revived somewhat. The night was cold but not too uncomfortable. My feet, however, allowed of little sleep.

A five-mile ride the next morning brought us to the first settlement, the King of Chiala's palace, a low unimposing aggregation of stone buildings. The king evidently had had very simple tastes in palaces, for this one was little different in construction or extent from any other average Tibetan house. Here our ullah stage ended and no other animals were available that day, no matter how we threatened, bribed, or pleaded. They had all been driven far down the valley to graze for the winter to escape the snow.

It was November 2nd, just a month since we had started the campaign against the Konka. I spent the day lying on a camp cot beside the fire in the kitchen of the "palace." Moore whiled away the time photographing the natives and bargaining for their silver-and-turquoise jewelry.

Only three horses turned up the next morning. Gaomo finally persuaded the local populace to "bai" our kit on foot, allowing us to ride the horses.

It was usually three days' travel from here to Tatsienlu across the Djezi La—forty-two miles of rough mountain trails. We hoped by forced marching to make it in two. Those carrying loads on foot could not hope to keep pace with us, so we rode on ahead at a faster rate, hoping that they might catch up to us after nightfall.

All day long we rode up the Yulong Valley into the pass. A trot or canter proved decidedly aggravating to me, as I could put no weight in the stirrups. Still, if we were to make our stages it had to be done. A short rest for lunch, for which the sole item of food was a dry crumbly piece of ancient yak cheese, then on again.

Towards mid-afternoon we rode into the face of a driving blizzard that swept down out of the pass. The cold wind was numbing and the trail was all but obscured by the flying snow.

We had hoped to find lodging with a nomad whose encampment had been in the upper valley during the summer. To our consternation we found that he too had moved to the lower levels for the winter.

By nightfall we were still riding on into the teeth of the storm. The blizzard increased so much that danger existed of our becoming separated. Gaomo, fortunately, knew the terrain well, as this was his native heath, and not once did he lose the track.

We were now at an elevation of 15,000 feet, far above timber line. Our baggage was miles behind and we had no hope of seeing it that night. We had no blankets nor any food save two uncooked cornmeal cakes and a freshly plucked chicken.

A train was formed with the halter ropes of our mounts to keep from getting separated in the darkness, and, though each man was only ten feet away from the next, he was nearly invisible through the blackness.

At last through the murk we all but stumbled over a small Tibetan encampment beside the trail. Our hopes rose that here they would at least have a tent we could share.

But our fond hopes of shelter were speedily dashed. We found that they were traders who had just crossed the Djezi La in deep snow with a caravan of bales of hides. They had no tent, but simply built a wall of the bales as a wind-break and lay down behind it.

We threw ourselves from our horses and lay on a

rubber poncho while Gaomo tethered the horses. The traders, five men and a woman, attempted to make a fire with some furze bushes and dry grass. They got it started with some trouble and its flickering flames brought joy to our hearts. The raw chicken was got out and we vainly tried to roast it in the flames, while the Tibetans heated their buttered tea. After five minutes the fire died out completely, never to be resurrected. The chicken was scarcely singed on the outside.

Our hosts, when the repast was at an end, proceeded to retire. This evolution was, under the circumstances, most interesting to watch. A yak's hair saddle blanket was placed on the snow. On this the individual knelt on hands and knees with his head bowed in the attitude of a Mohammedan devotee praying. He then drew a similar blanket over his entire person completely touching the ground all the way around. Provided he did not succumb to the aroma imparted to the blankets by several generations of yaks, his breath kept him warm beneath the upper blanket and thus he slept through the night.

The next morning there would not be a person in sight, only a number of rounded mounds of snow scattered over the plain. One after another they would miraculously explode, revealing a tousled Tibetan. The whole procedure was carried off in a most casual way, as though such a manner of living were quite in order, which no doubt was the case. One never ceases to wonder at the hardihood of these Tibetan people, who eke out a precarious living under such strenuous circumstances.

The blizzard continued unabated. After the failure of the fire, Moore and I lay huddled together on the poncho for warmth. He generously insisted on my wrapping my feet in the only available saddle-blanket in an attempt to keep frost-bite from recurring. Thus we prepared to spend one of the most dismal nights one could well imagine. There was no sleep for either of us.

From time to time we would sit up and shake the snow from our clothes, and then lie back, shivering. Several hours passed. I began to feel a lethargy creeping over me.

Suddenly we strained our ears. Was that a faint shout borne on the wind? Our porters? Impossible. It had been dark now four or five hours. Our ears had played us false. Hope dies hard, however, and we raised a shout in unison, as lusty a one as our unhappy condition would permit. There was no answer.

The snow lay deeper and deeper upon us. Another hour passed like an eternity. I was seized with a bad chill and shook from head to foot. Again we imagined we heard a cry, much nearer now. There could be no mistake about it this time. Our hearts leaped within us, scarcely crediting our ears. Again we raised a shout.

It was answered!

Moore scrambled to his feet and, taking a flashlight from his saddle-bag, strode off down the valley. The light dimmed and faded out in the gloom. Five minutes passed. Ten. Then through the veil of flying snow dim figures stumbled into view. Two men and two women. The loads had arrived. Brave, strong-hearted people, how we loved them at that moment!

With uncanny skill they had fought their way on and on through a black, snow-filled night, hours on end, over trackless wastes of drift. Unerringly they had found us after nearly fourteen hours on the trail. It was all in the day's work to them.

Surely there is no finer race on earth than these simple nomad folk. Their pay a paltry half-rupee a day; their faithfulness and devotion beyond all price. It may be that to them we owed our lives.

Gray clouds enshrouded us the next morning, though it had stopped snowing. Over a foot had fallen during the night. I was lifted on to my pony and we rode away breakfastless at the first light of dawn, leaving our baggage to follow when it might. Tatsienlu lay twenty-five miles ahead across the pass.

The pass high up was even deeper in snow, and the ponies' legs were so short that our feet dragged in it on either side.

As we reached the top (15,685 feet) and began to descend, a cold fog blew up from the valley, freezing on our faces and clothes in a white crust. For pure unmitigated discomfort I don't think this moment had its equal on the whole expedition.

At last we got below the fog belt and things went better. Then the trail crossed a snow-covered boulder-field. My pony stumbled frequently, going down twice. Each time I was able to clear my feet, and each time he was able to rise without my dismounting, though I feared once that he had broken a leg. He was not in the least trail broken and continually wandered from the track, wedging himself between boulders, making no allowance for his rider. I never wished anything as much harm as I did that incorrigible animal.

By noon, on reaching timber line the snow vanished. I began to feel decidedly faint and once or twice caught myself slipping from the saddle. We had eaten scarcely any food for thirty-six hours and I had had little or no sleep for six nights, having been on the road four days.

Late in the afternoon we reached Yulongkong, the first little settlement on the Chinese side of the mountains. Here we stopped at a farmhouse to cook and eat part of our chicken. The food worked wonders and we felt considerably refreshed.

Moore's horse was fast giving out and fell much behind. We had yet six miles to ride to reach Tatsienlu. At length, when Moore was abreast of a small hovel beside the trail where a man was selling peanuts, his horse stumbled up and leaned against the door in a most abject pose. He refused to move farther.

It was growing dark. I told Gaomo to ride back to Moore's assistance while I rode on, being so nearly done in that I was afraid of giving out, as the poor horse had done, if I were delayed.

It had been over three months since we had left Tatsienlu. As I rode into the narrow winding streets I became confused. The sensation of being lost in an oriental town at night on horseback in narrow, crowded streets without light, was novel, to put it mildly, especially so as I knew I could not dismount but must ride on until I found the mission. I only hoped friend horse would not follow the bad example set by Moore's, for then my predicament would have been grave, if not so ludicrous.

Finally I rode over a covered bridge, scattering pedestrians to right and left, and ducked beneath a low arch into a street that I recognized. There at last was the gate of the mission. Riding up to it determined to make my return with a flourish, I bellowed, "Kai men O!" "Open the gate!" in as commanding a voice as I could. The gates swung in and I rode through them, past the astounded gateman and up across the compound to the very steps of the house.

Here I slid from the pony and crawled up the steps. My plans for a triumphal entry were, at this point, utterly ruined, for I was caught in this informal pose by one of the Cunninghams' Tibetan maids. Conquering heroes do not, as a rule, crawl on all fours to their seats of honor!

The woman uttered a shriek and dashed into the house in terror, where she told the missionaries that a devil was crawling up the front steps.

When I saw the rate at which she disappeared, I knew there was no necessity of knocking. Nor was I mistaken. I had barely time to recover my composure and assume a more dignified pose when Dr. and Mrs. Cunningham, several other foreign missionaries, and numerous Tibetan retainers came rushing out to investigate this devil situation.

I was speedily carried upstairs in triumph and put

to bed amid a storm of questions, just as Moore arrived, followed by Gaomo. Thus after three months
and a half "out in the blue," we had again reached
the fringe of civilization.

How wonderfully welcome it was!

Chapter XVII

ROADS AND RIVERS

DURING our absence in Tibet, a fierce civil war
had broken out in Szechuan Province between
two rival war lords, Liu Wen Whei and his nephew,
Liu Hsiang. Field-guns, airplanes, and all the modern
implements of war, save gas, were used. One hundred
and fifty thousand troops were involved and the province was in a turmoil.

The roads to the "outside" were all blocked and
we were virtually cut off from the coast. Even the road
from Tatsienlu to Yachow was filled with troops going
into the war areas.

To further complicate matters, the military element
was "lau fu-ing" or impressing all available transportation, both men and animals. Rumor had it that there
were a hundred carrying-coolies locked up in a near-by
teashop under guard, awaiting troop movements. We
were effectively prevented from going farther for the
present.

My condition became worse. Gangrene set in badly
and increased materially the danger of infection. There
was no doctor in Tatsienlu, the nearest one being our
friend, Dr. Crook, in Yachow, under favorable conditions an eight days' march away.

It would be impossible for me to travel over this

road for we knew not how long. The only alternative was to send for help, for it was felt by the missionaries that my condition required immediate medical attention, and they were wisely reluctant to take the responsibility for my welfare upon themselves.

Fortunately there was a military telegraph line to Yachow. A wire was sent to Dr. Crook, asking him to come in to Tatsienlu. For two days there was no reply. We concluded that he must be away on a medical itinerary, and that I had best try to make the trip to the Yachow hospital without him. The prospect of such a journey was not very encouraging.

Then came an answer. True to the highest concepts of the unselfish service of these stalwart missionaries, Dr. Crook wired that he was taking to the road immediately.

If he could get through at all, we could not expect him for another seven or eight days. Meanwhile the Cunninghams waited on me hand and foot, doing everything humanly possible for my comfort.

The Sisters of a small French Jesuit mission in Tatsienlu came and ministered to me with their traditional tender sympathy and skill. They had but little knowledge of medicine, but they treated the feet expertly from their small store of medical experience. Though I could only converse with them in a patois of French interspersed with Chinese, no one ever felt more strongly than I the tremendous power for good to which these people were giving their lives.

Burdsall turned up four days after our arrival, bringing with him the main caravan. He was rather a pitiable sight, for his seven fingers were painfully blistered and swollen. He was still suffering somewhat from the effects of the campaign. Indeed, we were all a rather depressing aggregation with our various aches and pains, but the Cunninghams bore the inconvenience of our presence with true Christian fortitude.

November 5th, radio-operator Moore tuned our short-wave receiver to Manila. The landslide for Roosevelt resounded even to this far corner of the globe. The election returns came in "play by play" only a fraction of a second after they were announced at home.

We dared not use our portable transmitter, for fear of arousing distrust amongst the irresponsible military factions, and so had to content ourselves with sending dispatches by land wire.

A wire was sent to Shanghai about the ascent, and we optimistically hoped it would get through relatively ungarbled. After a week, somewhat to our surprise, confirmation came that it had arrived.

Late one evening, a weary dust-covered traveler knocked at the gate of the mission. It was Dr. Crook, two days ahead of schedule! He had marched an eight-day trek over the mountains in six days, having covered thirty-five miles uphill on the last day between dawn and late evening!

My relief at his arrival was inexpressible, and I think the others shared in it. His strong, capable hands and reassuring smile gave me a new lease on life and my troubles seemed to evaporate. That night I slept for almost the first time in a fortnight. It had been seventeen days since that fateful night on the Konka.

His examination of the feet revealed that their condition, while serious in the extreme, was not so bad as we had feared, and he felt that a good portion of them could be saved. He advised my immediate removal to the Yachow hospital.

Two days later we bade farewell to Tatsienlu and our delightful hosts, of whom we had become very fond. By one means and another a motley crew of twenty coolies was collected. I have never seen a more dejected lot, but they were all that remained in the wake of the troops.

I was carried in a litter high on the shoulders of two of the most woebegone individuals, a third alternating with them. In this way I traveled out over the same road by which Burdsall and I had first reached Tatsienlu.

Twelve to fourteen hours a day the men struggled up and down over rough, stony roads, through arid valleys and up over snowy passes. At times they skirted cliffs high above the river, where the litter swayed towards the yawning abyss below. Horrid thoughts assailed me as to what would happen should one of the coolies stumble.

It was again imperative that we make the stages between towns set for each day, for the coolies must be sheltered and fed. My men were so slow that only on one occasion did we get in before dark, and several times the opium-famished coolies did not reach the required town until nearly midnight.

One of these late arrivals was especially memorable. The men had been stumbling along in the dark for an hour, the lanterns being with the party ahead. The trail skirted a cliff and I could hear the roar and faintly see the white foam of the Tung River several hundred feet below. Twice the coolies stumbled in the dark and swayed alarmingly towards the edge. There was no wall, and each time I fancied my finish was at hand. At length we halted and I sent the spare man ahead to get a light, though when it was brought it did little more than blind the men.

At last towards midnight the lights of Lutingchiao came into view—"The Town of the Iron Chain Bridge." Here the Tung was spanned by such a bridge (see p. 41), whose flooring consisted of a narrow catwalk of loose and rotten planks. On the way to Tatsienlu, Burdsall had paced off the span at 112 yards.

The town lay on the far side and the bridge must be crossed that night. My coolies, weakened by a long hard day and the lack of their habitual evening smoke of opium, demurred. To be sure, this was the first time they showed lack of nerve, though there had been many a place ere now where they could have scarcely been blamed for faltering.

Finally they plucked up courage, and with the spare man carrying a dim, smoky lantern in front, we started over. The footing even in the daylight was treacherous enough, but at night the chance of stepping on a rotten board or where one was entirely missing was much too great for comfort.

We reached the middle of the river and the bridge began to sway badly. The men staggered crazily in the darkness and my litter swung violently from side to side with the gyrations of their shoulders. They began to shout hysterically to each other in a panic of fear.

I looked down at the boiling torrent below, determined to make a last desperate effort to save myself by grabbing at the low chain which served as a hand rail. Wedged between two heavy bamboo poles and laced into a sleeping-bag, my chances of survival would not have been worth much.

The men, despite their panic, had sense enough to halt, and slowly the bridge stopped swaying. Again they proceeded, and when the chains began to swing, stopped a second time. In this way, after what seemed a veritable eternity, we got safely across.

That night our bedding loads didn't reach us until we had spent several hours on a filthy inn "kang" trying to get a little much-needed sleep, having relegated their arrival *that* night to the realm of the impossible.

Each night was spent in some such inn within the walls of a town. Each night, after Dr. Crook had shooed away the legion of curious onlookers and numerous livestock, he dressed the feet, a procedure under these trying circumstances fraught with the ever-present danger of infection. The filth of these inns does not bear description.

Due to his extreme care, no infection developed, and after eight days of continuous travel we reached that pleasant haven of refuge, the American Baptist Mission in Yachow, on the 24th of November.

Here again every care was lavished upon me by these generous folk. The 25th was Thanksgiving, a day on which I felt doubly thankful. It was celebrated with a dinner in the true New England tradition, even down to the celery and cranberry sauce—within the shadow of those distant peaks, halfway around the world from where the Pilgrims had celebrated the first Thanksgiving Day.

Yachow was destined to be my home for seven months while my feet underwent renovation and my toes were removed. One could have gone much farther and fared far worse in the matter of cheerful and sincere friendship than with these fine men and women. I was more than fortunate in my choice of a place in which to recover. And recover I did, thanks to the excellence of Dr. Crook's surgery and the fine care I received from Miss Shurtleff and her staff of Chinese nurses.

One never fails to marvel how, under the crudest of conditions and the absence of many of what are considered essentials in modern medicine, these isolated medical missions accomplish the wonders of treatment and cure they do.

The hospital, though small, was well appointed when one considers that all supplies for it must be ordered from Shanghai at least a *year* ahead. I was the first white patient there for something like eight years.

Jack Young returned to Tatsienlu after a most successful hunting trip into the wild Lolo country, producing a formidable array of large game, described later. Finding that we had left for Yachow, he took a small caravan and made the trip out, joining us on December 3rd. Once again the Sikong Expedition was united— for the last time until nearly a year later, when we met once more on a New York steamship dock 12,000 miles

away, whence we had sailed on high adventure bent two
years before.

Our three objectives had been accomplished. The
mighty Konka had gone down in noble defeat—the
second highest mountain in the world whose summit
has been reached. We had much valuable survey data
and many photographs, and there were numerous specimens of big game, as well as a collection of birds, to
our credit.

Ours had been some of the finest adventures imagina-
ble. We had sweated and frozen, starved and feasted,
faced hardship and danger, together. We had learned
the value of teamwork. If friendship and faith in a fellow man were ever put to the test, it was here—and we
emerged from a wonderful adventure, friends for life.

And so we come to the end of our tale. Minya Konka
still reigns in majesty, alone and indescribably beautiful,
over that remote land. The glory of the slow-dying day
still bathes its snowy battlements with fiery gold. Still
the wind flaunts its banner streaming from an icy summit against a cold black sky. Borne on some vagrant
breeze to those lone lamas in the valley, still comes the
rumble and shudder of an avalanche cast down by
Dorjelutru in his wrath, to set them droning their "Om
Mani Padme Hums" in fear and awe.

But even to those lamas the dread God of Thunder
must seem less terrible and less fearsome, for have they
not with their own eyes seen men, fellow mortals, who
have dared his wrath and probed his mysteries, who
have scaled his sacred heights and looked down from
his high abode upon the earth beneath?

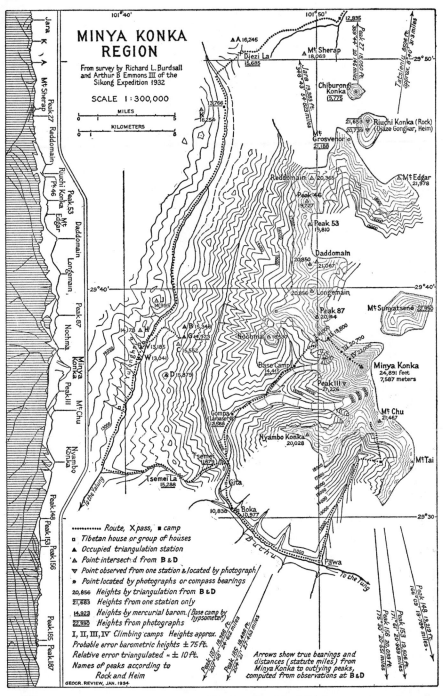

Map of Minya Konka. Above the snowline (heavier dotted line) contours are shown by dotted lines. The panoramic sketch is from station B: the area below the snowline is shaded. (Courtesy of the *Geographical Review* published by the American Geographical Society of New York.)

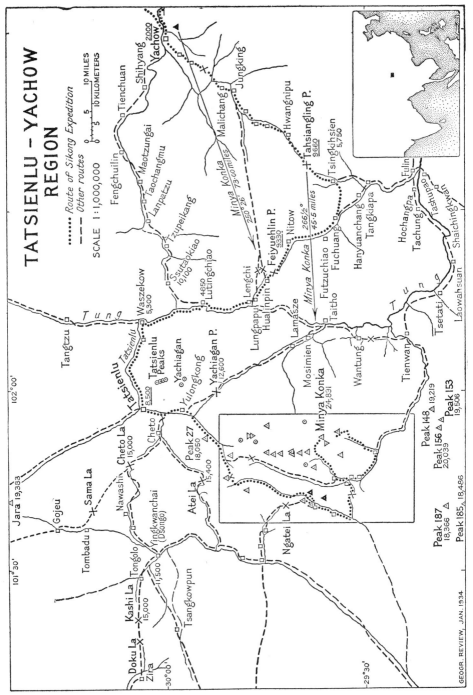

This map was compiled from Survey of India 1 : 1,000,000 sheet 100 and "Kartenskizze von Tatsienlu und Minya Gongkar-Gebirge, 1:275,000," by Heim and Imhof, with a corrected grid and a few other changes and additions by the Sikong Expedition. Symbols are the same as on page 235. Peaks were given numbers corresponding to their magnetic bearings from station B. The position of Peak 156 agrees roughly with that shown for Tzumei Mt. on the Survey of India sheet. (Courtesy of the *Geographical Review* published by the American Geographical Society of New York.)

Appendices

A. HUNTING NOTES

BY JACK THEODORE YOUNG

I

AMONG the big game found in western China and highly prized by scientists are the giant panda; the takin, a queer half-goat, half-antelope creature of cow size, which has fallen under the rifles of not more than half a dozen sportsmen; the chiru, whose beautiful horns are greatly valued; the golden-haired, snubbed-nose monkeys, pride of the Chicago Field Museum, which is the possessor of the only habitat group in the world; blue sheep or bharal, goral, sambhur, and serow, all of which are rare specimens.

Our secret ambition was, however, to get a species of bear which had often been mentioned by travelers in Tibet but which had never been seen on display in any museum. It is the brown, or grizzly bear, known to the scientists as *Spelæus lagomyiarius*, Severtzow. I first saw the skin of the animal four years ago when a native Tibetan brought it to Kermit Roosevelt in answer to a general call for a panda skin. To the best of our knowledge, only once had it been shot (by Wallace, author of the well-known book, *Big Game of Western China*). Unfortunately, it was made into a rug!

Should we fail in getting the grizzly bear, we next would turn our attention to the giant panda. First discovered by the French Jesuit father, Père David, more than sixty years ago, it had not been successfully hunted until 1929. The Roosevelt brothers, whom I accompanied on their hunting trip in western China, were the first ones to kill a giant panda, and this after great difficulties.

The panda, from its appearance, ought to be a bear, but is a distant blood relation of the raccoon. A normal one weighs about two hundred and fifty pounds and is recognizable, as far as sportsmen can see to shoot, by its black legs, black shoulder wedge, black throat, ears, and eye patch, all set upon a dense furry coat of white. The grizzly bear might, however, be mistaken for the panda, because both are about the same size and have a white patch over the shoulder.

For shooting we had two British Lee and Enfield .303 rifles and one Mauser sporting-rifle, chambered for U. S. Government 30-06 ammunition. We found that both kinds stood the dust, soaking rain, and roughing far beyond expectation. Though the Enfield rifles were heavy, they had the advantage of being almost fool-proof, even to the Tibetans, whose sense of curiosity often proved to be destructive. We also carried two .22 rifles for small game and one .410 shot gun for bird collecting.

II

Moore and I, arriving together at Camp Boka, late in September, were warmly greeted by Emmons and Burdsall, both looking very distinguished with their manly beards and tanned faces. They warmed my heart with the information that they had seen forty-two blue sheep the week before. I immediately announced that I was going to take a native hunter with me and climb the rocky cliffs for some blue-sheep hunting.

Known to the Chinese as "Pan Yang," the blue sheep has horns not unlike those of the East Caucasian tur and differs from the goats by the absence of a beard and of the strong odor that is peculiar in the males of the goat family. The most distinctive features are the comparatively smooth, olive-colored horns, which curve at first outwards and then backwards from the sides of the head. The female has short and almost straight horns. An adult animal stands about three feet tall and weighs about 130 pounds. The general color of the upper parts is a brownish gray, tinged with slate blue, the flanks, stomach, and legs being handsomely marked with black and white.

Blue sheep are common throughout the Sino-Tibetan border on the high ranges above the timber line, records showing that they are never found at an altitude lower than 8,000 feet. During summer months they sometimes frequent the alpine regions of 17,000 feet altitude. They are fairly easy to hunt, for when fired upon they never fail to halt and look around at their enemy. However, the nature of the country and the rare atmosphere usually render the work tiring and arduous.

My call for native hunters and guides was answered with great enthusiasm, an unusual experience for me. As a rule the natives are very suspicious and will often interpret collecting efforts as a disguise for some ulterior motive, and a long-winded and tactful explanation becomes necessary. However, Burdsall and Emmons had long established a firm friendship with the Tibetans; they had come to look upon us as members of their own little community.

My guide was a husky Tibetan. In many ways he reminded me of a Cherokee Indian, with his erect posture, his bronzed complexion, and his high cheek bones. I called him Shu. Like all Tibetan servants, Shu wanted his money before he started; but I told him plainly that he had the cart before the horse. He would get his money, and perhaps an extra reward, when he came around early next morning.

The day was surprisingly warm and beautiful. Shu came early. Together we made for the mountains overlooking the Büchu Valley. We stopped first at his house for a Tibetan breakfast consisting of ground roasted barley mixed with buttered tea, the ever-present Tibetan dish. As we approached his hut a huge woolly Tibetan dog barked at us, clanking a heavy chain which was drawn around his neck. One never fails to see one of these brutes guarding a Tibetan house, no matter how poor a family may be.

For three hours Shu and I climbed, finally reaching a little pinnacle where we could command a good view of the surrounding country. We were now about 12,000 feet above sea-level. I scanned high and low with my field-glasses to get a bearing of the country, which was unmistakably the home of blue sheep. The view was superb. We could see the Tsemei La (pass) faintly painted with new snow here and there. Further back lay the Tibetan plateau. Above us rose the mystic snow-capped peaks of Nyambo Konka, revealing in the morning sun secrets that no man had ever probed. A glacial stream roared down the valley and disappeared like a white snake into the dense birch and rhododendron forest below. Two tiny specks below turned out to be our tents on the bank of the Büchu River. A long wisp of smoke issuing thence told us that Burdsall was having his lunch, and I hungrily devoured my two chunks of ten-days-old bread.

By 4 P.M. we had covered a large territory, but had not sighted any blue sheep. While waiting for the sheep to make an appearance, I sat down and read my book of O. Henry's short stories. Nothing came into view except a few screaming eagles, who seemed to be jeering at us. Shu reported that he had seen musk-deer droppings and had come upon numerous serow tracks that were a week old, but of the blue sheep he had seen nothing. Reluctantly we turned back home, a very dejected pair.

Another hunt for sheep the next day again brought us no better luck, though I managed to bring home a white eared-pheasant (Crossoptilon crossoptilon crossoptilon) for the pot. During our trip we shot at least ten of these birds, bringing one out alive for a zoo for the first time.

Tired, discouraged, and disgusted, I had almost no energy to drag my weary, aching bones up the cliffs for a third try. Burdsall, seeing my disappointment, cheerfully asked if he might join me on the next day's hunt. With renewed enthusiasm, I slapped him on the back and said, "Yes, come along!"

We engaged Shu again and promised anew to give him the reward of two rupees if he would show us the blue sheep whether they were within range or not. Anticipating his hesitancy, I brought forth an empty tin of Libby's bouillon cubes. "This I will give you in advance," I said to him, "if you will take us to the blue sheep." Tibetans prize tin cans highly; sometimes when money fails to win them, a cracker-can alone will do the trick. Extending a greedy hand for the box, he grunted his assent.

Instead of going to the places covered by my previous unsuccessful attempts, Shu led us farther down the Büchu Valley. I would stop continually to scan the surrounding mountains for sheep, but nothing greeted my eye. About four miles out, we met an amiable old Chinese carrier. Only a few hours ago he had seen a great flock of blue sheep, oh, several hundred of them, he said, sunning on the shrub-clad slope of the mountain a few miles further down. Being a Chinese myself, I was fully aware of the fact that the natives had a great habit of exaggerating their speech, and I refused to let my imagination run wild. Nevertheless, we lost no time in investigating. After a half hour of climbing we saw the herd, silhouetted against the sky, about a mile away. Through my field-glasses I estimated there were about fifty in the group. However, the going was by no means easy; between us and the sheep stood several rocky, thorny ravines and gullies which radiated from the high ridge above us like the ribs of a giant fan. The slopes dropped precipitously into the Büchu Valley. On hands and knees we edged our way slowly over the boulders. Neither of us could match Shu's ability and speed. He jumped over the rocks like a jack rabbit, and calmly ran across the steep moraine, giving no heed to the clatter of stones which his feet hurled down. Burdsall and I watched him in utter amazement. Three hours of this rough going brought us to the spot where we had last seen the sheep; but to our disappointment they had all disappeared. We scrutinized the countryside from here with our field-glasses, but in vain. We felt another day had been wasted.

The descent was twice as difficult, though to our native hunter it did not seem to make much difference. Suddenly Burdsall, who was a few feet ahead, came unexpectedly upon a herd, about fifty in number, hidden in one of the ravines. The sheep broke into a run and were soon dashing wildly all over the slope. I seized my rifle and fired at a huge male running not eighty yards away from me. I missed, and then, as though to stamp a grand finale on the day's luck, my rifle jammed as I tried feverishly to push the second shot in. It took me two minutes to get the shell clear and to reload my gun. By that time the sheep had gotten quite a head start. I spied ten of them just as they were about to disappear below the ridge. I fired as quickly as I could and dropped one of them, but he picked himself up and joined the crowd. Meanwhile Dick was firing, but had made no hits. Again the range was empty; nothing but barren hills for us.

Just as I was cursing my rifle I saw a number galloping two hundred yards above us. They were at three hundred yards' range when I shot and dropped a male. He fell and rolled headlong down the mountain-side. Dick had also found a target, which rolled down after mine.

It was with a new spirit that we descended to claim our prizes. Both animals had rolled quite a distance down the steep incline, but, fortunately, the horns remained intact. The measuring and skinning took over an hour; darkness had fallen when we started for camp. Gaomo and Tsong, our Tibetan servants, came with lanterns to meet us.

Our first job was to complete the habitat group of blue sheep, which I later succeeded in doing by bagging five more, two of which, unfortunately, fell into a deep narrow canyon and could not be retrieved. Bad weather prevented hunting for a few days, and by the time the weather cleared up, our mountaineering project had begun in earnest, demanding the services of all hands available. When I returned to my collecting work again the three mountaineers had everything well established above the base camp for the hazardous attempt to conquer the Konka.

III

The rhododendron and beech forests of the Konka Gompa Valley offered one of the most fascinating hunting-grounds, in both quality and quantity. Returning from a reconnaissance trip one afternoon, Emmons and Moore had seen five huge black bears. A careful and exhaustive inquiry revealed that "ma shung," or grizzly bear, roamed about the forest "in great number." My discovery of a mask made from this bear in the lamasery offered additional encouragement. I made a survey one morning and came upon numerous, day-old bear tracks of enormous size, and at places the ground was literally covered with bear droppings. On my way back to camp a musk-deer flashed across my trail with lightning rapidity, but I found no further signs of grizzly bear.

Killing was strictly forbidden by the head lama of the lamasery and ruler of the valley, although he and his followers were, upon occasion, the greatest meat-eaters I had ever met. But fate stepped in to aid us. The lamas left on a pilgrimage to some far-away lamasery. It was my chance.

The next day, a glorious one, I sat upon the lamasery steps, scanning the forests below with my field-glasses. There had been a heavy snowfall the night before, and I had great hopes of tracking down a bear. Nor was I disappointed. I soon caught a glimpse of two dark spots coming across the deep and thickly wooded ravine. They were emerging from the rhododendron forest and slowly making their way up the slope covered with fresh snow. It was difficult to tell what they were at first, as a thin veil of mist obstructed the view. A few moments later, I could make out that they were bears, and very large ones. They appeared now to have a white patch around the shoulder. I immediately ran to get my rifle, an ice-ax, and a pocket full of ammunition. My Tibetan guide, Shu, refused to accompany me, although I offered him my spare rifle. It had something to do with his religion, he explained. But I suspect it had more to do with the wading of a knee-high, ice-cold stream necessary to get over to the region of the bears; moreover, the prospect of facing the creatures at close range did not offer him such an inviting picture.

It took hours to reach the spot where I had first caught a glimpse of the bears, for plowing through the fresh snow and thick rhododendron shrubs was tedious work. Several times I was persuaded to give up the search, for the freshly made bear tracks which I was following seemed to lead me around in circles, getting me nowhere. Just as I was about to abandon the hunt I came upon fresh droppings that were still warm. With doubled zest I continued to pursue Mr. Grizzly. The sun was now high in the sky, and the snow was beginning to melt rapidly. Progress was made more laborious by the weight of my shoes, which were now thoroughly saturated with water. Then the scene began to shift with kaleidoscopic rapidity. The cold thick mist came like a sea from the east and settled in the valley, shutting everything from sight. This is one of the unfriendly characteristics of Minya Konka, for which hunters have to suffer. Knowing that it was useless to track the animal any longer, I sat down for a much-needed rest. The water squashed uncomfortably in my shoes as I tried to wiggle my benumbed toes back and forth. I heaved a deep sigh, such as only sheer weariness can bring forth.

The fog had now become so thick that it was almost impenetrable. I decided to return to the lamasery, fetch my sleeping-bag and a few of Mrs. Cunningham's cookies, and spend the night under the big boulder across the stream near the Konka Glacier; this would permit an earlier start the next morning.

The sun came out the next morning dressed in all its splendor. I discovered the two bears prowling about at the same spot. Losing no time, I scrambled within thirty yards below them and dropped the larger one with the first shot. The bullet went clear through him two inches above the heart and sent a puff of snow and dirt off the ground behind. He rolled within several feet of me, dead. I fired six times in rapid succession at the cub, who was looking down at me dumbly, with great amazement. The first few shots did not move him, but the last one apparently found its target. He gave a loud grunt, started to roll, but picked himself up nicely, then dashed out of sight among the tall shrubs. To my greatest pride and satisfaction, the bear turned out to be the answer of our secret desire, a perfect specimen of a large female brown, or grizzly, bear.

Referring to this animal, the Roosevelts wrote in 1929:

The brown bear, known by the natives as ma hsiung, or horse bear, is by no means as numerous as the black, but we saw masks made from their head skins in several lamaseries, and were told by the lamas that the animal lived in the neighboring forests. We also saw a number of hides. As far as we know it has never been collected. It is not mentioned in such accounts of animals of the district as we have read. As well as we could determine, it does not exist south of Szechuan. It is much feared by the natives and is unquestionably a disagreeable customer for a woodcutter to meet. It seems possible that there may be more than one variety. A good series would be of great value to a museum, and would deserve careful scientific study. They vary markedly in coloration, some being so light a brown that it was to these that the natives thought we referred when inquiring for beishung (white bear).

When my enthusiasm and rejoicing had subsided, I began to realize that there were other problems to work out. My first thought was to get men and porters to help me in skinning and transporting the animal. This necessitated a fourth crossing of the stream, which I so dreaded; however, the elation that was mine spurred on my feet as I forced my way across the rapids. When I reached the lamasery, I found Shu, the two lamas, Gaoma, and three other Tibetans ready with baskets of all sizes and shapes, awaiting my arrival. Evidently they had heard the firing and were now lining up expectantly to receive their share of the bear steak!

I ordered them to put away their baskets and return with me to get the bear. After making me promise to give them the bear's gall, which constitutes a very rare and valuable Chinese medicine, they willingly followed me.

It was hard work skinning in the cold with numb fingers. In cutting open the stomach to examine its contents, we inhaled a heavy, not unpleasant odor of musk, and saw handfuls of gray musk-deer hair. Undoubtedly some unfortunate musk-deer had been part of the bear's dinner not long before. While I directed the measuring and skinning of the grizzly, Shu and Gaoma went around to look for the wounded cub. They followed the bloody trail for two hours and then gave up only because evening approached.

The lamasery was a scene of riot that evening. No doubt the gods were rolling their eyes in horror at the unabashed display of sin and transgression; all religious pledges were suspended, for the night, anyway, while the lamas and Tibetans feasted on bear steak.

This feasting lasted for several hours until, filled with rice wine and flooded with that happy feeling which usually follows an over-indulgence in food and drink, the lamas started to dance. Swinging around in dizzy circles, they cut such silly figures that even the yak, who stood outside the lamasery, could not resist poking his head through the window to see what was going on. Finally, in a state of sleepiness, they wrapped themselves up in blankets and fell fast alseep.

Within the next few days I added a large female adult black bear to our collection. I came upon her tracks one morning in the newly fallen snow. Though they were partly obliterated, I knew they could not be very old. Two hours of trailing through the dense forests brought me to the spot which she had selected for a home. I shot her as she was about to get up from her nap.

The last day of my bear-hunting brought a still greater surprise, for Moore, after an absence of ten days, suddenly made an appearance. His fuzzy beard, weather-beaten face, and shabby clothing reminded me of the jungly Kashmiri shikarries we had had on the Roosevelt Expedition. Our handshake lasted several minutes. And why not, since the mighty Konka had at last bowed down to us in defeat!

Porters and animals had to be engaged for the three record-making men in order to hasten their trip to Tatsienlu, for Emmons, whose feet had been badly frostbitten, was in need of immediate medical attention; moreover, Moore and Burdsall were showing signs of great fatigue.

IV

Left alone to continue my collecting, I spent three more weeks, accompanied by my Tibetan cook-porter Su-ling, following parts of the old Roosevelt trail into the Lolo tribe country, circumambulating the Konka Range back to Tatsienlu, and making stops at places where there were good hunting prospects.

On November 4th Su-ling and I bade goodby to the Konka community, which we had learned to like so much. However, nice as the place was, we took away with us a rather unpleasant souvenir of our sojourn there, an annoying little animal that infested my sleeping-bag and caused me no end of discomfort. I determined to have a flea-cleaning campaign on my arrival at Chow Kuo!

No sooner had we left the lamasery than we met a rice-carrier coming from the direction of Chow Kuo, carrying some takin meat. Upon inquiry, we found out that some native hunters had trapped a baby takin at a place thirty miles distant. We hastily continued on our way.

We made twenty miles that first day, spending the night under a big rock, with high mountains and rocky cliffs towering above us. The country was wonderful in its natural beauty, a perfect paradise for botanist and zoologist. One glance at the gigantic mountains and the lofty trees made one feel small and insignificant. Fifteen miles out of Pawa, Su-ling pointed out a huge rock to me. Originally this rock had been carved with many characters, but the years that it had been exposed to wind and rain had practically wiped out all legibility. Its only significance now is that it used to be the boundary line between the Chinese and the Tibetans years ago.

As part of our itinerary we had not anticipated spending two interesting and profitable days with a Chinese musk-deer trapper whom we discovered by accident. It was our second day's march toward Chow Kuo. We were passing by a crude tumbled-down shack, a not unusual sight in these uncivilized parts, when suddenly I caught sight of a peculiar, roughly-made altar at its side, upon which was placed a large pile of musk-deer hair. This, I knew, was a sort of religious belief of the musk-deer trappers, that whenever they kill an animal they must offer its hair at the altar of the Hunting God. Of course, I was curious to study the methods used by these hunters to ensnare the animals. Upon looking into the hut, I found it quite empty; not stopping to find out if we were trespassing on some one's hunting-grounds, Su-ling and I set about making a lean-to under a neighboring cliff.

Later on in the day the musk-deer trapper returned and was not a little surprised to find us building a lean-to right next to his hut. Evidently he was doubtful of our character and hesitated to approach us. Then my porter raised his hand and hailed him, assuring him that we meant no harm, though we did plan to spend the night there. The hunter came up to us, and, in kindly though shaky tones, told us that we were welcome to stay as long as we wanted. In the conversation that ensued I explained to him that I was also a hunter and that I was greatly interested in the type of traps he used. At the mention of traps, his manner immediately changed; native hunters, as everyone knows, guard their secrets very jealously, and he was no exception to the rule. However, impressed by our firearms and persuaded by our friendly tones, he finally took us into the hills and pointed out to us the different spots where he had laid his traps.

Upon closer inspection these traps turned out to be quite ingenious affairs. A strong, flexible branch, about seven feet long, had been planted in the ground, arching over a small ditch and held down loosely at the opposite side by another looped branch, about the size of the wire arches used in croquet. So insecure was this fastening that at the slightest touch the larger branch would spring up into the air; the noose, which was tied to its end and which was cleverly disguised under a pile of fallen leaves and grass, would then tighten by itself around the paw of the unfortunate creature who had stepped into the snare, flinging him up with the branch. There would hang your prize, neatly roped and very much alive!

I marveled at the hunter's cleverness, and, with his approval, proceeded to make a trap in the same fashion. Our stay there netted us one more blue sheep and a beautiful musk-deer, both of which we snared with ropes and later killed with a .22 rifle.

The musk-deer is a pretty animal. An adult male seldom grows over three feet in length from nose to root of the tail; the female rather less. It stands much lower on the forelegs than on the hind. Its hair is of singularly spiky texture, dark glossy amber in color. On either side of its mouth two dagger-like tusks project, slender, sharp, ivory white. These are employed by the animal in digging and scraping up scanty herbage on the steep rocks and beneath the snow.

The natives trap and snare but rarely shoot them. Without dogs, hunting them would be particularly difficult, since they live where the forest of spruce, silver fir, and larch is at its thickest. If it were not for their insatiable curiosity, which often lures them into the open, it would be almost impossible to shoot them.

This deer is relentlessly persecuted by the natives throughout the Orient for its musk, which commands a high price as medicine and for the manufacture of perfume. This secretion is stored during the rutting season in a skin gland situated in the genital organ of the male. The whole gland, about the size of a small hen's egg, is removed and constitutes the "musk pod." From Tatsienlu alone the annual exports of musk are valued at tls. 300,000, or $100,000 gold. Until recently, some of the leading Paris perfumeries maintained agents in remote mountain villages of the Tibetan frontier for the purchasing of musk.

We pushed on again to Chow Kuo, a small village located at the junction of the Büchu and Tung rivers. It was a forty-mile trek and took the better part of two days. The trail was poor, and all the while we were in a gorge. Walls on both sides of us towered to dizzy heights. Rocks of fantastic shapes hung over us, draped with graceful ferns. Streams fell in floating mists from the cliff. Beneath us the Büchu River roared angrily. Precarious rope bridges spanned the water; one would almost have to perform a circus act to cross over them! These and many others like them were the scenes that inspired the flowing pens of Chinese classical poets. As I stood there, breathing in the beauty, a feeling not unlike a poet's surged into my own soul.

Much to my surprise, a great delegation of natives awaited my arrival in Chow Kuo, affording me a warm welcome. Evidently the fame of the "three holy fathers and a Chinese monk" had spread over the countryside. This honor was bestowed upon the manly beards which Burdsall, Emmons, and Moore had acquired and the flying helmet that I wore. The entire village turned out to see their queer-looking visitor. And a funny picture I did make, I suppose, with my poncho, my monk-like helmet, my enormous hob-nailed shoes, and my unbecoming mustache! Moreover, the rifle on my back attracted much comment, as did the four-foot snake which I had tied to a pole and slung over my shoulder. (I had shot it with my pistol outside of Gego, a native village ten miles away.) The village children scrambled for cover when they spotted me coming in their direction, and the women peeped curiously from behind half-closed doors. When the head man, Chang, heard of our arrival, he hospitably invited us to make our headquarters at his house, which invitation we gladly accepted.

The history of Chow Kuo is interesting. Ten years ago Lolo outlaw tribes came, three thousand in number, from the neighboring mountains and made a clean haul of the place. Nothing was left intact, not even the Tibetan Lamasery, the ruins of which still stand pathetically near the river banks, a reminder of the tragedy that had occurred. Now at every strategic point, the villagers have built guarding-towers.

The chief occupation of its inhabitants, and their means of existence, is hunting. With the aid of dogs, native guns, and ingenious traps they not infrequently bring home with them takin, panda cats, tufted deer, gorals, bears, and huge snakes from the dense jungle of the surrounding mountains, which, to the best of my knowledge, has never been touched by either zoologist or botanist. Snakes were especially plentiful in this region. A native informed me that he once saw a snake whose circumference was about the size of a frying pan. To be sure, I had no desire to bump into one of these reptiles! It was raining that morning and I had thought of staying in to finish up some skinning; but late that afternoon an old farmer came in with the cheerful information that he had seen two gorals asleep across the river. Together we crossed the long suspension bridge and climbed for fifteen minutes before we came to a little hut situated halfway up the mountain. Suddenly the farmer clutched my sleeve and, pointing a finger towards a cliff well over two hundred yards away, said, "There they are, lying down on the grass!" I studied the spot for over ten minutes but failed to see anything approaching the form of a goral; visibility was poor, for long gray fingers of mist creeping up from the valley persisted in blocking the view. We sat down comfortably on the soft grass, waiting for the weather to clear up. Meanwhile I kept asking the farmer, whose eyesight seemed to be very keen: "Do you still see them? Are they still there?"

By this time quite a gathering of villagers had collected around us, anxiously awaiting the shooting. The fog was beginning to lift; I could barely make out one of the gorals hidden in the tall grass. It was a little thing with enormous ears but no horns. At the crack of my rifle the goral turned over. Then amidst loud cheers of the natives, the second goral suddenly arose from the grass and dashed down the cliff, full speed, bouncing from rock to rock like a rubber ball. I emptied my magazine as he staggered and disappeared into a cave among the rocks. We later found that two bullets had penetrated him, one breaking the hind leg and one boring neatly through the body.

The villagers received the meat with great glee, but were puzzled over my generosity. No Chinese hunter ever did that. I carefully explained to them that I only wanted the skins to make "medicine" with. Any attempt to explain the real purpose would arouse suspicion and might prove disastrous, for science and museum display meant nothing to these natives. They accepted my explanations and were quite satisfied.

The goral is sometimes known as "goat-antelope" because of the intermediate position which it holds between the true antelope and the goats. Its horns curve regularly backwards and are conical in form, marked by small irregular ridges. The shabby, stringy hair is dark brown in color, tending to grow lighter towards the face. Its chief characteristic is a black line running from the nape of the neck to the end of the tail, and a dark stripe running down the front of each leg. These animals are quite common throughout China. During the summer time the gorals around the China-Tibetan border live at an altitude of 8,000 feet, coming down lower in the winter. They make their homes in the shrub-clad country and are seldom found in the forest. They feed early in the morning and late in the evening, except in rainy or misty weather, wasting most of the day in napping. When alarmed, they make a curious, sharp, hissing sound, but they are not easily frightened. The natives usually study their runways and snare them, or else use men and dogs as "beaters" to drive them out from the bushes and shoot them.

v

On November 13th I headed for the Lolo country. My original plan was to visit the little town of Yehli, where the Roosevelts bagged the first giant panda, but local warfare compelled me to alter my itinerary. Instead, I spent two delightful days in a tiny village several miles south of Tzetati (see map, p. 236). The Lolos were very hospitable towards me, remembering well the visit of the Roosevelts and especially mindful of their generosity.

The Lolos are an independent people, who seldom mix with other tribes and never intermarry. They are mountaineers for the most part, depending on their hunting for a living; some even have the reputation of being head-hunters. In features they are hard to distinguish from the Tibetans, having the same dark complexion, the same sturdy build, and wearing similar dress.

The Lolos were extremely keen on hunting and were anxious to have me get rid of the wild pigs that ran amuck over their cornfields, causing tremendous damage to their crops. I armed my guide and another Lolo hunter with my spare .303 Enfield and a .22 Remington, giving them instructions to take the dogs far away from my position. We had barely parted when I heard two shots fired in rapid succession. Turning back, I saw an enormous wild pig plunging forward from the bushes in the cornfield, with ten dogs hot on his trail. The pig staggered for a minute, then, snorting angrily, tore madly down the field, heading directly for the house of my host. Not stopping for doors, he rammed clear through the mud wall of the house and came out the other end. The whole episode was screamingly funny, and I was almost helpless with laughter. Meanwhile there was a violent commotion within the house. A Lolo woman rushed out hysterically, comb in hand and hair floating wildly behind. Evidently she had been at her morning toilet when the early visitor had made his unannounced arrival. I hastened to calm her, though all the while I could not control my laughter. We entered the house together, and what a sight met our eyes! Tables turned over, chairs knocked down, teakettle squashed, chinaware broken to pieces and scattered all over the floor. The poor woman almost collapsed as she gazed at what used to be her home.

We held the wounded pig at bay behind a tree and, with three more shots, finished him.

My last day with the friendly Lolos was spent in an interesting monkey-hunt. These lively creatures live high up in the cliffs above the forest, coming down occasionally to the cornfields in search of food. To get within shooting range one had to climb difficult cliffs and struggle through jungly forests that were close, thick, and dark. The branches met overhead, shutting out the blue sky, so that one seemed to be moving up an endless, shadowy tunnel. Only the loud squeaks of the monkeys as we neared them brought me back to reality. We saw seven that day and gave them wild chase. As we emerged from the forest, making a sharp turn, we came face to face with a venerable old monkey; behind him was his troop. He stared at us with wide, startled eyes. My guide, upset by the unexpected meeting, threw up his arms, turned back, and slipped feet first over the rock into a mass of thorns and shrubs. The monkeys jumped ahead of us and were almost two hundred yards away before I gathered myself to shoot. I shot two of them, sending them hurtling through the air like two dark balls to crash many feet below. They were beautiful specimens, resembling the golden monkey with long brown hair. We carried them home as trophies of my last day's hunt in the Lolo tribe country.

The Lolos begged me to stay longer. They offered to take me where takin were to be found in great quantity and where we could get giant panda for a certainty. However, my anxiety to return to Tatsienlu to hear further news of my three companions prevented me from accepting their kind invitation.

The day before Thanksgiving, Su-ling and I arrived in Tatsienlu with six loads of skins and skulls. The Cunninghams welcomed me heartily, as they had been somewhat worried over my prolonged stay alone in the Lolo country. A few days later I made my departure with a small caravan to join the expedition at Yachow and to see how Emmons was progressing.

———————

The specimens which Jack Young collected were: five blue sheep, a grizzly bear, a black bear, two wild boars, three gorals, a musk-deer, a monkey, and a live white eared-pheasant. These, together with Burdsall's collection of thirty-eight birds, also two mice, a small viper, and a few high-altitude plants, were presented by the expedition to the Metropolitan Museum of the Academia Sinica in Nanking.

In order to complete the zoological work of the Sikong Expedition, Young made another trip with native hunters while Emmons was confined in the hospital at Yachow. This trip took him to Muping and through the wild country north of Tatsienlu, and resulted in the acquisition of a specimen of the giant panda (now at the American Museum of Natural History in New York City), and of two live Tibetan grizzly bear cubs.[64] The latter were kept on exhibition for some time at the zoo in Nanking. They were then brought across the Pacific and arrived safely, in February, 1934, at the Bronx Zoological Park in New York City.

These cubs, and the large bear shot by Young which is probably of the same species, are undoubtedly the most interesting and valuable specimens secured by the expedition. Dr. W. Reid Blair, director of the Bronx Zoological Park, prefers to wait until the cubs are older before giving his opinion as to their exact classification.

Mr. Arthur de C. Sowerby, of Shanghai, well known explorer, naturalist, and author, writing about these cubs in the *China Journal*, of which he is editor (vol. xx, no. 2, February, 1934, p. 109), says:

Recently we have had further opportunities of examining specimens of what may be called Asiatic grizzly bears. Mr. Jack Theodore Young last summer brought back with him two bear cubs which he had secured in the Szechuan-Tibetan border regions, depositing them with the Metropolitan Museum authorities in Nanking while he visited America. On his return to China recently he shipped the cubs, a male and a female, to the United States, bringing them to Shanghai for the purpose. This gave us the opportunity of examining them, and we have no hesitation in identifying them as belonging to the species *Spelæus lagomyiarius*, Severtzow, which some authorities claim is identical with the Himalayan blue bear (*Spelæus pruinosus,* Blyth), but which we maintain is a distinct form, and call the Tibetan grizzly. The species, amongst other things, is characterized by a pronounced white shoulder band, while the hair of the ears is very long, that of the body long, dark brown or black and grizzled all over, the grizzling being most pronounced on the flanks. In the skull of this species the muzzle and jaws are long and the forehead inclined to be high, owing to the development of the frontal bones. In the brown bears of the genus *Ursus* the muzzle is not so long, although the skull may be narrow, while it is the occipital region that tends to be high, giving a very different profile. The skull in the Asiatic black bear group, genus *Selenarctos*, Heude, is much wider and the muzzle and jaws much shorter than in either the *Spelæus* (grizzly) or *Ursus* (brown bear) groups.

In a later number (*China Journal,* vol. xxi, no. 2, August, 1934) Mr. Sowerby writes:

We examined these cubs when they were in Shanghai and only a few months old, and it was our opinion that they represented a species of bear found on the Chinese-Tibetan border which has been classified by us as a grizzly rather than a brown bear. This species was originally named *Ursus lagomyiarius* by Severtzow, having been secured by the famous Russian explorer Przewalski in Kansu, probably in the southwestern part of that province. We based our diagnosis of Mr. Young's specimens on the presence of the white shoulder band, a characteristic of what we call the Tibetan grizzly and refer to scientifically as *Spelæus lagomyiarius,* Severtzow.

R. L. B.
A. B. E.

B. SURVEYING NOTES

By Richard L. Burdsall

Barometric Observations

THE results are given in Table I, and details of those at Camp Alpine are shown on pages 260 and 261, to which the following remarks apply:

Curve 1. The Zikawei Observatory in Shanghai publishes a daily weather map for China, showing isobars at 6 A.M. Upon my return to Shanghai I was kindly supplied with these for each day of our observations. Their nearest station was at Chungking, about 275 miles east of our camp, so the isobars for our location can be only approximate. However, they seem to offer the best values obtainable, and I used them to get the sea-level pressure, interpolating for the time of our observation and making a correction for diurnal variation, which was assumed to have an amplitude of .108". Leveling had been carried up the Yangtze only as far as Hankow, but from a long series of barometric observations the zero mark on the river gauge at Chungking is considered to be 546.5 feet above sea-level. The mercurial barometer of the Customs Office, which reports to Zikawei, is 165.9 feet above this, or 712.4 feet above mean sea-level.

Curve 2 shows the barometric pressure at Station G by mercurial barometer reduced to standard conditions. The barometer remained set up inside our tent throughout the period.

Curve 3 shows dry bulb temperatures taken with a small sling psychrometer outside the tent at the times of the barometric readings.

259

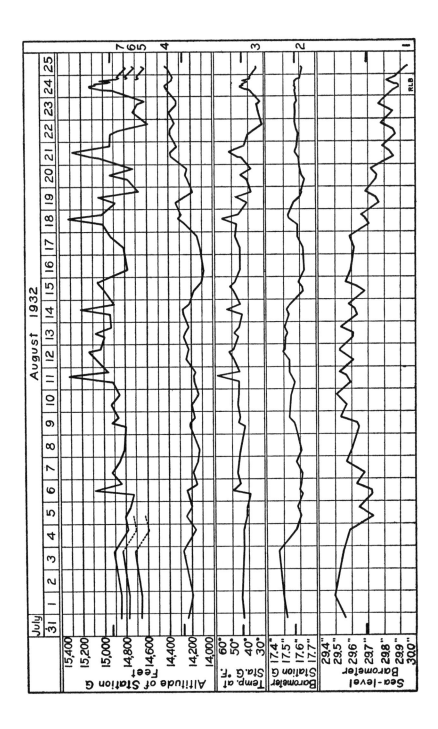

BAROMETRIC OBSERVATIONS MADE AT STATION G (CAMP
ALPINE) FROM JULY 31 TO AUGUST 25, 1932

The altitudes were computed separately for each of the seventy
observations by the Smithsonian Meteorological Tables, with
the following results, which are plotted on the opposite page.
For further explanation and comments see pages 259 and 263.

Curve		Maximum	Minimum	Range	Mean
1	Sea-level barometer (inches).	29.947	29.498	.449	29.705
2	Barometer at Station G.....	17.626	17.476	.150	17.571
3	Temperature at Station G (°Fah.).................	59	31	28	43.8
4	Approximate uncorrected altitude...................	14,440	14,089	351	14,272
	Temperature correction.....	897	88	809	459
5	Altitude corrected for temperature.................	15,098	14,427	671	14,731
	Humidity correction........	152	79	73	117
6	Altitude corrected for humidity....................	15,250	14,506	744	14,848
	Correction for gravity and latitude................				56
	Correction for gravity on air.				11
	Further temperature correction...................				11
	Height of barometer above station.................				−3
7	Final corrected altitude (feet)	15,323	14,581	744	14,923

TABLE I—BAROMETRIC HEIGHTS RECORDED JULY TO DECEMBER, 1932

Station	Date and Time	No. Observations	Feet Above Sta.[4]	Air Temp. °F. Mean	Air Temp. °F. Range	Pressure (Reduced to Std.) Mean	Pressure (Reduced to Std.) Range	Pressure at Sea Level[2] Mean	Pressure at Sea Level[2] Range	Altitude of Station,[3] Feet Mean	Altitude of Station,[3] Feet Range	Altitude Meters
Chengtu	July 12 22:40	1	17	87	……	27.901	……	29.602	……	1,756	……	535
Yachow	July 15 18:30	1	15	85	……	27.699	……	29.687	……	2,044	……	623
Yachow[1]	Nov. 28 11:45 / Dec. 1 11:15	2	8	54	2	28.177	.079	30.243	.108	1,957	30	596
Tahsiangling	July 18 15:30 15:40	2	2	74	2	21.334	.002	29.520	.004	9,665	46	2946
Feiyuehlin	July 20 16:05 16:35	2	2	60	0	21.386	.006	29.540	.003	9,332	4	2844
Tatsienlu	July 24 to July 27	11	15	69.6	16	22.139	.198	29.602	.186	8,533	545	2601
Tatsienlu[1]	July 25 to Sept. 6	28	3	62.2	21	22.205	.315	29.786	.599	8,480	363	2585
N. E. Djezi La	July 29 18:35	1	2	46	……	18.758	……	29.494	……	12,835	……	3912
Djezi La	July 29 10:45-13:40	4	2	47.7	7	17.111	.022	29.532	.032	15,685	232	4781
Upper Yulong	July 29 18:20	1	2	47	……	18.184	……	29.481	……	13,766	……	4196
Station G	July 31 to Aug. 25	70	3	43.8	28	17.571	.150	29.705	.449	14,923	744	4549
Tsemei La	Aug. 26 9:30 9:45	2	2	41.7	1.5	17.420	.016	29.880	.000	15,288	23	4660
Tsemei[1]	Aug. 26 13:05	1	50	55.5	……	19.865	……	29.829	……	11,670	……	3560
Konka Gompa	Aug. 26 18:20	2	2	49	8	19.174	.012	29.807	.076	12,588	304	3837
Boka House	Aug. 27 11:00	1	15	53	……	20.281	……	29.773	……	10,977	……	3346
Boka Camp	Aug. 27 18:45 / Aug. 28 to Sept. 19	5	2	53.2	15	20.451	.064	29.861	.128	10,838	179	3303
Base Camp[1]	Oct. 5 19:00	1	0	31	……	17.745	……	29.957	……	14,415	……	4394
Camp I[1]	Oct. 7 19:00	1	0	28	……	15.015	……	30.008	……	18,078	……	5510

[1] By hypsometer; other readings by mercurial barometer. The series of hypsometer observations at Tatsienlu was made by the Rev. R. L. Cunningham, using our spare thermometer in his hypsometer. This was checked by comparison with our hypsometer and gave the same reading.

[2] From weather maps of the Zikawei Observatory corrected for time of observation and diurnal variation.

[3] By Smithsonian Meteorological Tables using temperature gradient of 0.30° F. per 100 feet.

[4] Height of the barometer cistern above the station. At Tsenei the barometer was set up at some distance from the two houses.

The station at Chengtu was the Campus of the West China Union University; at Yachow, the house of Dr. R. L. Crook, American Baptist Mission; at Tatsienlu, the building of the China Inland Mission.

Curve 4 shows altitudes obtained from the data of curves 1 and 2 with no corrections applied.

Curve 5 shows the altitudes corrected for air temperature. For the mean temperature of the hypothetical air column I used the temperatures of curve 3, and assumed a temperature gradient of 0.30° F. per 100 feet to get the sea-level and mean temperatures. The suitability of this figure was confirmed by correspondence with the U. S. Bureau of Standards and the Weather Bureau, and sea-level temperatures computed by it are fairly consistent with records at Chungking. A change of 0.014 in the value of this gradient will give a change of 1° F. in the mean temperature of the air column and a change of 30 feet in the resulting altitude. With the gradient used the sea-level temperatures were 44° higher, and the mean temperatures of the air column 22° higher than those of curve 3.

Curve 6 shows the altitudes corrected for humidity. Although both wet and dry bulb temperatures were taken, the corresponding data for sea-level were not available, so the correction used was the average one given by the tables.

Curve 7 shows the altitudes of curve 6 with the addition of 75 feet, made up of minor corrections, as shown in the table. The addition of 11 feet as a further temperature correction arises from the fact that the actual altitude was higher than that assumed, and that with a gradient of 0.30° per 100 feet, the sea-level temperatures should therefore be increased 0.74° and the mean temperature of the air column 0.37° F.

The chief error in the final result is probably attributable to the corrections for temperature and humidity. The unsatisfactory nature of these is shown by the fact that, while the uncorrected altitudes (curve 4) have a range of 351 feet, the corrected altitudes (curves 6 and 7) have a range of 744 feet. Observations taken at midday when the temperature was high usually gave higher altitudes than those taken in the morning or evening. The corrections are based on the mean temperature of the "air column" which extends from sea-level up to the elevation of the station. This "air column" does not really exist, its location being within the plateau under the station, and its temperature gradient and mean temperature are therefore mere hypothetical quantities impossible to obtain by observation. The corrections based on the mean temperature of this hypothetical air column must, however, be applied, and the assumption that it is the mean of the station and sea-level temperatures seems to be the best that can be made.

Although the range in the final altitudes (curve 7) is considerable, there are few observations near its limits, and the mean of the 70 observations gives a value whose probable error is considered to be ±0.5 per cent, or ±75 feet. This figure, 14,923 feet, was therefore accepted as the altitude of Station G (Camp Alpine) and all of the altitudes obtained by triangulation were based upon it.

TRIANGULATION

Referring to the diagrams on opposite page, V-W represents the base line, 3185.15 feet long, in the Yulong Valley. This was measured twice with a steel tape, the discrepancy being 0.56 feet. It was extended by triangulation to B-D, all of the angles being measured by repetition at each corner of the quadrilateral. The extended base B-D was 13,775.7 feet (2.6 miles) long. From its ends at the high stations B and D, horizontal and vertical angles were measured to 25 peaks, including Jara, 50 miles away to the north. All readings were taken face right and face left, bubble corrections being applied to the verticle angles. Sixteen altitudes were taken of Minya Konka, and six of Jara, and the horizontal angles to these peaks were measured by repetition.

Station G (Camp Alpine), where the barometric readings were taken, was not visible from B or D, as parts of the ridge intervened. A small triangulation was therefore used to connect it with Station B. A base line, E-F, 307.346 feet long, was measured three times with the steel tape, the greatest discrepancy being .003 feet. The horizontal angles at E, F, G, and B were measured by repetition and the vertical angles at

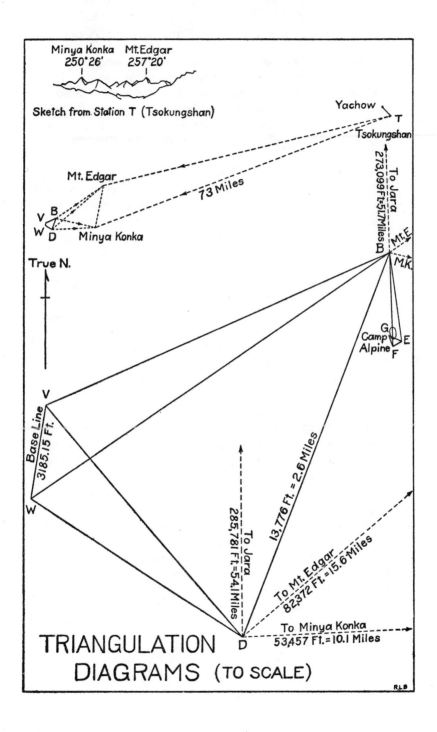

Minya Konka   Mt.Edgar
250°26'   257°20'

Sketch from Station T (Tsokungshan)

Yachow
T
Tsokungshan

Mt. Edgar

73 Miles

V B
W D   Minya Konka

To Jara
273,099 Ft.=51.7 Miles

Mt.E
B
M.K.

True N.

G
Camp   E
Alpine F

V

Base Line
3185.15 Ft.

13,776 Ft. = 2.6 Miles

To Jara
285,781 Ft.=54.1 Miles

W

To Mt. Edgar
82,372 Ft.=15.6 Miles

To Minya Konka
D   53,457 Ft. = 10.1 Miles

TRIANGULATION
DIAGRAMS (TO SCALE)

RLB

each point were observed several times. The calculation showed that Station B was 423.5 feet higher than Station G. The difference in elevation between B and D was computed directly, and also through V and W, the final result showing Station D to be 532.5 feet higher than Station B, or 956 feet higher than Station G. In all altitude computations the value .60 was used as the index of refraction.

The altitude of Minya Konka above Station G was found to be 9,963 feet, the calculations through B and D showing a discrepancy of 11.5 feet. Judging from the angles involved and from photographs taken on the summit, 5 feet seems the right amount to add to this figure for the height of the true crest above the point of tangency of our sights. This sum, 9,968 feet, added to 14,923 feet, the altitude of Station G, gives 24,891 feet (7,587 meters) as the altitude of Minya Konka above sea-level. We believe that the probable error of this result is about ±85 feet, and as a round figure call the altitude 24,900 feet, or 7,590 meters.

On November 28th I measured the vertical angles to Minya Konka and to Mount Edgar from the side of Tsokungshan overlooking Yachow (point T in the upper diagram). The resulting altitudes were both lower than those obtained at our survey camp by 262 feet and 177 feet, respectively. These results are based on our figure of 2,000 feet as the elevation of Yachow. Because of the distance (73 miles) and the uncertainty in the elevation of the instrument the only value attached to these observations is that of a rough check.

It may here be worth while to comment on the Szechenyi Expedition's figures for Minya Konka and Jara, as the figure for the former is nearly correct, and for the latter (7,800 meters or 25,592 feet) very much in error. The account of the determination, which was made by Lieutenant Kreitner, is contained in *Die Wissenschaftlichen Ergebnisse der Reise des Grafen Bela Szechenyi in Ostasien 1877-1880* (Vienna, 1893-1899). Describing his method, Kreitner says (as translated in the *Geographical Journal*, vol. 75, 1930, pp. 347-348):

... I determined the position of conspicuous peaks and summits of mountains and other prominent objects by compass bearings, and, as far as practicable, from several, or one other, similar bearings, plotted the angles graphically. I thus obtained a distance, within the possible limits of accuracy, for the fixed object from my position, in order to ascertain the relative difference of height by measuring the vertical angle. On a rapid journey on public roads, it is possible only occasionally to set up the theodolite, so a few only of the determined heights were measured with that instrument. I generally used for sighting the corners of my rectangular survey-box, on the reverse side of which I had constructed a quadrant with a 5° scale, or else the compass of the expedition's geologist, fitted with a contrivance for reading vertical angles.

In his table of altitudes Kreitner does not state whether the theodolite or the rougher instruments were used. Bo Kunka (Minya Konka) was measured from Dsongo, which is the Tibetan name for Yingkwanchai. Its elevation is given as 3482 meters, the distance to the mountain 16,000 meters, the vertical angle 14° 30′, and the resulting altitude 7655 meters, which is rounded off to 7600 meters. According to Heim's map the true distance is 55,500 meters. Kreitner's angle would therefore indicate an altitude of 18,100 meters! Using our altitude for Minya Konka and Heim's altitude (3500 meters) and distance for Yingkwanchai, the vertical angle there should be 4° instead of 14° 30′. As Kreitner's figures are consistent, there does not appear to be a typographical error, and the position on his map is in agreement with them. Misidentification suggests itself, but his sketch from Dsongo (p. 703) is obviously the same as Stevens' sketch from the same place. Stevens gives another sketch of Minya Konka in nearly the same aspect from Haja La. Here he had his back toward Kreitner's position of the mountain, which, according to Edgar, is occupied by "rolling downs with excellent pastures." Kreitner's measurement of Jara was made from Kashi La. Its elevation is given as 4474 meters, the distance to the mountain 33,000 meters, vertical angle 5° 35′, and resulting altitude 7774 meters, which is rounded off to

7800 meters. According to Heim, the true distance is 47,600 meters, and Kreitner's angle would indicate an altitude of 9400 meters. Using our altitude for Jara and Heim's altitude (4600 meters) and distance for the Kashi La, the vertical angle there should be 1° 23'.

DETERMINATION OF POSITION

While in camp we were unable to ascertain our position, because our wireless set had not arrived, the sun at noon was too high for observation with our transit, and at night we were always enveloped in cloud. We did, however, take time and azimuth observations from the sun, using an assumed position. As the position is now known, these sights have been reworked, and the four azimuth observations show a range of only 4' 34''. A single compass bearing taken with the transit showed a magnetic variation of 0° 36' W. Thirty-three bearings taken with a pocket compass at B showed variations of 38' E. to 1° 57' W., the mean of all being 53' W.

On our return journey we obtained the position of Yachow, using the John Ball adaptation of the Marc St. Hilaire method, observing six stars and taking six altitudes of each. The stars used were Benetnash, Arcturus, Spica, Sirius, Betelgeuse, and Capella. We consider that the location obtained from the six lines of position is correct within one-quarter of a mile. For the purpose of this observation, Moore obtained time signals by wireless, on a wave length of 33.8 meters, from Station NPO, Cavite, Philippine Islands. A good watch was used, and its rate was determined by a series of receptions before and after the observation.

From the side of Tsokungshan (point T in diagram) the angles were measured between Minya Konka, Mount Edgar, and a line to a point in Yachow. Later the direction of this line was determined by two sun azimuth observations, which agreed within one minute. The distance from the station on Tsokungshan to the point in Yachow was 12,300 feet measured roughly by stadia. Our work at Camp Alpine gave the distance from

Minya Konka to Mount Edgar and the direction of the line joining them. This, with the angle at Tsokungshan and the directions from there, allowing for convergence of meridians, gave sufficient data to solve the triangle and to compute the position of Minya Konka (see Table III). We consider the resulting location to be correct within one mile, and believe this to be the first instrumental determination of the latitude and longitude of Minya Konka.

INSTRUMENTS USED

Transit. Keuffel and Esser, reading to minutes with full vertical circle.

Steel tape, 100 feet long, tested after our return by the United States Bureau of Standards.

Mercurial barometer. Fortin type, loaned by the American Geographical Society. Its index error and that of the attached thermometer were determined by the Zikawei Observatory in Shanghai, before our departure for the interior.

Hypsometer, with two thermometers graduated to read pressure in millimeters of mercury. We compared the thermometers and found that they read the same. We compared the hypsometer with the barometer by ten simultaneous readings at Station G (Camp Alpine) and two at Tatsienlu. The hypsometer read low by amounts varying from .017″ to .074″, a range equivalent to 88 feet at Camp Alpine. The mean of the differences was .028″ and all hypsometer readings in the table have been corrected by this amount.

Sling psychrometer. Small size Tycos, used to take air temperatures simultaneously with barometric observations. This instrument was checked after our return by the U. S. Bureau of Standards.

Wireless. A short-wave, three tube receiving set was used for time signals.

TABLE II—TEMPERATURES RECORDED (1932)*

Place	Altitude	Date	Remarks	Temperature °F.
Station G............	14,923	Aug. 23	Minimum	29.5
Base Camp..........	14,415	Oct. 6	”	31
” ”	”	Oct. 14	”	20.5
” ”	”	Oct. 15	”	21
Camp I..............	18,000	Oct. 8	8:00 a.m.	15
”	”	Oct. 16	Minimum	14
Camp III............	20,700	Oct. 25	9:00 a.m.	5

* These were the only temperatures recorded in addition to those of the barometric observations. Using a gradient of 0.30° F. per 100 feet, the corresponding temperatures at the summit of Minya Konka would range from 0° to −11° F.

TABLE III—POSITIONS DETERMINED

Place	Latitude (N.)	Longitude (E.)
1. Yachow.....................	29° 59′ 38″	102° 58′ 55″
2. Minya Konka...............	29° 36′ 32″	101° 52′ 12″
3. Station B...................	29° 38′ 20″	101° 43′ 05″
4. Station G...................	29° 37′ 53″	101° 43′ 05″
5. Jara.......................	30° 23′ 22″	101° 41′ 26″
6. Tatsienlu (Approx.)..........	30° 03′ 30″	101° 58′ 50″
7. Tahsiangling Pass (Approx.)...	29° 38′ 44″	102° 37′ 40″

The first position (tennis court of Dr. R. L. Crook, American Baptist Mission, Yachow) was obtained from six stars and is considered correct within one quarter mile. The next four were derived from it by azimuths and triangulation and are probably correct within one mile. The last two may be two miles in error; that of Tatsienlu is based on topography shown on photograph from summit of Minya Konka and upon our route to the mountain; that of Tahsiangling Pass is based on pocket compass bearings to Minya Konka and neighboring peaks and photographs of them taken from the pass.

C. MOUNTAINEERING NOTES

By Arthur B. Emmons, 3rd

Equipment. A few words here may not be amiss as to the equipment used by the climbing party, both in the reconnaissance and in ascent of Minya Konka itself. Unfortunately, some of the equipment obtained in the United States was lost on arrival in the Orient, and we were forced to substitute for it as best we could from whatever resources Shanghai was able to provide.

High-altitude Tents. Makeshift ones had to be made in Shanghai, where, unfortunately, proper cloth was unavailable. These were constructed after the pattern of the Mount Logan type, 7′ x 7′ x 7′, pyramidal shaped with an eighteen inch wall, tunnel door, curtain type ventilator (we found it difficult to keep snow from sifting through), sewed-in floor, and jointed bamboo pole. White canvas used made these tents about eighteen pounds with pole—very much too heavy. We had two of this type which would hold four men. These tents did excellent service as high as 22,000 feet on an exposed ridge with constant terrific winds and zero temperature.

Two-man Tent, 5½′ x 7′ x 5′, pyramidal in shape, with an eight inch wall at the back, peak offset toward the door, tunnel door, sleeve-type ventilator (better adapted to high winds and drifting snow than the curtain type), sewed-in floor, and single-piece bamboo pole. This canvas was even heavier than on the larger type and was light green in color (more desirable for snow work than plain white because it is more easily seen against a white background and reduces the glare when one is inside). This tent weighed fourteen pounds with pole—far too heavy for two-man tent. This tent was primarily designed for the

271

reconnaissance and would hold two men comfortably or three in an emergency. It was ideal except for its weight. We had only one, and that was never taken above the 18,000-foot camp, due to its weight and small size.

Both the foregoing types were constructed to present a minimum of surface perpendicular to the direction of the wind, thus reducing the strain on the tent. We also found that there was less danger of ripping the cloth in a wind if the tent ropes were not pulled too tight, for, although there was much slapping at times, the strain was taken at a better mechanical advantage.

Sleeping-bags. Woods Arctic Senior Eiderdown sleeping-bags with zipper fastening (thus enabling the bag to be opened out flat—almost a necessity in a country like China or Tibet, where vermin are easily picked up, though, as a matter of fact, we were never thus troubled), and special eyelets to enable two bags to be opened out and laced together, thus forming one large bag. In this way two 90″ x 90″ sleeping-bags could be made to accommodate four men, thus obviating two sleeping-bags and their added weight when desirable, and two 78″ x 84″ would hold three men, obviating one bag. Our bags were in both sizes, 78″ x 84″ and 90″ x 90″, the latter being capable in an emergency of holding two men, as they did on several occasions. Having these two sizes gave us great latitude of arrangement and proved most valuable.

These sleeping-bags at altitudes up to 22,000 feet kept us comfortably warm when used with 3 x 4-foot air mattresses in a tent, in exposed situations with winds up to 100 miles an hour and temperatures running as low as −15° F. They were excellent and deserve the highest recommendation.

Primus stoves. Two types, the small- and large-base types. The small ones were nearly useless above 18,000 feet and caused us much trial and tribulation. The large ones, however, proved as remarkably efficient as their lengthy history on many previous arctic and mountain expeditions would seem to indicate. We used them as high as 22,000 feet, where they burned satis-

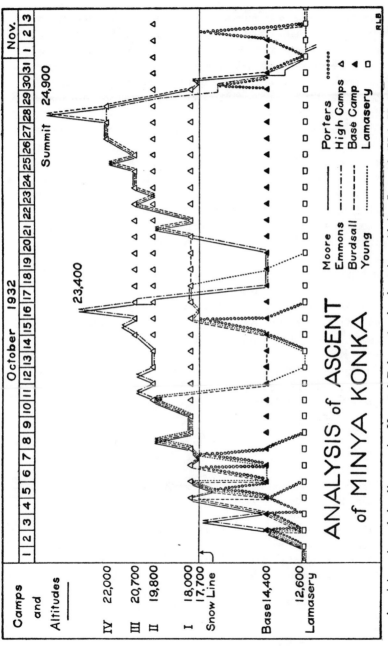

ANALYSIS of ASCENT
of MINYA KONKA

An elaboration of the diagram by Howard Palmer in the American Alpine Journal (Vol. II, No. I, 1933).
See photograph No. 43.

factorily. We found, however, that, contrary to a somewhat
general belief that at high altitudes gasoline would burn better
than kerosene, our experience showed just the opposite to be the
case. This may, however, have been somewhat due to the inferior grade of gasoline which we had acquired in western China.
A considerable quantity of Meta (patent) fuel was also used,
although this solid fuel necessarily made cooking much slower.

Instruments. The climbing party had two max.-min. thermometers which saw some service, but one at length was broken and
the other left at the base camp, so a small sling psychrometer
was used for temperature observations at the higher camps, although no complete record was kept, our energies being bent in
other directions. A hypsometer was carried as high as the
18,000-foot camp, but as there were many points in the vicinity
whose elevation had been previously determined by theodolite
in the course of the survey work, there was little trouble in
arriving at good estimates of our various positions, and this
instrument was taken no higher.

Cameras. Two 3¼" x 4¼" cameras, a Zeiss and a Kawee,
and one 2¼" x 3¼" Kawee were used with Verichrome film
packs. These cameras gave excellent service, except that the
larger Kawee developed a serious light leak.

Clothing. A list follows of what was worn at high altitudes
when conditions were at their worst. This list was subject to considerable variation, however.

    Three pairs long wool underwear
    One pair thin cotton socks (next to feet)
    Three pairs heavy wool socks
    Two pairs felt insoles
    One pair leather-top rubber boots (size 12 E)
    One light turtle-neck wool sweater
    One heavy flannel shirt
    One light wool sweater (on top)
    One pair wind-proof Gaberdine pants (ski pattern)
    Two wind-proof parkas
    One leather flying-helmet

Two pairs wool mittens
One pair leather over-mittens
One pair snow glasses
One leather wool-lined face-mask

It will be noticed that an effort was made throughout to keep each item light, the theory being that, for instance, two light sweaters were warmer than one heavy one. This idea seemed later justified by our experience with severe conditions at great altitudes.

High-altitude clothes and equipment were taken to supply three porters, but were not used. This included parkas, boots, socks, mittens, goggles, crampons, and ice axes similar to our own.

Wind-proof trousers were fine and were made very large to give freedom of action and included plenty of large pockets.

Wind-proof parkas by Beebe and Co., San Francisco, were excellent and were warm in the strongest winds. I used an additional parka with a fur-lined hood in which I found very great face protection in the sand-blast of ice particles we encountered, driven before the terrific gales of wind.

Snow glasses. We found that dark glass in snow glasses need not be overdone, the lighter tints being more in demand. In fact, on several occasions just plain glass was worn in full sunshine at 22,000 feet with no ill effects. The main thing, however, is to have the glass supported well away from the face to prevent undue fogging. Slit metal goggles were also tried, without great success. They were always carried, however, as a precaution in case the others were broken.

Mittens having removable linings were essential, as the combination could be taken apart and dried separately. As two pairs of these woolen mittens were worn at a time, one set was larger than the other and each size had a distinguishing color for identification. The same system of identification should be used for woolen socks. The thin leather over-mittens worn outside wet through quickly, but, more important, they also dried quickly, and hence were better than those of heavier leather. *Boots* were of the type made by L. L. Bean & Co. of Maine, and had a new and most excellent design, having flat heavily reinforced rubber soles instead of old rounded type, thus fitting snugly on to crampons. We had two sizes, twenty-five inches high and twelve inches high. The low variety were found preferable in this work. The insoles were removed every night and dried out to prevent freezing. Crampons were always worn with these boots when on snow.

Crampons were of the Eckenstein ten-point variety and were universally used in spite of a tendency to clog more than the eight point model in certain conditions of wet snow. We had no breakages, although they were several times used on stretches of bare rock.

A small rubber *hot water bottle* was carried by each man under his belt beneath a parka to keep it from freezing, providing drinking-water while on the climb during the day. This system worked admirably.

In addition to the above, each climber carried in his pocket a magnesium flare for emergency signaling at night. A small pocket first-aid kit was always at the highest camps, the main medical supplies being left at the base.

Willow wands were used on the upper ridge on open stretches, one every one hundred feet, to serve as trail marks in case of storms or clouds reducing visibility.

FOOD

In general there was little to differentiate the food used in the higher camps from that of any similar mountaineering expedition. It ran largely to dried items such as fruits (figs, dates, apricots, etc.), dried soups, milk, and so on, a quantity of which had been brought unopened from Shanghai. These items were supplemented by local produce such as yak butter and cheese, Chinese bread and mein (noodles). One rather interesting local product which we found not only palatable, but very sustaining, was tsamba (parched barley flour), which required only the addition of boiling water. Malted milk, both the tablets and the drink, and sweet chocolate found great favor. Our hot-water-bottle canteens were usually filled with sweetened lemonade made from lemonade powder, thus not only mitigating the flat taste of the snow water and more effectively quenching the thirst, but also yielding valuable energy in the form of sugar when it was most needed.

Our appetites in general became lax, due to the altitude, and eating was more of a duty than a pleasure. Certain things became extremely tiresome, such as oatmeal, and all of us were united in disclaiming this particular dish, although we continued to eat it for its food value.

On the whole our menu could have been more varied and would have been enhanced by the addition of a greater number of specially prepared foods. Our diet, while it at times grew tedious, nevertheless kept us energetic and in good health under rather abnormal and trying conditions.

FROSTBITE

It may be of interest to some to append here a short discussion of cause and effect in cases of high-altitude frostbite. This type of frostbite is especially insidious because its attack is apt to come on unannounced. There are several reasons for this subtlety. First, at great heights the mental perception of the mountaineer is much reduced through lack of sufficient oxygen. Therefore the initial stages of frostbite may set in unnoticed.

Secondly, where a man's attention and energies are so completely concentrated on the problems confronting him in attaining his objective, and where physical discomfort and hardship are taken as a matter of course, small attention is often paid to minor ailments such as the loss of sensation of one or two toes, unless a man is more than casually awake to the danger at hand.

Thirdly, few people realize the profundity of the physiological changes which take place at great elevations. The *laissez-faire*

278 MEN AGAINST THE CLOUDS

attitude of mind is one very easily conceived up there, and a man, if he has faith in the suitability of his clothes and equipment, is apt to assume that he is safe, an assumption which is seldom justified.

Although we were constantly alive to the danger of frostbite and were continually on guard against it, in my case there is little question that my feet were frozen for the three days at 22,000 feet without my having perceived the fact.

I attribute my lack of perception to a number of factors. First, after getting my feet unpleasantly cold on October 26th after establishing Camp IV, I massaged them until the circulation and sensation had apparently completely returned, without, however, removing *all* my socks. Therein I believe lay my fatal mistake—in not *seeing* as well as feeling that the feet had returned to normal. One of the primary factors which differentiate high-altitude frostbite from that at lower elevations and renders it so much more deadly is that of the increased viscosity of the blood due to the lack of oxygen, and hence a reduction of circulation. High-altitude frostbite, once initiated, rapidly compounds itself, and even when circulation is reëstablished, there is very little revival in the affected tissue, compared with that at low-altitude.

Secondly, I was misled by my apparent security while at Camp IV during the ascent. I wore three pairs of heavy loose wool socks, inside an eiderdown sleeping-bag of great warmth, in turn inside a tent where, at least while the stove was going, the air could not have been much below freezing. The frostbite most probably started before reaching Camp IV and was fostered by my inactivity there. The feet could not have frozen after abandoning the high camp on October 29th, for the 29th was comparatively warmer than usual, and on descending, the circulation is, if anything, enhanced by the increased activity.

I had been living for over five weeks on the snow, and the continued cold and altitude may have induced a chronically poor circulation which needed just a small initial activity to start the frostbite cycle. From Burdsall's experience on the summit, it may be seen how a severe frostbite can develop in only a few seconds of exposure to high winds at great elevations where circulation is poor.*

A further consideration is possible. During the three days I spent in the tent at Camp IV, the Primus stove was kept going for considerable intervals. The tent was purposely constructed of non-wind-proof material to insure good ventilation. In addition, when the stove was going the door or ventilator was kept open whenever the weather outside made such a measure at all endurable.

Despite these precautions, it may have been possible that, due to the low oxygen content of the air, although the stove apparently burned perfectly, a certain amount of carbon monoxide gas was generated. The amount could not have been great, because we felt none of the usual symptoms of monoxide poisoning such as headaches or dizziness. There may have been enough, however, to induce a chronic poisoning to the point where, augmented by a general oxygen-lack, a partial asphyxiation set in; hence the inception of frostbite, or at least the aggravation of any tendency towards it which may have been acquired prior to reaching Camp IV. This would be brought about by the monoxide reducing the capacity of the available oxygen-carriers in the blood under circumstances where they were already scarcely capable of properly supporting metabolism.

If breathed over a period of some hours, carbon monoxide can become dangerous to life if present in air containing only 0.1 per cent. In air of less than one-half the usual density it need only be present to the extent of 0.05 per cent of the original total volume. Carbon monoxide has approximately two hundred times the affinity of oxygen for combining with the hæmoglobin of the blood.

In this connection it is interesting to note that by one of the latest theories, the disaster of the Andrée Arctic Expedition of 1897 was brought about through carbon monoxide poisoning produced by a Primus stove in an improperly ventilated tent

* "A sixty mile wind at 0° F. feels colder and does more damage than a fifteen-mile wind at —30° or a calm at —50°."—Steffansson, *My Life with the Esquimo.*

after the balloon in which they were attempting to cross the Pole had been forced down.

Yet, I wore exactly the same clothes, the same size of boots, and the same number of socks as the other men. I took the precautions they did of drying out socks and insoles every night to get rid of perspiration moisture—a well-recognized cause of freezing. I was in fully as good condition physically as either of them on October 27th. Here again I was misled by a feeling of false security, believing that, as they were all right, I must be equally so.

The freezing of my feet may not have anything to do with the cut in my hand, as has been suggested, though had I not become a "noncombatant," I should probably have discovered my condition sooner.

It is interesting to note in this connection that one of the Sherpa porters on the Rutledge Everest Expedition of 1933 froze his entire hand without knowing it. It was saved only through administering oxygen to him for an entire night, in itself an innovation in frostbite treatment.

TREATMENT

A word as to the treatment of frostbite once it has been discovered. Contrary to a common fallacy, rubbing snow on the affected area is decidedly contraindicated.*

Frozen tissue is delicate in the first place, and when rubbed with some rough substance, such as snow, is easily torn and bruised. Furthermore, the aim is to thaw out the frozen part slowly, so of what use is it to apply snow, which itself is below the freezing point and only leads to further loss of heat? A rhythmic massage of the portion above the affected area is excellent, but direct rubbing of the frozen zone is to be avoided.

Excessive heat should never be applied, but rather a gradual thawing process should be induced; otherwise the damage may

---

* "Naturally we had learned from Steffansson that the sane thing to do when we were frostbitten was simply to warm up the affected part— never, never to accentuate the condition by rubbing snow on it."— Laurence Gould, *Cold*.

be increased. The frostbite should be allowed to correct itself as much as possible.

When I discovered the damage I did not rub snow on the feet, but massaged the ankle above the frozen area and replaced my boots. Unfortunately in my case, I was forced to walk a considerable distance, which no doubt aggravated my condition, and later, when I had to spend a night out in the snow, the frostbite may have recurred.

Upon reaching the base camp on the second day, I kept the feet well away from the fire, soaked them for intervals of twenty minutes in water just above the freezing point, and kept them supported as high as possible to aid the return of circulation.

The grave danger in frostbite, and that which caused us so much haste in trying to reach a doctor, is that of infection setting in when gangrene develops. Had we known it, however, the danger was not as imminent as we suspected. We might have spared ourselves much of the exhaustion and exposure engendered by our hasty retreat to Tatsienlu, an exposure which may well have caused an even more extended injury to the feet, for it was not until two weeks after the initial injury that the danger of infection became patent.

It is well to remember then, that once frostbite has set in, there is but little that can be done, save to get the man down to lower altitudes as fast as possible, taking especial care to keep the frostbite from advancing, which it will do far more easily upon a second exposure. Medical aid should be obtained as soon as possible, but not, as in our case, to the further detriment of the condition.

New and startling results have been obtained in frostbite and gangrene cases by the administration of oxygen gas and by a new type of pressure pump now being experimented with.

It is seldom, however, that a mountaineer can readily avail himself of the apparatus that such treatments require. Prevention is by far the best cure, and on a high mountain one can never be too careful in guarding against this insidious foe.

ALTITUDE AND ACCLIMATIZATION

NOTE: The factor upon which the efficiency curve is based is an arbitrary one derived from the rate of climb, fatigue, sleep, and general physical efficiency at the altitudes indicated. It shows tendencies rather than a definite physical condition. It is based upon my personal observations and as much as possible upon the reactions of my companions. The nature and scope of these observations is necessarily very limited and the graph is included here for general interest rather than for any scientific value which may attach to it.

In the early stages of the campaign it will be seen how steeply the curve descends for a given increase in altitude as against the same change in altitude later on when our acclimatization was more perfect. The recovery part of the curve is correspondingly abrupt, showing a more rapid readjustment than later on. This readjustment carried over to the later phases of the campaign.

The curve for the high climbs of October 16th and 28th may at first seem inconsistent until it is remembered that on these two occasions we climbed without loads.

A marked reduction in efficiency is apparent from the date of our occupation of Camp IV. This decline is due not so much to the increase in altitude as to the fact that about this point symptoms of altitude deterioration began to be felt. No one point can be said to mark the beginning of this phase for any one individual, though this period was characterized in general by a decidedly increased loss of appetite and energy and by gastric disturbances, though breathing did not seem correspondingly more difficult.

Again, during the descent on October 29th-30th, though badly exhausted by altitude and exposure, we felt a surprising gain in physical and mental well-being as a lower level was reached. My own experience was that by the time I reached the snow-line at 17,000 feet, even though my frostbite was causing con-

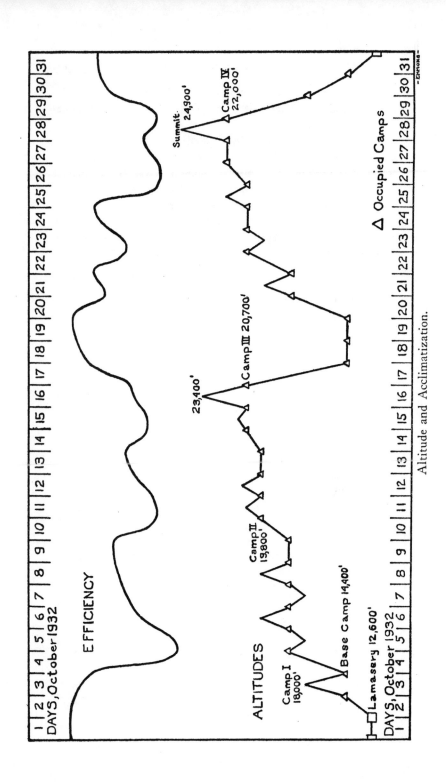

Altitude and Acclimatization.

siderable pain, the whole complexion of life took on a new and brighter hue not entirely attributable to the successful completion of our campaign.

The question has been often raised as to why we used no oxygen in climbing Minya Konka. The answer is that we relied solely upon the slower and perhaps more positive method, that of gradual readjustment to the severe conditions of oxygen deficiency at high altitudes. Oxygen as a physical aid to climbing has, for the present at least, been largely discredited. The increasing tendency seems to be, even on Everest, to rely solely upon acclimatization, and to carry oxygen only for medicinal use.

Epilogue

LAST SEARCH

by Terris Moore

A LONG succession of unforeseeable, world-shaking
events have receded into history since that day, in the
simpler world of March 1930, when Allen Carpé first called
my attention to "Mount Koonka 30,000?" and started us on
our search for a mountain higher than Everest. Of the ten of
us, only Jack Young and I survive, both at the biblical three
score and ten. In the pages that follow I relate the later lives
and fates of my companions, my recurring encounters with
Minya Konka memories—and the curious denouement of
our search for the world's highest mountain.

In mid-May, 1932—even before our expedition had departed Shanghai for the interior—my inspiring friend Allen
Carpé perished in Alaska at around ten thousand feet on
Mount McKinley's Muldrow Glacier. A noted scientist as
well as America's leading climber, in death he became
immediate page one news at the *New York Times*. We read
the cabled account on the front page of Shanghai's daily
English language newspaper. Allen had fallen into a
treacherous crevasse from which his body could not be
recovered. He was engaged, not in mountaineering, but in
cosmic ray research on his Carnegie grant for Dr. Arthur H.
Compton of the University of Chicago. (At that time a wide

In Cambridge, 1933: Moore, Burdsall, Emmons, and Young

program of investigations of cosmic rays at high elevations in different parts of the earth was centered under Compton.)

Years later we learned that the cosmic ray observations and measurements, made at so tragic a cost, had remained in Carpé's scientific notebooks in a lonely little tent at 11,000 feet at the head of Muldrow Glacier, rapidly becoming snowed up and in danger of disappearing forever. Because these were the only data of this particular kind that had ever been recorded, on a subject of great interest to the scientific world, an expedition was promptly organized for their recovery.

Subsequently the organizer of that expedition received a letter from Professor Compton that read: "... the cosmic ray datum obtained by Carpé and Koven [the assistant whose body had been found face down upon the glacier] in their measurements on Mount McKinley seems to be of unusual interest. It represents the only high altitude value of cosmic rays that is available at latitudes so far north. Contrary to the results obtained at lower levels [a control station had been simultaneously operated at the Kennecott railhead, a similar latitude], the intensity at that altitude seems to increase as we go north of the United States. This would indicate, if correct, that there are in the cosmic rays particles which are prevented by action of the earth's magnetic field from striking the earth at lower latitudes, an important point in connection with our theory of the nature and origin of these rays."

Film found in their cameras, recovered with the scientific records, shows Carpé in the foreground viewing a magnificent unnamed peak nearby to the east; this has since been measured as 12,550 feet high and permanently named Mount Carpé.

———

1934. Mao Tse-tung and his revolutionaries fought their way west—from the area on our 1932 frontispiece map marked "Communists shooting at the boats"—and controlled all approaches to the Chinese-Tibetan border ranges. Keeping south of the Yangtze, they finally were able to cross that river and turned north along the west bank of the Tung river. A key battle took place at Lutingchiao (our Tatsienlu-Yachow Region map page 236), "The Town of the Iron Chain Bridge" (pages 41 and 231-232), where the capture of this bridge greatly enlarged his opportunities.

Here Mao wrote a poem about the "snows of Minya" seen to the west; from this point on he fought his way along both sides of the torrent that he renamed the Ta Tu (Big Battle) River, and so north to Yenan and the caves where he headquartered. A small battle with the fiercely independent Ngolok Tibetan tribes to the west around the Amne Machin range, in which machine guns quickly settled the issue, promptly brought that region under Mao's control.

During World War II, American aircraft flights "over the Hump," where spectacular Minya Konka could at times be seen to the north, occasionally provoked newspaper accounts in the United States about pilots encountering "a mountain higher than Everest." But to the cognoscenti, either the pilots were "pulling the reporters' legs" for a spoof, or possibly a new pilot, coming out of a cloud and unexpectedly encountering Minya Konka, was suffering from oxygen starvation and was not quite sure whether his early-type Kollsman altimeter (in those years with pointers only for hundreds and thousands) was reading twenty-thousand-plus or thirty-thousand-plus.

After our 1932 ascent and publication of our complete 360° photographic panorama from the summit of Minya Konka, international cartographers in New York, London, Paris, and Zurich no longer had any doubt: Minya Konka is certainly the highest for at least a hundred miles around. Uncertainty still continued, however, about Pereira's and Rock's Amne Machin range some 200 miles to Minya Konka's north. For none of the World War II reports from flying over the Hump could have described the Amne Machin range, that far away on the *other* side of Minya Konka.

Of the several post-World War II expeditions that set out

to explore the Amne Machin, the first to publish and settle the question of its height was the flying expedition of Mr. Moon Chin, a Chinese pilot and small airline owner based in Shanghai, during the summer of 1948, a year before the Communist takeover. *Life* magazine invited consultants, of whom I was one, to evaluate the results that had been sent them for publication.

The startling photographs of Minya Konka's unmistakable shape—which I recognized immediately—anchored the rest of their account. Flying a large modern-cabin pressurized aircraft, with the navigator clearly knowing his position throughout, pilot Moon Chin flew the Minya Konka altitude of approximately 25,000 feet along the border ranges and right through the location of the Amne Machin range on a crystal clear day.

High glaciated mountains there were. But nothing within thousands of feet of Minya Konka's height. Cartography, geology, ethnology, and all the rest of ground-based exploration still to do: but no peaks "rivalling Everest in height" to discover. Great snow-capped mountains, "seen from a high pass at about 16,000 feet and rising much higher," can be most inspiring—as they were to Brigadier General Pereira and Dr. Rock—but are these mountains really a hundred miles away, or perhaps only fifty? Measuring the same vertical angle at that point, their exact distance away makes all the difference!

———

What about our original companions, Gene Lamb, Mrs. Lamb, and Major Logan: did they ever make it to the Amne Machin range and the Tibetan Ngolok tribes reported by

Dr. Rock, their primary interest? We think not, but really have little information. No published accounts of their travels, after (to our regret) they left us in Peking in early 1932, seem to have ever appeared. Their records at the Explorers Club end inconclusively in the middle 1930s, a time of great social turbulence for everyone. (During this time the Club itself, through a mortgage foreclosure, lost its original Clubhouse at 110th Street and Cathedral Parkway and later experienced yet a second move from rented quarters before finally settling into its present owned location.) Shortly after World War II a brief obituary notice appeared, without details, recording that Gene Lamb had died in China.

———

The next event for us, in this long half century, was the tragic, dramatic loss of Lewis Thorne in 1950. A successful medical student at Johns Hopkins, Lewy next specialized in psychiatry and engaged in practice as a staff psychiatrist at Yale University. He became a trustee of Yale-in-China, visiting China again shortly after World War II before the Maoists took Peking. Over lunch in Cambridge, Massachusetts, following his return, Lewy described to us his view that Mao's people were really just "harmless agrarian reformers, carrying out necessary reforms long overdue." He had been conferring with John Paton Davies and John Carter Vincent, State Department officials, and was in accord with their views – not shared by Jack Young! In New Haven a year later, Lewy found it necessary to have a certain student patient committed, who subsequently was released as harmless to others. The former student soon

sought out Lewy at home, shot him dead upon his own
doorstep, and gravely wounded his wife.

Dick Burdsall, a lifelong bachelor, returned from Minya
Konka to continue his career as a civil engineer at Port
Chester, New York. He was a member of the Society of
Friends (the only Quaker among us) and resumed his in-
terest in the service work of his church. Greatly respected
by his contemporaries in the small climbing fraternity of the
day, he served for years as treasurer of the American Alpine
Club.

Six years after Minya Konka Dick was a very welcome
member of the First American Karakoram Expedition, in
1938, which made an attempt on K2. Twenty years after
Minya Konka he was eager to become a member of the
1953 attempt and served very capably for some months as
expedition treasurer. The twentieth anniversary of our
Minya Konka expedition—October 28, 1952—fell during
this period. In Fairbanks, just after I had concluded my il-
lustrated lecture to a handful of mountaineering students at
the University of Alaska I was handed a telegram from New
York, signed "Burdsall and Emmons." It read: WE
COULD STILL DO IT COULD YOU? An amusing
whimsy, I thought, and I do not remember my reply.

But Dick evidently shared the sentiment; he was not too
old for the highest mountain in South America. Dick
successfully reached the near-23,000-foot summit of Mount
Aconcagua in Feburary 1953—the second North American
to do so. According to his biographer, Dick exhausted
himself in rescue efforts for an Argentine party then on the

mountain, and, quite simply, expired at about 21,000 feet while descending.

A bare-facts, conflicting account of the episode appeared in the March 3, 1953, issue of *The Standard*, an English-language Buenos Aires newspaper. The conflict still exists, unresolved.

ANDES TRAGEDY
How Mr. Burdsall Met His Death

Sr. Jorge Washington Flores of the Club Andinista Mendoza, who served as a guide to Mr. Richard Burdsall, the North American engineer who died after reaching the summit of Aconcagua, has given some details of the occurrence.

He said that he left Mendoza on February 11 with Burdsall and Miss Gwendolyn Foster and three days later they were at Plaza de Mulas. By February 16 they had reached an altitude of 6,000 metres and Burdsall apparently was already feeling the effects of the rarified air. The following day they reached an altitude of 6,600 metres and late in the afternoon reached the Juan Jose refuge where they found Cesar Fara and Leonardo Rapicarelli of the Club Alpino Italiano. These two were in a rather bad state of health. The five of them decided to try and reach the summit next day but due to bad weather had to postpone the ascent until February 20. They set out in spite of a strong wind and at 0500 the group was at the foot of the 'canaleta' at an altitude of 6,900 metres. First of all, the two Italians tried to reach the top and then Flores and Burdsall did the same, reaching their objective at 2100 the same day. The two Italians and the American were completely exhausted so Flores had to return to the refuge and prepare some food and hot drinks for his companions.

When Flores returned with the food, he found that the three men had disappeared. He started to look for them and went down to 6,700 metres where he fell asleep from exhaustion. He awoke at dawn and continued his search for Burdsall and the two Italians. He found the last two as they were descending with great difficulty, being almost blinded by the snow which had been whipped by the wind against their eyes. He took them down to Plaza de Mulas and then returned to look for Burdsall. He found him at an altitude of 6,300 metres and took the American down. Burdsall died just before being taken by mule to Puente del Inca.

———

My next encounter with Minya Konka memories occurred on December 9, 1957, a curious event that may be traced in pages of *The Alpine Journal* (London), with overtones that continue to this day. The unexpected setting for it was the occasion of the one hundredth anniversary of the founding of the Alpine Club, the oldest mountaineering club in the world. In the nineteenth century Queen Victoria had taken a publicly critical, thoroughly negative view of alpinism, especially after the 1865 disaster on the Matterhorn.

But by the fiftieth anniversary of the Club's founding, in 1907, she was gone and attitudes were changing; ex-President Theodore Roosevelt attended that anniversary's social event, representing Americans. Queen Elizabeth II and her husband Prince Philip, however, are enthusiasts; they had recognized and much appreciated the Hillary-Tenzing first ascent of Mount Everest in 1953 at the time of her coronation. It was announced that for the Centenary there would be a Royal Reception in the Great Hall of Lincoln's Inn. Along with the few other American members of the Alpine Club, I received my invitation and flew over to attend. Because at that time Minya Konka was still the highest mountain climbed by Americans, John Case, then president of the American Alpine Club, was invited to present me to Her Majesty as she progressed around the Hall.

Just at this moment, while we were all standing around in white tie and tails awaiting her arrival, an English member spoke to me: "Dr. Moore, what are you saying to the Chinese?"

"Well, I've read briefly that they climbed Minya Konka in June of this year but have not yet written them because I've not yet seen their account."

"Then you haven't yet read what they've written about you?"

... Thus I learned that a brief piece from China had just appeared in a Swiss mountaineering publication implying that the Chinese had made the first ascent in 1957 because on Minya Konka's summit they could find no rock cairn or other evidence of our visit of twenty-five years earlier!

Next morning in the clubhouse library in South Audley Street, Tom Blakeney, technical assistant to the editor of *The Alpine Journal,* began: "I seem to remember your party published a complete overlapping photo-panorama taken from the summit of Minya Konka. Can you locate it here in the library?" I could, of course, and did. "Here in our book *Men Against the Clouds"* – I handed him the London edition – "it's opposite page 180. But the best reproduction of our summit photography is found in the French journal *La Montagne,* Paris, October 1934 – 'La Premiere Ascension du Minya Konka,'" I added, handing him the latter also.

He intently examined the summit pictures, and I can still see the quizzical expression slowly spreading across his face as I pointed out: "The summit is a snow-covered small glacier cap, which at that altitude of course never melts; the nearest reachable rock outcrop is way back down the climbing route. And you may be sure that after we'd finally done the summit panorama photography with time barely left to make it safely to camp before dark, it never remotely crossed our minds that on the way back down we should try to pry up rocks at the outcrop, to take back up again for a cairn to set on that glacier cap snow! *Any* object left there would surely disappear completely in a few years; and who's likely to be visiting that place again for decades? Well, I'm now looking forward to seeing *their* summit photography — 360-degree panorama like ours — *plus* the rock cairn their summit party has erected there!"

Most eagerly did Art Emmons, Jack Young, and I await their detailed accounts, especially their photography. When these did appear we carefully studied the eleven photographs and fifty-six pages of English text, by a Peking translator over Shih Chan-chun's name. The first ten of these photographs were immediately identifiable as unquestionably the same photogenic places we also had visited, up through to the top of the 20,500-foot Hump — but none beyond that. No photograph of their high camp, nor of the summit party on the final 4,400 feet of climbing ridge; and the eleventh picture, titled "At The Summit" in one account and "Atop Minya Konka At Last" in another, merits careful comparison with our own summit photographs. Their single picture (much less any 360-degree panorama) reveals no horizon in the background, nor indeed any other mountain or mountain features; behind the climbers only sky, and in the foreground only snow, with nothing remotely resembling a rock cairn!

During the ensuing years until Art Emmons died in 1962,

he, Jack Young, and I fully discussed the details of the
photographs and accounts of the 1957 Chinese expedition
and the controversy in the international mountaineering
journals that the Chinese-published accounts generated for a
while.

My opinion has often been asked about the Chinese
climb, especially about the probable location of their famous
five-star-red-flag photograph "Atop Minya Konka." No
photographs in their published collection can be identified
beyond the 20,500-foot Hump—specifically, that is, to com-
pare with our #53, The Hump—Looking Back Across the
Gap; or with our #60, Camp IV—Nochma; or with our #63
and #62 summit photography. But we accept their claim to
have reached the summit of Minya Konka, despite the
absence of such photographic proof, because we suppose
that all their high-altitude pictures were lost with the bodies
of the three members of their summit party, who are described as falling to their deaths.

The motives as well as the success of our 1932 Minya
Konka expedition were also challenged by the Maoists. In
their fifty-four-page book *The Conquest of Minya Konka,*
published by the Foreign Languages Press of Peking in
1959, the following appears: "Let us take a look at the
American explorers.... According to their report, they
spent three months in conquering this high mountain, the
like of which cannot be found on any other continent. They
claimed that Moore and Burdsall reached the summit where
they planted the American flag amidst a violent snowstorm
and that the flag was left there as evidence of America's
success in distant conquest.... It is regrettable that we were
unable to discover any traces left by the Americans on
top.... It remained for our youthful mountaineering party—

the All-China Trade Union Mountaineering Party, in June 1957, to triumphantly conquer this world-famous peak, and eradicate the blank spot on the map of the motherland."

Initially I expressed surprise to Young and Emmons over these factual misstatements about us: that Burdsall and I reached the summit "amidst a violent snowstorm," when in fact we reported clear weather and our summit photography confirms it; that we had left an American flag planted, when we had left nothing; and that our motive was "America's success in distant conquest," when in fact we *first* flew and photographed the national emblem of the Republic of China in salute and recognition of the sovereignty of the Government that had extended us its official permission and given us financial support via its "ullah" transportation subsidy. This unique summit photograph had been widely published in China at the time.

But Young and Emmons, pointing to the inside title page, observed: "You're not reading the words of *Shih Chan-Chun*, the leader of the expedition who is listed as the book's author. What you're reading are the words of *translator Huang Kai-Ping*, who, if you check the names of the climbers, apparently was not even on the mountain with them. You're reading what the Foreign Languages Press in Peking, in the year 1959, wants the readers of its book in English to believe. You and Dick committed the crime in 1932 of putting up the wrong flag: the one that's now in exile on Taiwan!"

By this time the mountaineering editors had long since read all the Chinese Minya Konka reports and had re-examined our 1932 summit photographs; American and West European editors fully accepted our account. A London editor had written, as far back as November 1958:

"... Indeed the tables have now been turned, for although Terris Moore is quoted in *Appalachia* as accepting the ascent by the Chinese party, doubts are introduced [about the Chinese] over the burying of a container under a stone cairn, since the Americans found no rocks within one thousand feet of the summit...." After that, Chinese accounts omit any reference to a stone cairn: in 1959 the Peking translator has their leader saying (page 39 of *The Conquest of Minya Konka*): "... I inserted into a tin can a record of our ascent and *buried it in the snow*." (Italics supplied!)

In early 1962, while on a consulting mission in Washington, D.C., I stayed the night with Art and Evie Emmons at their pleasant home. Art had reached the top echelon in our State Department, Class I, qualifying him for ambassadorial rank. He had just been diagnosed as having cancer, but at this point it was thought to be controllable. We enjoyed a happy evening together and indeed casually talked about the possibility of their starting to build a retirement home on an island near our summer place in Maine that they had visited in 1960 and 1961.

That evening, perhaps contemplating the possibility that he might lose his struggle with cancer, Emmons said: "In case anything happens to me, do you know about Eduard Imhof and his mapping?"

My reply was, "Well, I remember that a year or two before we arrived in China, the Sun Yat Sen University of Canton sent out an expedition with government support, with purposes very much like our own. They had engaged three Swiss surveyors, with two Chinese graduate students, to map the Minya Konka region, but had very bad luck with the weather. And I remember that in 1932, when we were reorganizing after the Lamb expedition fell apart, their work was one reason for our turning away from the Amne Machin to Minya Konka as our objective. Dr. Arnold Heim, their leader, later wrote a book in which he used the spelling Minya Gongkar; and in 1933 he sent each of us a copy of it with a pleasant inscription. But their figure for the height of the mountain was several hundred feet higher than ours, wasn't it?"

Art replied: "True; but when Dick Burdsall visited them in Switzerland, he found that because of their difficulties with weather, they came to regard our data as superior and accepted our altitude for Minya Konka in preference to their own. They, however, had made route surveys where we had not gone, and Heim had circumambulated the whole range, which we of course never did, providing further route survey data. We, on the other hand, had the high altitude photography that they did not.

"So Imhof's idea was to fit the two sets of data together, using the best from each, and come out with a still more complete and more accurate map of this last important blank spot on the map of Asia. I've been expecting the Sun Yat Sen University to publish it. But what with the Japanese occupation during World War II, and then the Communist revolution and the University fleeing to Taiwan, I guess they've had more important projects than this one!

"But the point is that if Imhof ever published such a map, he would incidentally be proving independently beyond any doubt that you and Dick had taken our summit photographs from the very top of Minya Konka. The Swiss had the most modern of photo-theodolites, more accurate even than our Keuffel & Esser transit. To integrate their survey triangles with ours they resected the angles between the other peaks in the range that appear beneath the horizon in yours and

Dick's 360-degree summit photographic panorama. In this way they could and did prove that our summit pictures could only have been taken from the very top of Minya Konka."

I returned to New England and my consulting work; but six months later I received an urgent message from Orville Emmons that said: "My brother's cancer has become terminal.... He fully understands his situation; and very much hopes you can come down to Washington for a farewell visit."

Next day at Emmons's home again, this duty became the most poignant, the most strangely moving experience of my life, because of his remarkable calm and composed manner. I promptly recognized the same gallant, courageous spirit with whom thirty years earlier, for three days and two nights, in the open where darkness happened to catch us, I had ridden horseback from the base of Minya Konka back to Tatsienlu. Then he had been tortured by the excruciating pain of frozen feet thawing out, jolted by our riding, and we had had no means whatever to deaden it. Now there was little or no pain but instead the overwhelming certainty that at 3 p.m., the time set for me to go, it would be goodby forever. Numb with sorrow, I left the choice of conversation to him.

Not until days later did I really begin to think about what we discussed. We mused about the importance of that year in China to our later lives. The greatest influence had been upon his own; the least, among the four of us, upon mine. He had started at Harvard as an engineering student; but from our China experience his interest had moved to diplomacy, and some years after graduation he had entered the State Department's Foreign Service School.

Initially he had been balked by the regulation that individuals with his walking disability (he had lost all his toes from frostbite) could not be accepted into the Foreign Service. But he pointed out that the country's then highest ranking foreign service officer, Franklin D. Roosevelt, was even more crippled, a polio victim in a wheelchair, and this was not deemed sufficiently incapacitating to interfere with *his* diplomatic duties!

Perhaps the fact that Art had been an active member of the 1936 British-American Himalayan Expedition that made the first ascent of 25,645-foot Nanda Devi (then the highest peak climbed) helped persuade the admissions officers. (He could not be in the summit party, though he had specially made short boots.)

Thereafter followed an interesting career with many foreign assignments, including Canada, China, Korea, Uruguay, Spain, Australia, Ireland, and Malaya. He was in the American Consulate in Seoul, Korea, at the time of Pearl Harbor, and while interned in Tokyo witnessed the Doolittle Raid from his place of detention. Following this, he said his Japanese captors' attitude became noticeably more polite! He was repatriated on the *S.S. Gripsholm* with Ambassador Grew and returned again after the war as Political Advisor to the Commanding General occupying South Korea. During the Korean War he was Officer-in-Charge of Korean Affairs at the State Department, Washington; from this he was finally promoted to Deputy Chief, Southwest Pacific Affairs.

At last, when three o'clock arrived, Art got up and escorted me outside the door. He offered his hand, and in a perfectly calm voice said: "Goodby, Terry; thank you for coming down. It's going to be a little rough now." I was speechless, gripping his hand, unable to let go; finally I turned and walked away. At the corner I looked back. He was still standing there; we both waved. I walked out of sight into the side street, tears coursing down my cheeks.

———

Minya Konka memories continued to emerge. In December 1967, I received a letter from Dr. Fouad Al Akl in Brooklyn. He had returned to the United States from China in 1932 by continuing on around the world and then quickly resumed his medical career. We had met once during World War II: a very brief encounter in Washington, D.C. In the post-war years he had developed a substantial practice in the Egyptian-American community about New York and had produced several medical research publications.

Now his letter said: "Is it conceivable that after living together on the Tai Ping Yang, then with Gene Lamb and Major Logan, that we can ever forget one another? For years I have looked for your address to inquire where I could find a copy of the book you wrote when you tried to reach MaChin Shan via the Yangtze River, and only recently I found your address at the Explorers Club. Will you please remember our private phone [giving the number] when you come to town. Peggy and I would love to see you. Always faithfully, Fouad."

I of course promptly sent an inscribed copy of *Men Against the Clouds*—he had not yet made the switch from the Amne Machin—and we enjoyed a pleasant correspondence, with every expectation that we would meet and reminisce. But fate decreed otherwise: before this could come about, he had died.

———

I remember Jack Young in so many essential roles on our Minya Konka expedition that is is difficult to know which was the most important. Without him we could never have made more than a tourist visit to Shanghai, Peking, and perhaps a European missionary post or two in Szechwan province and the Tibetan border. But beyond his essentiality to us he should be seen in perspective, historically, as the first modern Chinese mountain explorer: reaching twenty thousand feet while doing his share in establishing his expedition's camp there. Viewed in this way, Jack Young's life will long be remembered by those interested in exploration mountaineering in China and Tibet.

Jack was born in the Hawaiian Islands of Chinese parentage and brought up from age two in Canton, the scion of an old and very well-connected Chinese family. Supporters of Sun Yat-sen (leader of the Han, true Chinese, revolution of 1911 that finally overthrew the centuries-long Manchu imperialism), they were disappointed in the ensuing "warlord" regime in north China, which seemed to worsen following that leader's death in 1925. Consequently Jack, at seventeen, was operating as a zealous clandestine "agit-prop" agent behind warlord lines during the 1927 military drive north by Sun Yat-sen's followers; Chiang Kai-shek and his Wellesley graduate wife were their leaders.

In the brief open-society period for China that followed, Jack—recommended by the Chinese Legation in Washington—was invited to join the Roosevelt brothers' Giant Panda expedition of 1929. Since this took him to the very "Mount Koonka" region of our own subsequent expedition, he came ideally prepared for his indispensable role with us. And his New York University education in journalism, which he somehow fitted into all this, made him culturally one of us, a most welcome member of our four-man partnership.

After Minya Konka, Jack lived through one wrenching experience in China after another, involving him and his people continuously from the mid-thirties through the end of World War II, and beyond. The Japanese invasion of China, which had temporarily slackened while we were in Szechwan and Tibet, gradually escalated into a full-scale war of aggression. In 1934–35 the Japanese military, who had fully consolidated their control of Manchuria, installed Henry Pu-yi there as the puppet Emperor of a renamed "Manchukuo." Born in 1906, Pu-yi had been the last of the millenia-long continuous line of Emperors of China, in whose name from 1908 a Manchu Regency had ruled in Peking, until the end in 1912.

Two decades later Chiang Kai-shek, fighting the invading Japanese while simultaneously struggling with the Mao communists to his west and north, was forced in late 1937 to move the capital of free China from Nanking to Chungking. Years of this, in which Pearl Harbor in 1941 was but the incident that drew the United States into the hostilities in China, found Jack Young at the end emerging with a chest full of ribbons (every one of them earned in the field). He served as General George Marshall's aide and interpreter during Marshall's historic post-war conference with Mao Tse-tung. Among his many accomplishments Jack had spent, at different times, a total of a year behind Japanese lines with a radio transmitter. The United States awarded him two Silver Stars for gallantry in action, the Legion of Merit twice, and the Bronze Star three times; and the governments of the Republic of China and South Korea awarded him a number of similar decorations. If ever a man's autobiography would be worth writing, and being read, it is his: but to date at least, he has declined all persuasive efforts.

Jack is retired now as a Major General in the Chinese Army for service with the Republic of China prior to Pearl Harbor, and at Brigadier General level in the Army of the United States for services since Pearl Harbor.

There is a touching incident about Minya Konka that is forever in my mind when we meet to reminisce. At the infamous sack of Nanking by the Japanese Army on December 13, 1937, Jack Young was the last officer of the Republic of China to leave the Metropolitan Museum of the Academia Sinica, retrieving what few precious items could be removed in the last-minute rush to safety. The final item he rescued was the flag of the Republic of China that Jack had passed to me at our twenty-thousand-foot Minya Konka camp, and that Dick Burdsall and I five years previously had flown and photographed on the summit.

———

My life following Minya Konka could be summed up in the classic: "he went home, married his sweetheart, and they lived happily ever after"! Katrina had been editor of the campus newspaper and Phi Beta Kappa in her Vassar class of 1930. After graduation she went to work at Harper &

Brothers book publishers in New York, and also moon-lighted a little as a successful freelance writer. She and I had become engaged just before the expedition left New York for China in November 1931 and corresponded as best we could throughout. But mail required two months for an immediate reply round trip between Shanghai and New York – and one-way was the only possibility from far up the Yangtze along the Tibetan border – so we did not lack for subjects of conversation when, fifteen months later, she and Lewy Thorne met my Ford Trimotor airliner at Newark airport!

Unlike my more colorful companions, I never resumed Himalayan-scale mountaineering, nor did I revisit China; instead I pursued an essentially conventional professional life and for avocation took to nearby mountain flying in-stead of mountain climbing. I think the reason was a wish to live, work, and play near my growing family so we might do things together.

After my master's and doctorate (in finance; thesis subject in money and banking) I interned for the better part of a year, running securities, etc., for a New York Stock Ex-change firm in financial Boston; then came a teaching ap-pointment as Instructor in finance and accounting at UCLA in California, 1937–39.

When Pearl Harbor occurred my life – with millions of other Americans – was thoroughly disrupted. Secretary of War Henry L. Stimson had for years been a member of the tiny, three-hundred-person American Alpine Club, and thus fully understood what specially trained and equipped moun-tain troops – hitherto unknown in the U.S. military – might be able to do. I was already on that Club's Council and was Assistant Editor of the *Handbook of American Mountaineer-*

Moore on the summit of Minya Konka with flag of Republic of China

ing, which the War Department in the winter of 1940–41 had commissioned the Club to produce as a prototype for part of the Army's first "Mountain Operations" Field Manual. From all this I was drawn to Washington full time as Consultant to the Quartermaster-General. Many of the country's mountaineers were involved, in an overall effort well related in the *American Alpine Journal, 1946, Special War Number.* My own first-person account of the U.S. Army Test Expedition of 1942, in the high basin on Mt. McKinley, appears in the last chapter of *Mt. McKinley: The Pioneer Climbs.*

Just before the war my close friend Bradford Washburn had become Director of what today is the Boston Museum of Science; and in early 1940 I had been invited to join the Board of Trustees. Late in 1945 I was asked to take the responsibilities of president of the Trustees and of the Society that operates the Museum, specifically charged to carry out some drastic changes: to sell the existing building and site and develop a modern educational museum on a new, more appropiate site. The initial steps for this were accomplished in the late summer of 1948.

Meanwhile in Fairbanks, Alaska, the University of Alaska's first president, Dr. Charles E. Bunnell, was retiring after twenty-seven years; and a call was issued for candidates to succeed him on July 1, 1949. My administrative experience and my familiarity with Alaska from extensive visits since 1930 encouraged me to apply for the position. As there appeared to be no organized search committee at the University in those years, I decided to fly to Alaska during the late winter in my 65 horsepower ski-equipped little Taylorcraft, to campaign actively for votes among the widely scattered Board members. Two months later, at their May 1949 meeting, I was elected President.

Beginning in 1954 I had other academic employment and consulting engagements in New England. But the years when I was the University's active head, and my family and I were Alaskans with our daughter and son in the public schools there, certainly remain in memory as the most inter-

esting and stimulating of my professional engagements
anywhere.

———

Our final enlightenment about the possibilities for a
mountain higher than Everest—which so long ago had sent
us upon our quest to the Chinese-Tibetan border—came
about gradually. After it had finally been proven that there
could not be anything higher in that border region, the only
remaining possibility lay in Antarctica; but by the time of
the International Geophysical Year, 1957–58, it had become
clear that there are no peaks in Antarctica rising higher than
between 16,000 and 17,000 feet.

About that same time (1957) artificial satellites were
placed into orbit around the earth, which in little more than
a decade resulted in the manned lunar landings of 1969. As
the astronauts watched the earth turn before them on their
homeward journey, new ways of thinking about earth
emerged.

Viewing earth from space, as some of us now do, the con-
cept that the farthest out point on the earth's surface is its
"highest mountain" becomes realistic. For those who look at
earth this way, Mount Everest is not "the world's highest
mountain." Instead it is Mount Chimborazo, in the Andes
of Ecuador on the other side of the world: its summit by the
latest calculation (using orbiting satellite data for the exact
shape of the "figure of the earth") is some 2,000 meters
higher above the center of the earth than is the summit of
Everest. And the runner-up—its summit only 23 meters
lower toward earth's center than Chimborazo's—is not a
peak in the Himalaya or Karakoram but is in fact Mount
Huascaran in the Andes of Peru.

Actually, however, the small difference between these two lies within the limits of computational accuracy. The definitive determination of whether Chimborazo or Huascaran rises the higher from the center of the earth must wait until someday when gravimeters can be taken to the two summits, there to measure the strength of gravity with the exquisite accuracy these instruments make possible, and thus determine the world's highest peak above the center of the earth.

Why not accept the simple idea that Mount Everest is the highest mountain in the world above sea level? Its summit surely reaches up into a thinner atmosphere than any other peak in the world. On the basis of barometric pressure alone it is unquestionably the world's highest; and so also on the basis of an artificial, theoretical sea level even where no sea exists.

But the barometer everywhere is notoriously changeable and has to be corrected for local weather conditions; and at high altitudes, increasingly as one goes up, it becomes subject to even larger corrections for latitude and season of the year (because of the peculiar and seasonally changing shape of the upper envelope of the earth's atmosphere). And sea level itself is not level, curving away as it does at the rate of eight inches to the mile, with the curve forever bending yet farther downward as the distance increases; worse yet, the curve is different if you are going north and south instead of east and west, because the sea is flattened about 13¼ miles toward each of the poles by the centrifugal force of the thousand-mile-an-hour spin of the earth at its equator.

As Allen Carpé put it: "Standing on the summit of Mount Fairweather, 15,300 feet, and looking right down to salt water only a dozen or so miles away, and looking north a hundred miles to St. Elias, 18,000 feet high and itself only about sixty miles from the ocean, I have the feeling that 'height above sea level' for these and nearby mountains means something to which I can relate. But when it comes to peaks way off in the middle of the humped-up Asian land mass hundreds of miles out of sight of the ocean, and when you realize the summit of Everest is not even as high above the Tibetan plateau as Mount Fairweather is above the ocean at its base—it makes you wonder: 29,000 feet above what? Well, theoretically, above where the ocean would be if you let it in by a tunnel. But I can tell you that if you did, the sea would not in fact level out 29,000 feet below the summit of Everest. It would rise measurably higher—no one knows by how much. Reason: the Bouguer Anomaly."

There had been scarcely any discussion of all this in New York; but it was resumed at our survey and climbing camps, and at our spectacularly beautiful Base Camp with the summit soaring up ten thousand feet in one clear sweep above us. Inevitably, of course, we asked Dick Burdsall, "What's this Bouguer Anomaly of Allen Carpé's, and his idea that even if one could let the sea in by a tunnel below the summit of Everest it would not come to rest 29,000 feet down below, but in fact somewhat higher?"

Dick's immediate reply was: "He's entirely right, of course. The principle is well known: it's the upward gravitational attraction of the vast mass not only of Everest and the other high nearby Himalayan peaks, but even more perhaps of the huge Tibetan Plateau, which would raise the sea water level there."

"Well then," one of us asked, "just what is it, 29,000 feet down there, from which you surveyors are measuring?" Dick smiled and said: "It's known as the *geoid*, or the *ellipsoid of reference,* an imaginary surface for the 'figure-of-the-earth' that the geodesists have worked out which all surveyors must start with.... Look, you young fellows are so eager to discover the world's highest mountain. Well, when we've completed our survey results you just may find that, in terms of height above base, it's Minya Konka. Your Alaskan Mount McKinley," he said, looking at Art and me, "is about three and a half miles high above the tundra twenty miles or so out, and you call it 'the highest mountain in the world above its base.' But it looks to me as if Minya Konka is going to prove to be about four miles high above its base, the Tung River, twenty miles or so out on the Chinese side."

For some years thereafter, we thought "highest mountain above its base"; but when we encountered the oceanographers we soon learned they will have none of it. To them the Mauna Kea-Mauna Loa *massif* on the Hawaiian Islands is the world's highest mountain. They "think under water" and trace its height up from a base 30,000 feet down in the abyssal deep of the Pacific Ocean. Yet a fourth way of defining the highest mountain: include sea-mounts!

Intrigued by Bouguer and his anomaly, I learned years later that in 1735 Pierre Bouguer and Charles de la Condamine were sent out by the French Academy to Quito, in what was then the Spanish Province of Peru. Their mission was to measure a meridian of arc of the earth's surface near the equator, for comparison by astronomy with one in Lapland, to determine for the first time the true figure-of-the-earth, whether it is indeed flattened toward the poles as had been reasoned by Sir Isaac Newton. And it was against the great nearby mountain mass of Chimborazo that Bouguer conducted the first gravity experiment describing the anomaly which ever since has borne his name.

Bouguer and la Condamine seem to have been the first scientists to regard Chimborazo as the world's highest mountain, a view widely held for over a century. When Alexander von Humboldt in 1802 decided to try to climb as high as a human could go, after consulting with other scientists of his day, he selected this double-domed mass on the equator (and reached about 18,900 feet, the record for the next thirty-six years). Even as late as 1856 Chimborazo as the world's highest was still the received wisdom. In *Aurora Leigh* Elizabeth Barrett Browning tells us:

> I learnt the royal genealogies
> Of Oviedo, the internal laws
> Of the Burmese empire... by how many feet
> Mount Chimborazo outsoars Himmeleh.

Last search? At this point the light-hearted lady whose lines Dick Burdsall published on page 58 (and whom I was fortunate enough to persuade to marry me—even more fortunate to have had her stay with it these forty-six years), when she had read all the foregoing, laughed. "So relax, there *is* no highest mountain on earth!"

To this your author replied: "Well, all right all *right*, so I'll give you the famous quotation about science from Aristotle!" No doubt, dear reader, you also know it; but for those who may not, here's how it goes in English:

"The search for the truth is in one way hard and in another easy; for it is evident that no one of us will ever master it all, nor miss it wholly. Each one of us adds a little to our understanding of nature, and from the facts assembled there arises a certain grandeur."

Last search? Of the original ten, Jack Young and I alone
survive. In memory he and I step outside our Base Camp
tent in the meadow. Under the brilliant starlit heavens, and
startling us by its closeness, Minya Konka's spectacular
pyramid soars chalk-white into the night. In the presence of
this vision, ellipsoids of reference, Bouguer's Anomaly, centrifugal force from the unfelt thousand-mile-an-hour spin of
the earth's rotation, all seem to vanish into unimportance:
there before us rises our reality.

E. BIBLIOGRAPHY

ACCOUNTS OF THE MINYA KONKA—TATSIENLU REGION

GILL, CAPT. WILLIAM, R.E., *The River of Golden Sand*. (London, 1883.)

Die Wissenschaftlichen Ergebnisse der Reise des Grafen Bela Szechenyi in Ostasien 1877-1880. (Vienna, 1893.)

KREITNER, GUSTAV, *Im Fernen Osten*.

ROCKHILL, W. W., *Land of the Lamas*. (1891.)

DAVIES, MAJOR H. R., *Yun-nan the Link between India and the Yangtze*. (Cambridge, 1909.)

WILSON, EARNEST HENRY, *A Naturalist in Western China*. (London, 1913.)

TEICHMAN, ERIC, *Travels in Eastern Tibet*. (Cambridge, 1922.)

GREGORY, J. W., and C. J., *To the Alps of Chinese Tibet*. (Philadelphia, 1924.)

ROOSEVELT, THEODORE and KERMIT, *Trailing the Giant Panda*. (New York, 1929.)

EDGAR, J. H., "The Gangka—a Peak in Eastern Tibet" (*Journal West China Border Research Society*, III, 1926-1929).

"The Mountains about Tatsienlu" (*Geographical Journal*, LXXXV, No. 4, April, 1930).

STEVENS, HERBERT, "Sketches of Tatsienlu Peaks" (*Geographical Journal*, LXXXV, No. 4, April, 1930).

ROCK, JOSEPH F., "The Glories of the Minya Konka" (*National Geographic Magazine*, LVIII, No. 4, October, 1930).

HEIM, ARNOLD, "The Structure of Minya Gongkar" (*Bulletin Geological Society of China*, XI, No. 1, 1931, Peiping).

HEIM, ARNOLD, "Szechuan-Tibet-Expedition of Sunyatsen Uni-

315

versity, Canton," (*Zeitschrift der Gesellschaft fur Erdkunde zu Berlin,* 1931).

HEIM, ARNOLD, *Minya Gongkar.* (Berlin, 1933.)

STEVENSON, P. H., "Notes on the Human Geography of the Chinese-Tibetan Borderland" (*Geographical Review,* XXII, 1932).

EDGAR, J. H., "Notes on the Mountains about Tatsienlu" (*Geographical Journal,* LXXXII, No. 3, September, 1933).

ACCOUNTS OF THE SIKONG EXPEDITION

YOUNG, JACK THEODORE, "My Experiences in Tibet" (*The Chinese Republic,* II, No. 15, February 11, 1933).

MOORE, TERRIS, "An American Climb into Tibetan Skies" (*New York Times Magazine,* May 28, 1933).

MOORE, TERRIS, "The Minya Konka Climb" (*American Alpine Journal,* II, No. 1, 1933).

EMMONS, ARTHUR B., 3rd, "The Conquest of the Minya Konka" (*China Journal,* XIX, No. 1, July, 1933).

MOORE, TERRIS, "The Ascent of Minya Konka" (*Alpine Journal,* November, 1933).

EMMONS, ARTHUR B., 3rd, "Conquest of Minya Konka" (*The Sportsman,* XIV, No. 6, December, 1933).

BURDSALL, RICHARD L., "The Altitude and Location of Minya Konka" (*Geographical Review,* XXIV, No. 1, January, 1934).

EMMONS, ARTHUR B., 3rd, "The Reconnaissance of the Minya Konka" (*American Alpine Journal,* II, No. 2, 1934).

MOORE, TERRIS, "La premiere ascension du Minya Konka" (*La Montagne,* No. 262, October, 1934).

LITERATURE REFERENCES SINCE 1935

BURDSALL, RICHARD L., and MOORE, TERRIS. "Climbing the Mighty Minya Konka, Landmark of China's New Skyway" (*National Geographic,* May 1943).

IMHOF, EDUARD. Five professional periodical pieces in German, more fully covered in his 1974 book below (1947, 1948, 1950).

"The Conquest of Minya Konka" (*The People's China*, Peking, October 1957).

SHIH CHAN-CHUN. "Die Besteigung des Minya Konka" (*Berg, Schnee, Fels*, Internationale Alpinisten-Zeitschrift Lausanne, Nr. 7, 1958).

"Alpine Notes—Minya Konka" (*The Alpine Journal*, London, May 1958, page 130).

SHIH CHAN-CHUN. "The Second Ascent of Minya Konka" (*The Alpine Journal*, London, November 1958).

"Climbs and Expeditions, China—Minya Konka" (*American Alpine Journal*, 1958, page 125). Letters, editorial comment about the controversy.

SHIH CHAN-CHUN, translated by Huang Kai-ping. *The Conquest of Minya Konka* (Foreign Languages Press, Peking, 1959). A 54-page book in English with illustrations.

MOORE, TERRIS. "Keeping the Record Straight on Minya Konka" (*American Alpine Journal*, Climbs and Expeditions, 1964, page 235).

Mountaineering in China (compiled by the People's Physical Culture Publishing House, Foreign Languages Press, Peking, 1965). Begins with chapter "Conquering Minya Konka" (including their best-quality photograph titled "Atop Minya Konka at Last"), followed by chapters on exploring the Shule Mountain; the ascent of Mustagh Ata; the ascent of Mount Jolmo Lungma (Everest) "on May 25, 1960"; the ascent of Amne Machin, 7,160 meters, in May 1960; the Chinese Women's Expedition ascent of Mount Kongur Tiubie Tagh; and the Conquest of Mount Shisha Pangma, 8,012 meters, May 2, 1964. The latter "is situated in Myenyam County, Tibet Region, China."

MOORE, TERRIS. "Great Mountains of the World: Not the Height You Think" (*American Alpine Journal*, 1968).

MOLENAAR, DEE. "Minya Konka" (*Summit* magazine, October 1971).

MOORE, TERRIS. "Search for the World's Highest Mountain" (*Appalachia,* June 1972).

MOORE, TERRIS. "Last Search for the Highest Mountain" (*Explorers Journal,* June 1972).

IMHOF, EDUARD. *Die Grossen Kalten Berge von Szetschuan* (Zurich Orell Fussli Verlag, 1974). In German. 227 pages, many maps, paintings, drawings, and photographs. Much the most complete single publication on the subject of Minya Konka. A typescript translation into English by Katrina H. Moore is on deposit with the American Alpine Club library in New York; and publication of this by the Club is scheduled for 1980–81.

Of eighteen chapters, number eight is devoted to the American first ascent in 1932; and number nine is devoted to the Chinese ascent in 1957. The P.R.C. Chinese doubts about the American 1932 ascent are dealt with in detail; four photographic plates from the American expedition are reproduced. Plate #28, on page 78, reproduces in largest size and greatest clarity our key summit photograph, over the caption "View from the summit of Minya Konka-North.... This picture proves that Burdsall and Moore in 1932 reached the summit."

The very large foldout end map at back, by Eduard Imhof, embodies the survey work of both American and Swiss expeditions. On it the claim for Minya Konka as "the world's highest mountain above its base" may be accurately examined. All three rivers receiving Minya Konka's entire 360-degree unique drainage pattern meet in confluence 37 kilometers (23 miles) to the southeast, at 1100 meters altitude only. The summit thus rises 6500 meters (4 miles) above a specific base.

INDEX

319